The First World War in North Devon

Peter Christie BA(Hons), MPhil

First published in 2023 by Christie Publishing

ISBN 978-1-3999-5637-6

Typeset, printed and bound by
Short Run Press Ltd, Exeter, Devon

Contents

The First World War in North Devon

Foreword

This book has been many years in the making. Over the last 40 years I have been reading my way through the complete run of both the *North Devon Journal* (1824-present) and the *Bideford* (later *North Devon*) *Gazette* (1856-present) – and making notes on many different topics as I went. In late 2022 I looked at my files covering the First World War and decided to write them up, with the emphasis being on how the war affected North Devon and its people. This is different from the many parish histories which often cover the First World War, if at all, with a condensed biography of the men recorded on the war memorial who generally died far away. Such coverage is valuable in itself but I wanted to examine what was happening at 'home'.

Newspapers have been my main source but the many photographic illustrations used herein have come from a wide variety of people to whom I say a heartfelt thank-you. I have published some of these illustrations before on the 'Yesteryear' page of the *North Devon Journal* over the last 17 years and although I have endeavoured to contact as many of the people who originally sent them to me I haven't always succeeded in every case so please accept my apologies now.

I am indebted to the following:

I.Andrews	C.Darch	A.Green	B.Leworthy
N.Bailey	R.Davis	S.Harding	R.Mitchell
M.Bennett	J.Eastley	Rev.J.Harris	H.Murch
A.Berriman	C.Edwards	P.Harris	F.Ovey
P.Blackmore	C.Fulford	K.Hearn	S.Rookes
D.Blackmore-Heal	D.Gale	A.Hockin	S.Vass
B.Burgess	J.George	P.Isaac	J.Wood

I also need to thank the staffs of the Ilfracombe Museum, Braunton & District Museum, South Molton & District Museum, Bideford & District Community Archive, North Devon Athenaeum and the North Devon Record Office. Also a special thank you to Richard Morris who knows more about North Devon military history than anyone else and who kindly read through the typescript before publication. On a personal basis I would like to dedicate the book to Bob & Monica Kelly of Bideford.

Peter Christie BA(Hons), MPhil
May 2023

A note on money – under the old Imperial system each pound (£) was made up of 20 shillings (20/-), each shilling being made up of 12 pennies (12d) with pennies further broken down into halfpennies (½d) and farthings (¼d). The metric equivalent is 1p = 2½d, 25p = 5/-, 50p = 10/-.

In the text NDJ = North Devon Journal; BG = Bideford Gazette

This book is dedicated to the North Devon men and women who lost their lives during the First World War – and to the many who died after the war from the effects of hostilities and yet whose names do not appear on the war memorials.

The First World War in North Devon

August 1914

The First World War broke out on August 4th 1914 when Britain declared war on Germany following that country's invasion of neutral Belgium. The arrival of the news in North Devon was reported as being met with 'patriotic fervour'. At Ilfracombe, for example a 1000 strong audience watching a show in the Victoria Pavilion joined in an unscripted rendering of the National Anthem.

Initially of course many thought hostilities would soon be over, with the Mayor of Bideford S.R.Chope saying at the town's Horse Show that he 'trusted it would soon pass away.' This may have been the hope of many but more pragmatic locals were rushing to establish voluntary groups to help the families of men who were leaving for the fighting.

In Barnstaple a Devon Patriotic and Local Distress Fund was rapidly collecting money to help the families of servicemen, with Earl Fortescue giving two stags to be sold in aid of its targets whilst the Barnstaple Picturedrome cinema put on a special show, which the Mayor attended, to raise funds for the group. In Bideford a 'War Committee' was up and running by the second week of the war. Similar groups sprang up in all of the area's towns with even villages such as Bishops Tawton, Shirwell, Beaford and Dolton having their own auxiliary groups.

In addition to these funds local branches of the Foresters, a self-help charity group, offered to pay the weekly contributions of all members 'now on active service' whilst in Bideford local doctors said they would give free treatment to the families where the husband was in the forces. Also in August A.L.Christie of Tapeley Park announced plans to set up a Red Cross hospital in a house he owned in Bath Terrace, Instow which was to become one of the main wartime medical centres in North Devon. At Georgeham the building attached to the Rifle Range was being converted into a hospital whilst in Braunton and Barnstaple the Red Cross also opened emergency hospitals.

This all sounds as if everyone was working and pulling together but even in the first weeks of the war both the Mayors of Barnstaple and Bideford were appealing for people not to 'panic buy' food. This was to be expected, perhaps, when in the same issue of the *Journal* reporting this call was a note that at the Barnstaple Corn Exchange, where local farmers sold their produce, prices experienced a 'sensational advance'.

By the next week things had got so bad that the Barnstaple Trades & Labour Council were calling on the government to take over food distribution to

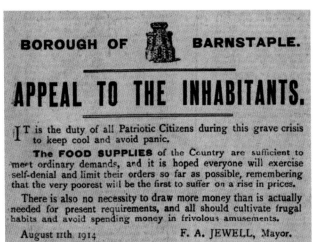

1. An 'Appeal to the Inhabitants' NDJ 13.8.1914 1a-b

ensure fairness and stop prices escalating. At the monthly meeting of the Bideford Rural District Council the chairman W.Harris asked locals 'to have a balanced and unselfish opinion with regard to the purchase of provisions and all necessaries of life.' Within a week or two, however, when it became evident there was to be no immediate scarcity of food, prices returned to their pre-war level.

The first actual military activity was the call-up of the local Territorials – both the infantrymen in the 6th Battalion of the Devonshire Regiment and cavalry men in the Royal North Devon Hussars.

2. The Royal North Devon Hussars assemble at their Barnstaple HQ.

It was noted of the former that 'Every man turned up promptly'. Their assembly point was in Barnstaple and a huge crowd gathered to see the men arriving. Many of the 6th Devons were actually at Woodbury training camp in South Devon and they were hurriedly brought back. The Bideford area territorials and Naval Reserve men from Appledore gathered and marched across Bideford Bridge to travel by train to Barnstaple whilst 'a great cheering crowd accompanied them' with the Mayor wishing them 'Godspeed' adding 'He hoped to have the pleasure of welcoming them back home again, when he assured them they would have a cordial welcome.'

When the Territorials gathered at Ilfracombe they were mobbed by so many people that they found it difficult to leave.

3. The Royal Naval Reserve men gather on Bideford Pill.

4 & 5. Scenes at Ilfracombe.

6.7.8.9.10. The Hussars at Torrington – was Michael Morpurgo's 'War horse' here?

11 & 12. The Hussars attend church service in South Molton before leaving.

At Torrington the 130 men of 'D' Squadron of the Hussars gathered in the Square to be addressed by the Mayor and Vicar from a hastily erected dais before entraining, this being the first troop train ever to leave Torrington station.

Meanwhile at South Molton the Hussars paraded in the Square prior to a Church Parade service.

The Hussars, who were mainly local farmers, brought their own horses but the Army began purchasing horses in large numbers.

The first groups of local reservists began leaving the area – whilst those left behind began forming new reserve bodies along with other unofficial

13. Territorials leaving Braunton by train.

Last week about 200 horses for the Royal North Devon Hussars were purchased in the district. In the Southmolton area Mr. Dudley J. O. Bush, J P., secured the finest lot of animals ever brought together in the town. Twenty of the horses purchased by Mr. Bush were hunters from the Exford stables, and many other horses accustomed to hunt with the Devon and Somerset Staghounds. The Lynton purchases also included many hunters which have been used in staghunting and in the Exmoor Hunt country. Four very valuable polo ponies were cheerfully parted with by Major Greig at a nominal price. The purchases in the Bideford and Torrington areas were also eminently satisfactory. In the Barnstaple district 137 horses were purchased, the average quality being very high.

14. The purchase of horses by the Army. NDJ 13.8.1914 5c

15. Horses brought to Bideford Market Place for purchase by the Army.

groups. In Bideford, for example, 43 members of the Church Lads Brigade aged between 17 and 25 joined the new Local Civil Volunteer Corps, with 17 younger ones enrolling as 'Messengers'. In Barnstaple 100 men signed up to a body calling itself the Civic Guard for Barnstaple – but as the War Office didn't sanction this body recruiting was hastily stopped. At Northam 300 enrolled into the District Emergency League, with the Vestry room in the Square being used as a recruiting office. Again this body was only semi-official and never seems to have become an active military formation. The men in this unit were old – but at least they had their own firearms.

16. Horses similarly brought to Hatherleigh.
(Copyright Beaford Arts)

17. *The Northam volunteers.*

One official government-sponsored body was the National Reserve and this had 140 members in Barnstaple within 3 weeks of it starting. Posters urging men to enlist were pasted up all over the area and one was found many years later at Braunton railway station.

Even North Devon Boy Scouts were helping the war effort patrolling railway bridges though when the local Education Committee started complaining about absenteeism from school this had to be curtailed – but not before three Braunton Scouts tracked 'a man of foreign appearance' who 'gave the impression that he was engaged in some form of espionage.' Unfortunately this mysterious individual gave them the slip. 'Spy-fever' wasn't confined to Braunton, however, as rumours (later proved false) swept South Molton that the local reservoirs had been poisoned by German agents.

There were, of course, enemy aliens in North Devon at the outbreak of war and those of military age were

18. *The poster at Braunton.*

14 GERMANS ARRESTED IN NORTH DEVON.

ILFRACOMBE AND LYNTON WAITERS AMONG THE NUMBER.

Considerable public excitement was aroused by the arrest on Tuesday of fourteen Germans by the Barnstaple Division County Police. At Ilfracombe five waiters, &c., were apprehended in the course of the morning, and in the afternoon were taken to Exeter Higher Barracks by P.C.'s Clarke, Hosgood, and Bradford. At Barnstaple the train was met by Capt. Holford Thompson, Superintendent of the County Police, who gave instructions to the office in charge. At Lynton nine Germans were arrested, most of whom were waiters in the large hotels there. One of them, however, was a wealthy gentleman, who, on being arrested by the police, temporarily handed over a large sum of money to the authorities. The prisoners were brought to Barnstaple by the last train by P.S. Champion, and P.C.'s Holman (Braunton Fleming), Perriman (Combe Martin), Hibbins (special constable, enrolled at Lynton), and Disney (Bickington). At Barnstaple Town Station a huge crowd awaited the arrival of the train. The party was met by Captain Halford Thompson, Serg'. Partridge, Assistant Scout Commissioner H. H. Williams (the latter rendering appreciated service in connection with the luggage arrangements for the prisoners.) At the Junction Station another crowd gathered, and a contingent of Territorials, armed with fixed bayonets, made a cordon around the prisoners until the Exeter train arrived. There was no demonstration of any kind whatever, and the Germans appeared to be in the best of spirits. As the train for Exeter left the station the crowd and the prisoners waved each other farewell. The Lynton prisoners were also taken to the Higher Barracks.

On Tuesday a number of Germans, employed in the town in various capacities, were handed over to the military authorities at Exeter, from Ilfracombe. Their names were Francis Gebhardt (Schwandorf, Germany), Hans Muller (Klineschaowitz), Paul Pommer, Gustave Ruske, Henry Kessler (Rine), and Hans Gerber. A number of other aliens have also registered at the Police Station.

A German waiter at Westward Ho was on Tuesday taken by the Police to Bideford Police Station for detention pending inquiries.

19. *Rounding up of enemy aliens. NDJ 13.8.1914 5d*

Reuben Johns, North Down Rd., Bideford.
Frederick Heard, Market Place, Bideford.
Ewens Clarke, Geneva' Place, Bideford.
William Shortridge, Torridge Mount,
  Bideford.
Philip Kelly, 15, Quay, Bideford.
Ernest Wilkinson, 8, Chanter's Road,
  Bideford.
Frederick Rendall, 15, Victoria Grove,
  Bideford.
William Henry Hopper, Honestone Street,
  Bideford.
Bertram Lake, Tower-street, Bideford.
Samuel Westlake, Northam.
Thos. John Westlake, Northam.
Ernest Arthur Jones, Northam.
Thos. Snell, Northam.
Sidney Kelly, Northam.
Henry G. Ford Trott, Northam.
Thomas Curtis, Northam.
Albert E. Vincent, Northam.
Alfred Paddon, Northam.
Frederick Arthur King, Northam.
William Lewis May, Northam.

20. Volunteers in the Bideford area. BG 25.8.1914 2e

quickly rounded up by the authorities. Some 14 Germans who were employed as waiters at Ilfracombe, Lynton and Westward Ho! were arrested and interned for the duration.

It was in this month that Lord Kitchener issued his famous call-to-arms and men flooded in to join the colours, with the *Journal* and *Bideford Gazette* patriotically printing lists of all these volunteers.

His call was echoed by both Earl Fortescue and his wife, the latter of whom wrote to the *Journal* requesting women to encourage their menfolk to enlist. Thus ended the first month of a war that began with high hopes that it would 'all be over by Christmas' yet was to drag on until November 1918 with the loss of millions of lives.

The First World War in North Devon

September 1914

The main news in the local newspapers for September 1914 was of a massive rush by young men enlisting into local military units. The *Journal* editor printed lists of these both by regiment and by place – with coverage even going down to street level.

Many young men joined after attending public meetings - as at Bideford.

Some surprising statistics were quoted about enlistment – as from the small village of Westleigh near Bideford where over 30 men or about 10% of the population were in the Forces including 5 brothers from the Parker family from the hamlet of Eastleigh in the parish who had enlisted en bloc into the 'New Army.' So great was this local influx of new recruits that the Royal North Devon Hussars had enough men to set up a reserve regiment with a separate detachment also being formed in Braunton. In the middle of the month, when asked, some 86% of the regiment volunteered for foreign service. At Torrington two recruiting officers arrived it being noted that 131 local men were already serving.

SOLDIERS FROM SILVER-STREET, BARNSTAPLE.

A small area in Silver-street, Barnstaple, has furnished no fewer than nineteen men to various branches of the Army. The soldiers are:—
J. Barrow, 1st Devon Res.
W. Barrow, 6th Devon Territorials.
J. Barrow, "
W. H. Beagen, R.N.D.H.
R. Beagen, 6th Devon Territorials.
B. Barrington, " "
P. J. Burrington " "
H. Bament " " "
W. Bament " " "
R. Cann, 2nd Devon Reserves.
O. Folland, 6th Devon Territorials.
J. Gabriel, 1st National Reserve.
R. Gabriel, "
W. Gilbert, 6th Devon Territorials.
J. Harris, " " "
W. H. Lewis " "
J. Woolway " " "
A. Woolway, " "
A. Braunton " " "

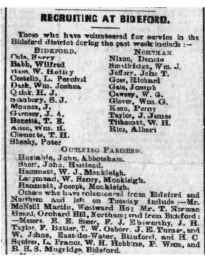

1, 2 & 3. Volunteers listed for Barnstaple, Ilfracombe and Bideford. NDJ 10.9.1914 2d

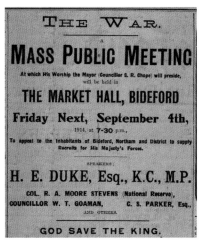

4. The advertisement for the Bideford meeting. BG 1.9.1914 2d-e

5. *Barnstaple recruits still in civilian dress.*

6. *Recruits on the steps of Barnstaple Quay railway station.*

9. *Torrington recruits outside of the town's Drill Hall.*

7. *Barnstaple recruits possibly pictured in Boutport Street and*
8. *In Gloster Road.*

10. *Volunteers at Swimbridge outside the village inn; it is thought the portly figure is a Major Munday.*

THE DEATH OF CAPT. WICKHAM, D.S.O.

TREACHEROUSLY SHOT BY GERMAN OFFICER'S ORDERLY.

Describing on trustworthy authority an incident in the campaign in Cameroon, of which no official account has been issued, "The African World" says:—

It is necessary to commence from the time war was declared, and when the Mounted Infantry on August 8 left Kano for the front. The march to Yola of 400 miles took only 17 days, which, taking all things into consideration, must be considered a splendid performance. To travel 24 miles a day in West Africa, and in the rainy season too, is no easy matter. Six officers of the M.I. accompanied the column, together with an intelligence officer and a doctor, and, upon reaching the River Benue they at once started for Tepe, the small frontier station just inside the Cameroons, and actually on the River Benue. This column of M.I. acted as the advance guard to the 2nd Battalion of the W.A.F.F.'s which was then at Yola, about 30 miles away from Tepe. On August 25 the M.I. came into touch with the enemy at Tepe, and repulsed them with the loss of three officers and a N.C.O. It was after this fighting, which only lasted about 25 minutes, that a most distressing incident occurred, in this way:—Captain T. S. Wickham, D.S.O., of the Manchester Regiment, had taken a German officer a prisoner, and, placing his hand on the prisoner's shoulder, he made the remark. "You are my prisoner." The German cried out for mercy, and begged that his life might be spared, and at the same time his orderly was told to respect the Englishman. Captain Wickham then turned round to ask his commanding officer what he should do with the prisoner, when the German officer's orderly brought up his rifle and shot Captain Wickham in the throat. Nothing more terrible could have happened. Needless to say, the German was at once shot, together with his orderly, in addition to which the village of Tepe was burnt to the ground.

11. The death of Captain T.Wickham BG 8.12.1914 8c

The first casualties began to be reported with one of the first of the war being a Bideford man. Captain Thomas Wickham of the 2nd Manchester Regiment, a son of a former Mayor, who was killed in Cameroon, West Africa on August 25th whilst carrying out a reconnaissance of this German colony. A later account described his death.

Captain Wickhams' medals and effects are on display at the Imperial War Museum. There is also a picture of him available on the IWM website.

Two other casualties are recorded – Pte.W.Burgess of the Royal Field Artillery from Ilfracombe had been hit by shrapnel during the Battle of Mons. This was a fighting retreat carried out by the professionals of the British Expeditionary Force in France – the first British soldiers to take on the Germans. His letter to his parents was printed in the *Journal* and clearly pre-dated battlefield censorship with its mention of retreating and the inactivity of the French – such letters would eventually be stopped.

Pte.John Ley of Braunton also wrote home describing how a soldier standing next to him 'had his head blown off' whilst he himself received a wound in his foot. Given the numbers who were to be killed or wounded it is odd to see so much space given over to these accounts – but hindsight is a wonderful thing.

As fighting began so more civilians organised themselves to support the Forces. Local distress funds to help the families of North Devon men away at the Front garnered more and more money whilst the first of countless 'flag' and badge days was held in Barnstaple where a group of women made badges displaying the flags of the Allies to sell in the Market with the money raised going to a Prisoner of War fund. Devon county council circulated a notice stressing that any teachers called up for service would find their jobs awaiting them when they returned although this did add the phrase 'as far as possible.' Interestingly the circular said this would apply to 'men or women' – an unusual example of sexual equality at this date.

AN ILFRACOMBE SOLDIER WOUNDED.

INTERESTING LETTER TO HIS PARENTS.

The following letter has been received by Mr. and Mrs. H. Burgess, of 10 Larkstone Crescent, Ilfracombe, from their son, Pte. W. Burgess, of the Royal Field Artillery, who is now lying wounded at the London Hospital, and who was present during the four days' severe fighting between the British and German forces:—

London Hospital,
Whitechapel-road, E.

Dear Parents,—I expect you will be glad to hear from me I have been badly wounded in two places by a shrapnel shell; I shall get better, though, in a week or so. I got hit in the right cheek and in the back. We had an awful time; lost a lot of men in our battery. The shells were flying all over the field. We had to retreat on Monday and Tuesday, and on Wednesday morning we met them about 3 in the morning. We killed hundreds of their men but the more we killed the more came up and took their places. We made arrangements to meet the French on that morning, but they did not turn up; there was a mistake made in the time. If they had come we may have done better, but the generals said it was the best bit of work England has ever done as regards fighting. We only had 75,000 men while the Germans had 200,000, so you can see what we did. I got taken to a French hospital, but in the morning the Germans started shelling it; they blew it to bits, and as they advanced they burst down houses, and killed women and children, and blew up churches. They are gone real mad. They were real cowards: as soon as we charged them they dropped their rifles and ran like mad. Well, mother, I wish you could send me a few little things such as books, to read . . . . I think this is all at present. With best love, From your ever loving son,

BILL.

12. A letter home. NDJ 10.9.1914 2e

As in all wars wild rumours spread quickly, with a local magistrate C.Darbyshire announcing at a recruiting meeting in Ilfracombe that '...it was now an open secret that a vast body of Russians had been landed in the North of France.' This story was backed up by a Barnstaple man who 'journeyed some distance with a party of khaki-clad Russian soldiers in a tramcar in London' whilst another Barnstaple man had injured himself 'whilst assisting to put Russian horses on board ship in an English port'. Such rumours came to nothing of course.

Again there were stories of German spies and espionage in general. P.c.Perriam of Combe Martin arrested a German caught 'sketching in the neighbourhood' though enquiries soon showed he was a 'naturalised Englishman' and so was released. At South Molton a 'German' was seen lurking around the railway viaduct at Castle Hill – but he turned out to be an innocent Englishman. In Bideford pigeon fanciers were told to keep the birds in their lofts as they 'run great risk of being shot by the military authorities, as many have already been' they being suspected of carrying messages from spies. At Hartland a suspected German 'spy pigeon' turned out to be just a normal racing bird. F.L.Schofield manager of the Barnstaple Gas Company wrote

ILFRACOMBE MAN WHO FOUGHT THE KAISER.

A SET-TO AT RAPPAREE IN 1878.

TAPPING THE "WAR LORD'S" CLARET!

There are not many men who can say that they have had a genuine set-to with the Kaiser, the arrogant "War Lord." There is, however, one man in Ilfracombe among whose memories figures a stand-up fight with that august personage when he was merely Prince Frederic William of Prussia. This historic battle took place in the month of August, 1878, and the scene was the Rapparee Bathing Beach. At that period the Prince was holidaying at Ilfracombe, and among the pleasures of the daily round was bathing at Rapparee. The party, of course, soon became known. One afternoon, they were on this beach, then in the tenancy of the late Mr. Price, who, with his brother-in-law (the late Mr. Tom Gibbs), was at the moment on the cliffs above the beach. The Prince's guardian and others went off exploring the neighbouring rocks, and the young Prince employed his royal leisure by making targets of the numbers on the bathing machines. This wanton mischief roused Mr. Price's son, Alfred, who said he should not allow his father's property to be damaged like that. The reply was "Do you know who I am?" but young Price, with all the Englishman's bluntness, said "I don't care a dash who you are."

Forthwith, the Prince, who appears to have had a little science in fisticuffs, landed Price a nasty one on the right jaw, knocking him down. But he got up at once, and though four years younger than the Prince (who was then 19) put up a good and game fight. For twenty minutes they were at it, hammer and tongs, Mr. Price, senr., and Mr. Gibbs, from the field above, enjoying the unwonted spectacle, no doubt with great gusto. There was a good deal of "claret," both blue and plebian, in evidence, but when the horrified tutor appeared on the scene, neither side had gained any advantage. The whole of this historic conflict was at the time kept nearly as quiet as news from the seat of the War now is, and during the battle the combatants had the beach quite to themselves.

Mr. Alfred R. Price, who still controls the Rapparee Bathing Beach, and is the popular host of the St. James's Boarding House, Ilfracombe, is perhaps the only man who ever lived who is able to boast (in the modest way in which he relates the occurrence) that he once gave the Kaiser a bloody nose!

13. The Kaiser beaten. NDJ 10.9.1914 8d

in to the *Journal* to refute claims he was a German whilst poor J.Paton of Parkham, a magistrate and retired Territorial Army captain, was alleged to be a spy as he spoke German fluently – a result of his having taken a degree at Heidelberg University.

One thing that was not a rumour was the arrival of Belgian refugees who were fleeing the German invasion of their country. The first group came to Lynton and hired a house in North Walk whilst a concert to raise funds for their countrymen was held in Barnstaple a week later – with the Mayoress of Barnstaple setting up a special fund for these refugees.

On a lighter note the *Journal* revisited a famous local story from 1878 when Prince William of Prussia, later to become the German Kaiser, came to Ilfracombe and got into fight.

The First World War in North Devon

October 1914

The third month of the war saw the reality of a pan-European conflict beginning to hit home. As in August and September large numbers of young men were volunteering for the Forces with the *Journal* continuing to publish lists of names settlement by settlement such as the two shown here. Amongst the recruits were 25 members of the South Molton Football Club who enlisted en bloc.

In addition the National Reserve was put on alert, many of these men having fought in one or more of Britain's many 'Colonial' wars.

The local infantry unit, the 6th Battalion of the Devonshire Regiment, was ordered to India and 800 men and officers began preparations before departing by train.

1 & 2. More local volunteers listed. NDJ 8.10.1914 2c + 5c

3. Men of the Reserves in Barnstaple after attending a church service – some wearing medals possibly won in the Boer War.

4. North Devon Territorials entraining at Barnstaple Junction railway station.

5 & 6. Men of the 2nd Devons pictured at Barnstaple Junction railway station after their short leave.

Meanwhile a Home Service Battalion of the same unit was set up and its 720 men billeted in Barnstaple where they trained in Rock Park and, as the *Journal* noted, gave Barnstaple the appearance of a 'garrison town'. The Territorial Royal Garrison Artillery units in Ilfracombe and Lynton both volunteered for foreign service and they began packing. The numbers of servicemen in the area were further swollen by the 2nd Devons who returned from Egypt and had a few days' leave before going to France. They were joined by two female nurses from Instow who received orders to go to Paris to care for the wounded.

The names of a few more local casualties were published in the *Journal* including Pte.Fred Delve of Barnstaple who had been an 'attendant' at the town's Picturedrome cinema. In addition two local men were listed as being prisoners-of-war following the Battle of Mons – Pte.Sutcliffe of Torrington and Sergt.Ridge from Braunton. The largest group of casualties, however, were Belgian troops who had been evacuated from the fighting to North Devon. - with some 50 arriving in Ilfracombe where feverish preparations saw then being distributed between various houses.

BELGIAN RεFUGEES Iε NORTH DEVON.

FREMINGTON AND BICKINGTON SCHεME.

During the past week a movement has been on foot in the villages of Fremington and Bickington to provide a homes for a family of Belgians, and the whole-hearted way in which the parishioners entered into the work is evidence of their sympathy with the homeless refugees. At a largely-attended meeting held at Bickington, over which the Rev. T. P. Dimond-Hogg (the esteemed Vicar of Fremington) presided, it was decided to accommodate a family of Belgian refugees of the tradespeople class. A point which aroused much discussion was as to whether they should link their funds with the Barnstaple Committee, but the majority ruled in favour of working entirely on their own. A subscription list was accordingly opened, under the superintendence of Mrs. Leaky (Hon. Secretary and Treasurer). As was exclusively reported in our last issue, it has been decided to rent the beautifully situated residence, "Home Place" (formerly occupied by the Rev. T. B. Williams, for some time Curate of Fremington, and now Rector of Monkohampton). The very gentleman has kindly consented to loo 'Home Place' at one half the usual rental. The house, which comprises eight large dwelling rooms, a bathroom (with hot and cold water), is lighted by gas, and has a complete system of electric bells; it was seen on Monday by our representative, who found every room well-furnished, whilst some thoughtful parishioner kindly placed a sewing machine in the kitchen. At the back there is a large garden, and an acre of land, which will be entirely at the disposal of the Belgians, whilst in the town's houses there are about a dozen fowls. All the furniture and household necessities have been lent by residents in the two villages, and more things are promised. The arrangements have been ably carried out by Mrs. T. P. Dimond-Hogg, Miss Ruth Dimond-Hogg, Mrs. Poynder, Mr. Smith, and Mr. Fred Holland.

7. Belgian refugees begin to arrive. NDJ 5.11.1914 3a

8. Wounded Belgian soldiers pictured at Ilfracombe.

9. Belgian civilian refugees at Home Place, Bickington.

These soldiers were joined by many civilian compatriots fleeing from the fighting.

Local people rushed to help them with families settling in Croyde, Fremington, Braunton, Combe Martin and Bideford. At the latter town Dr.Gooding of Bridgeland Street took in 15 with another 25 moving into Bath House (now the Youth Centre on the Pill). Their arrival in Bideford was noted in a diary kept by Rosalind Mounce nee Pennington, a seamstress at Chope's drapery shop in the town.

Two fund raising concerts were staged at Westward Ho! and Bideford.

Various Belgian Relief Funds were now up and running to help these traumatised people – examples of the many Home Front organisations that sprang up. At Torrington, Combe Martin, Marwood and North Molton, for example, clothing was collected and socks knitted to send to local servicemen whilst appeals in Barnstaple, Bideford and Northam saw large numbers of blankets being gathered in and sent off to the troops. At Clovelly 'silk bars' in the colours of the Allies were made and sold to help the refugees. Whilst much time was being expended on these practical efforts there was still time enough to listen and spread rumours with Belgian refugees being a rich source for 'Hunnish atrocity' stories. Striking a modern note a Braunton trader claimed to have seen the lights of an aeroplane over Hartland – the clear implication being that these were on a German plane! Also in Braunton harmless 'sketchers' were arrested as possible German spies carrying out espionage – though they were quickly released when found to be innocent.

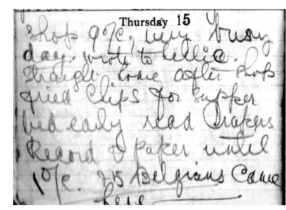

10. The Belgians arrive in Bideford 15.10.1914

More letters from serving soldiers were published including Cpl. Leonard Abbott of Ilfracombe who after writing that 'having marched 10 miles this morning, and we have marched over 200 miles in 12 days' asked his wife to send him some new socks. Pte. Joseph Shaddick of Barnstaple struck an optimistic note saying 'This fighting has lasted a week up to now, and I don't know how much longer the Germans are going to hang out.' Of more immediate interest to North Devonians was the requisitioning of two of P.& A.Campbell's Bristol Channel pleasure steamers for use as mine sweepers. Painted naval grey the paddle steamers would no longer bring tourists to North Devon.

One more development is worth recording as it hints at the realization that the war would not be 'over by Christmas' but could be a drawn-out affair. In this month the county council relaxed its rules on the employment of school children on agricultural work in order to release more men for the Forces.

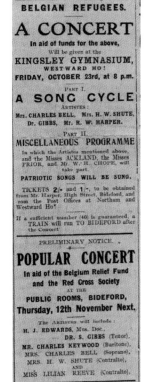

11. An advertisement for a concert in aid of the Belgians. BG 13.10.1914 2d

The First World War in North Devon

November 1914

Come November 1914 and the war was well and truly under way. Volunteers were still streaming in to recruiting stations – as the list for Bishopsnympton shows.

BISHOPSNYMPTON'S ROLL OF HONOUR.

The following are the names of those who are serving their King and Country from the Bishopsnympton parish:—Captain the Hon. G. W. W. Bampfylde. Assistant Paymaster Eric O. Tenton, Lieut. F. M. Merson. Messrs. Warren Bawden, Edward Bawden, Stanley Bawden, Ronald Bawden, John Bawden, junr., Joseph Blake, Charles Punchard, John Seatherton, junr., Henry Seatherton, William Kingdon, John Kingdon, William Tucker, George Westacott, Herbert Seage, Thomas Seage, Arthur Hussell, Edwin Ayre, Richard Elston, Wyndham Sydney Boundy, Percy Tucker, Henry Tucker, John Passmore, junr., Frederick Leeworthy, James German, Edwin Warren, Wm. Hawkes, Frederick Edbrook, John Edbrook, Henry Rodd, Henry Newcombe, Thomas Barker, W. A. Dart.

1. Volunteers from Bishopsnympton. NDJ 5.11.1914 5e

2. A Recruiting Sergeant and new recruits at Witheridge. (Copyright Beaford Arts)

By November some 352 Ilfracombe men had enlisted and as a gesture of support the town council there began to collect photographs of every one of them – wonderfully these still exist and are to be found in the town's brilliant Museum. Not to be outdone the South Molton town council formed a 'Recruiting Committee' to obtain more men. At Dolton out of a population of around 300 some 58 were in the Forces. These recruits were joined by retired officers who rejoined for the duration of the war – the *Journal* noting that virtually all the retired officers in Bideford had signed on again. A facsimile letter was sent to every borough in England from the Prime Minister encouraging recruitment.

Even at this early stage of the war voices were being heard calling for conscription to be introduced – though a long letter from R.Pyke in the *Bideford Gazette* denounced the whole concept reckoning that if Britain adopted it 'We should become materialistic, mechanical and unimaginative, no better indeed than Germany.'

By this time a steady trickle of German prisoners were being captured and men from the Bideford National Reserve were called up to guard these PoWs. At Lynton a Captain Field was forming a company of National Reserve men to guard railway bridges belonging to the Great Western Railway Company. The pre-war local military units had, of course, been posted away by now with the Royal North Devon Hussars being 'stationed on the East Coast' as the *Journal* put it – actually Clacton-on-Sea. The first volunteers for foreign service from

PARLIAMENTARY RECRUITING COMMITTEE.

12, DOWNING STREET, LONDON, S.W.

November, 1914.

Dear Sir or Madam,

We desire to draw your attention to the enclosed form, in which you are asked to state the names of those of your household who are willing to enlist for the War. By filling in and posting the Householder's Return without delay, you will render material assistance to the War Office. The names returned will be entered in a Register, and the nearest Recruiting Officer will arrange to attest those registered as their services are required.

There has been a generous response to the appeal for men for the new Armies, but the number of recruits, though large, does not nearly meet the Nation's need. In order to maintain and reinforce our troops abroad and to complete the new Armies which we hope within a few months to throw into the field, we need all the best the Nation can give us of its youth and strength.

If we are to repair as far as may be humanly possible the innumerable wrongs inflicted on our Allies, if we are to avoid for ourselves the ills which they have suffered, if we are to maintain for our children all that we hold dear – honour, freedom, our very life as a Nation – we must fight with the courage and endurance which won for us the struggles of the past

Every man, therefore, who is eligible will ask his own conscience whether, in this emergency, it is not his duty to hold himself ready to enlist in the forces of the Crown.

The difficulties and dangers which confront us have never been so great; we await the issue with confidence, relying on the spirit and self-sacrifice of our fellow-countrymen to prevail.

We are,

Your obedient Servants,

[signatures]

Presidents.

3. The Prime Minister's letter

the 6th Battalion, Devonshire Regiment, the North Devon Territorial unit, had reached India on November 11 and the *Journal* published an article entitled 'With the 6th Devons on active service' written by a Captain Pearce – which was doubtless lapped up by the men's relations.

All this activity was bolstered by a large number of eye witness accounts written by men at the Front whose families had allowed the local papers to publish them; censorship was still somewhat lax at this stage of the war. Thus letters from Pte.Arthur Turner and Cpl.H.Ashton of Barnstaple, Gunner Harry Barwick of Lynton, Pte.W.Snell of Swimbridge, Driver Albert Sharp of Ilfracombe and 2nd Lt.Alfred Hunt of Braunton were amongst those printed.

WE'VE LOOKED OVER THE GLOBE

LAHORE IS THE NICEST PLACE ON EARTH

A HAPPY CHRISTMAS

4. A postcard home.

BARUM TROOPER'S LETTER.

Corporal H. Ashton, of the 15th Hussars, attached to the Third Cavalry Division, who has relatives and friends at Barnstaple, has written as follows :—"It is slogging work and a ding-dong battle, but our lads show them what they are made of. They are the pure bull-dog breed. They go into the firing line happy and gay. Although we play the game, they (the Germans) don't by a long way. They abused the white flag not long ago, and a lot of our chaps suffered, but they made the Germans pay the penalty for it. We didn't half smash them up. . . I remember at one place the

5. A letter home. NDJ 5.11.1914 3e

DARING DEEDS AT THE FRONT.

Sir,
There have been many letters from the front telling of the work of British heroes, but I don't think that the magnificent work of Sergt. W. Wicketts, of Bideford, or better known to the troops as "Billie from Alwington," has been surpassed. Sergt. Wicketts is serving with the 4th Hussars. He has been to the front right from the beginning and my experience of him, although I have only known him a few weeks, is simply grand. He is a fine soldier, a splendid horseman and a born scout. He had already four medals having won the D.S.M. in South Africa and previously to my knowing him at the front he had won the V.C. and also been decorated with the Cross of the French Legion of Honour by the French Minister. No words that I can write can describe the splendid work of this lion-hearted hero, but I will give you a couple of my experiences. We had been fighting a terrible battle for eight days without either side gaining any advantage over the other. On the morning of the 6th day a battery of Artillery intended to come to our aid was rushing into a well planned German trap. We saw their mistake but under such a torrent of bullets we could do nothing to stop them. But Sergt. Wicketts swore he would save the battery or die in the attempt. So he rode away in the face of a storm of bullets and shells bursting in every direction. But he reached his mark, brought the battery into action and turned the tables of that terrible battle considerably in our favour. Another item I experienced. We had been fighting all day against big odds of about nine to one. We had lost very heavily, the 4th having lost all their officers and nearly being wiped out. Towards night the enemy got re-inforced with heavy guns and we looked like all going up when just in the nick of time Sergt. Wickett arrived with a troop he had collected together. He took in the situation at a glance. He turned to his men and shouting "Boys, we are not dead yet," he led his troop into a glorious charge, completely routing the enemy, taking a large number of prisoners and capturing 14 guns and we emerged victorious though with terrible slaughter out of that awful battle.
I am, Sir, your truly,
EDWARD BROWN, Sergt. Major
18th Hussars.
The Common Rest Camp, The Avenue,
Southampton, Nov. 9th, 1914.

6. A VC winner.
BG 17.11.1914 5d

Pte. Snell was in the Coldstream Guards in France and talked proudly of his regiment, 'Before we came out here they used to call us the feather-bed soldiers; now they call us the Coldsteelers, as the Germans cannot face the Guards when they charge.'

One letter described how Sergt. William Wicketts from Alwington came to win the Victoria Cross.

Where men had been wounded and were recuperating at home reporters published interviews with them, most having been wounded during the Battle of Mons. Thus L/Cpl.S.White of Heanton Street in Braunton, who had been wounded in the head, reckoned 'The Germans simply would not face the bayonet, and trenches the Devons had received orders to storm had been evacuated before our troops reached them. The German casualties had undoubtedly been appalling.' Casualties were, of course, growing in number with Cpl.L.Abbott of Ilfracombe and Pte.W.Ackland of Bideford

7. George Richards.

both being killed in action whilst Pte.J.Branch of Bideford 'died of wounds'. Another man came from Barnstaple he being George Richards who is shown here in his dress uniform as a member of the 19th (Queen Alexandra's Own) Hussars. Following his death his family sent out these black-edged death notices.

When L/Cpl.F.Norman returned to Combe Martin the whole village was decorated to welcome back the badly wounded man. A photograph of one of the early dead is reproduced here he being Francis Hoare, killed in action on HMS *Monmouth* off of Chile on 1 November 1914 aged 44.

Local papers also began to publish details of more PoWs in enemy hands with Pte.W.Branch driver of the Hartland mail cart being one of them. Five Appledore sailors had the misfortune to be in a Turkish port when that country sided with the Germans and thus they were interned.

Whilst all this was occurring Belgian refugees were arriving in ever greater numbers in the area. Barnstaple was housing some 21, Bickington 7, Bideford had 50 whilst some had even reached Beaford and Combe Martin. Local aid groups were now actively helping these displaced citizens

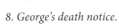

8. George's death notice.

whilst other groups were collecting warm clothing for both them and servicemen. The South Molton Ladies Sewing Party, for example, sent off 11 cwt of clothes with the Red Cross at Lynton providing 200 shirts.

Paranoia about suspected German sympathisers was less marked than earlier though George Tossell of Braunton had to publish a letter saying he had no 'pro-German sympathies' whilst Bideford-born Miss Constance Schmidt, a nursing sister at the North Devon Infirmary, had to publish a similar denial. Perhaps the oddest comment on the war in this month came from the Rev. Every of Holy Trinity in Barnstaple who wrote about the moral dangers to local young women from the presence of so many soldiers billeted in the town!

9. Francis Hoare

The First World War in North Devon

December 1914

The first Christmas of the First World War was a sombre time with many families having sent their menfolk off to fight for King and Empire. Appledore, for example, had sent 188, Northam 165, Winkleigh 39, Chulmleigh 92, Lynton 166 with even 3 coming from tiny Littleham and an astonishing 45 from St.Giles in the Woods. In Torrington a postcard commemorating the local men on the town's 'Roll of Honour' was published and featured 229 names. In Barnstaple Caroline Brayley had seen 6 of her sons join the Army whilst Thomas Parker of Eastleigh had 5 – with both receiving personal congratulations from the King.

1. The Torrington 'Roll of Honour' postcard.

2. Another postcard appeal to patriotism.

Even with these patriotic examples more men were still required and both the 6th Devons and the Royal North Devon Hussars were actively recruiting with the latter raising its third regiment. The Royal North Devon Hussars official designation was the Royal North Devon Yeomanry; but this was rarely used in the local press when referring to them.

The first overseas draft of the 6th Devons (1st/6th) had arrived in Lahore, India where they took the place of a regular battalion who had been redeployed to France. The '2nd Foreign Service Section' of the 6th Devons left for India in this month with 2000 people in Bideford lining the streets to cheer the local men on their way.

3. A group photograph of the Royal North Devon Hussars

4. Become a 'Soldier of the King'.
BG 8.12.1914 2c-d

Recruiting posters and advertisements were everywhere including the pages of the *Bideford Gazette* as the attached example shows.

Earl Fortescue even wrote to non-conformist ministers in North Devon asking them to encourage the young men in their congregations to join up – presumably the sixth commandment was a stumbling block. Not everyone, however, was convinced the war was a good thing as when a Recruiting Sergeant called to see his three sons of military age at Croyde Richard Miles, a road contractor, roundly abused him – and was subsequently fined 10/- (50p) for his outburst.

Generally though, most still firmly believed in the justice of Britain's cause even if more and more casualties were being recorded in the columns of the local newspapers. Thus L/Cpl. George Richards lost half his arm during the Battle of Mons whilst Chief Petty Officer Hiscock of Ilfracombe died when Submarine D2 was sunk and Cpl.A.Williams from Braunton was wounded by a 'dum-dum' bullet whilst serving with the Coldstream Guards. The unusually named Pte. Archelaus Curtis from Northam was killed on the 18 December aged 24.

5. Pte.Archelaus Curtis

Journal reporters interviewed some of the wounded who were being treated in the Miller Institute in Barnstaple (today's Yeo Vale School). Pte.H.Mock of Barnstaple had been wounded in the hand whilst serving with the Devons at Ypres where the British and German trenches had been only 50 yards apart. Mock reckoned 'Every day the Germans retreat more or less. The Devons had their share of the hardships, once spending 13 days in the trenches with water up to their knees, but they always "came up smiling".' The brutality of war was, however, rather casually indicated when he went on to say how he and his mates had found a German hiding in a haystack; he was 'found to be a sniper, who had caused no end of trouble among the Devons, and he was shot.' By now, of course, the whole of the Western Front was lined with trenches – only 3 months after the war had begun.

As North Devon's young men left for the Front so they were steadily replaced by Belgian refugees fleeing from the German invaders of their country. Seventy of them were given a Christmas tea by a Mrs.Kent of Ashford and fund raising to help all the Belgians in the area continued everywhere – thus a 'social evening' was held at Woolacombe along with concerts at Shirwell, Braunton and Torrington – and even carol singing at Parracombe. A Mrs.Clemson of Stevenstone offered 'Little Silver House' to a Belgian family with another house in Torrington's Castle Street also being placed at the disposal of the town's 'Belgian Committee'.

Our own servicemen were not forgotten with schoolgirls in Pilton knitting 'comforts' for soldiers. Other knitted goods came from Westdown, Eastdown and Dolton whilst villagers in Combe Martin collected enough funds to ensure all the local men in the Forces were sent an individual Christmas present. The Barnstaple 'Picturedrome' cinema invited all wounded soldiers to free matinees – where they could watch rush-released films such as 'The German Spy Peril' and 'By the Kaiser's Orders'. At Combe Martin Bowden Seed gave his motor car for use as an ambulance and the rector of Charles even set up his Rectory as a Red Cross Convalescent Home.

Perhaps the oddest comment on the war was noted in the *Journal* of 17 December when it was reported that there were no cases to be heard by the Barnstaple magistrates – a situation not seen for 40 years and even more remarkable given that some 2000 troops were billeted in the town!

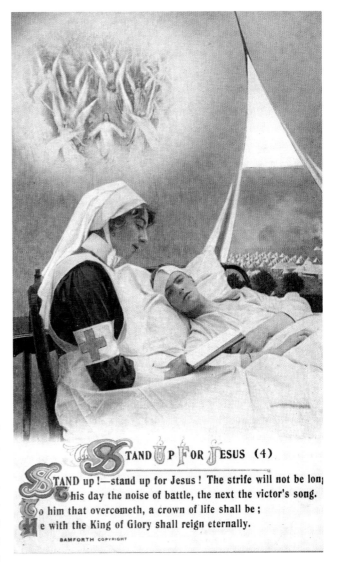

6. *A romanticised view of what being a casualty meant.*

The First World War in North Devon

January 1915

The war that many thought would be 'over by Christmas' now entered its second year and January 1915 saw a continuing call for men to enlist. The *Journal* continued to print names of new recruits such as in this section from Braunton's 'Roll of Honour' shown here.

1. Part of the Braunton 'Roll of Honour'.
NDJ 14.1.1915 6d

A novel way of obtaining more men came in this month when a detachment of the Devon Regiment arrived in South Molton and then set off on a route march around the district with a band, they managing to sign up 60 men en route. At Kingsnympton a Mr.Enfield in an excess of zeal, denounced a local farmer who refused to let his son join the Army saying 'if the Germans ever came to England, he hoped that that farmer's house would be the first to be burnt down.'

This lack of patriotism was compared to Lynmouth where an astounding 98% 'of those eligible to serve have joined the Army or Navy.' Possibly they had been encouraged by a series of cartoons published in the *Journal* and *Bideford Gazette* including these two.

More unexpected perhaps was the address in Barnstaple's Albert Hall by Miss Annie Keaney a prominent pre-War Suffragette who spoke on 'This War – Why men should join the Army.' One family who had answered the call was the Shaddicks of Green Lane in Barnstaple who had 6 sons in the Forces – and received a letter of congratulations from the King.

Some of their sons were in the local regiment the 6th Devons who were then settling down in their new posting in India whilst 180 men of the Royal North Devon Hussars (RNDH) Reserve Regiment were sent to help guard the coast at Exmouth.

2. BG 19.1.1915 7d-f

3. NDJ 28.1.1915 7c-d

4. The 6th Devons at Lahore Barracks.

5. Buglers of the 6th Devons in India.

6. An interesting mix of clothing worn by the 6th Devons in Lahore.

This photograph shows the new recruits waiting to board a train at Barnstaple Junction station in their Winter greatcoats.

7. Off to war.

8. Jack May of the RNDH pictured at Exmouth this month.

The *Journal* printed a selection of cheery letters from the local men in India along with a call from Lord Fortescue for a female boycott of shops employing men 'who were now engaged in nothing more profitable to the defence of the country than in selling ribbons and cottons and things of that kind.

As in previous months local papers published a surprising number of letters containing news from the Front including the legendary Christmas Day truce this being described in detail by Pte.H.Amy writing to his brother in the RNDH; 'On Christmas Eve our officer said "Don't shoot unless the Germans shoot" so all the night not a shot was fired. The Germans were singing and shouting "A merry Christmas to you". As day broke, a German would bob up and down, and, as we did not shoot, they plucked up courage enough to get right out. Soon their parapets were lined, and our chaps went out and met them and exchanged gifts of cigarettes etc.' He goes on to describe how the Germans seemed to have a better idea of how the war was going than did the British – one has to wonder how this letter got through censorship?

9. *HMS Monmouth.*

A more typical letter was from James Selwood of Barnstaple who was in the Navy and described his experience of the combined naval and air raid on Cuxhaven in Germany. His own vessel was attacked by German seaplanes and Zeppelins but received no damage. Perhaps the oddest letter came from Driver S.Hobbs to his parents in Lynton denying a rumour they had heard that he had been killed – indeed he was 'in very good health'. Of course some local men were amongst the dead. When HMS *Formidable* was sunk by torpedoes in the English Channel a boy-sailor from Northam called Curry went down with the ship, whilst Richard Adams a stoker from Combe Martin in HMS *Monmouth* was killed when his ship was sunk during the battle of Coronel off of Chile.

Poor L/Cpl.W.Holding from Parracombe had served unscathed in the Boer War but was killed on his first day in the trenches leaving a widow and child. He was one of 14 fatalities listed in the *Journal* this month, the worst figures for the war to date – but they were to get much worse. It wasn't all bad news as every serviceman got a Christmas present from the Royal family with all those from Berrynarbor also receiving a personal gift of tobacco and cigarettes from their fellow villagers.

One wonders what these villagers and others living in North Devon's coastal villages thought when news got out about the German Navy bombardment of Hartlepool, which killed over 100 people, whilst Zeppelins began bombing raids on Britain? Barnstaple town council immediately introduced a 'black out' from 8 p.m. each night whilst the Barnstaple cinema the Picturedrome publicised that 'Patrons are assured the necessary precautions have been taken in the remote event of a German raid' – though what these might have been is left unsaid. One definite result of the war was seen at Hartland where the carcases of horses washed up it being suggested they were 'those of horses which recently stampeded on a vessel in mid-ocean whilst being brought to this country from Canada' – presumably as part of the Canadian Forces. If these precautions and events were slightly surreal what are we to make of the order from the Chief Constable of Devon that homing pigeons in the county should not be shot, presumably because Army units were using them to communicate.

Domestic news was still heavily featuring Belgian refugees with an appeal for more accommodation for them in North Devon being put out this month. – with the offer of weekly rents to make the appeal more attractive.

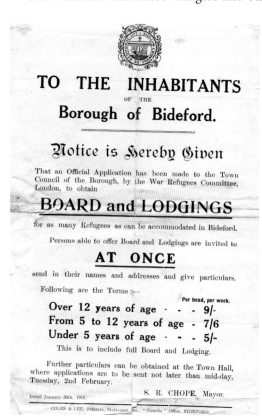

10. *A Bideford flyer appealing for refugee accommodation.*

The First World War in North Devon

February 1915

The sixth month of the war saw further emphasis on enlisting with more cartoons being published and further weekly lists of volunteers appearing including one for the Newport area of Barnstaple which added the men's addresses.

Although there were no local 'Pals Battalions' where large groups of neighbours or workmates joined up en masse it was noted in late February that about half, some sixty, of the Bideford Church Lad's Brigade, a 'paramilitary' church group, had enlisted.

Men in the 6th Devons undertook route marches in the Torrington area to attract recruits - with some 54 men signing up. Not every settlement answered the call. At Bradworthy a Colonel Griffen seems to have lost his temper when only one recruit came forward.

2. Bideford Church Lad's Brigade in camp at Saunton.

3. Bideford Church Lad's Brigade boys in the Devonshire Regiment.

1. Newport Volunteers.
NDJ 4.2.1915 6a

4. Recruiting in Bradworthy.
BG 2.3.1915 5a

Then Col. Griffen addressed the crowd, and remarked that no one of any intelligence could feel that the war was not justified, and that being so, the country wanted more men. "Why don't you come forward," he exclaimed. "Are you always going to look with your mouths open and let others do your work? Do not let the soldiers go away and leave Bradworthy in contempt. Are there none of you here with any spirit or enterprise? What will your sons say of you in years to come if you do not join the army? Will none of you make any self-sacrifice? You are content to die and have a decent funeral and you think you will get to heaven. The path to heaven lies through self-sacrifice. Good God, men of Bradworthy, are you content to stop here and let others do your fighting? Get up and show yourselves and do not for ever hide behind the women's skirts."

5. A famous cartoon. NDJ 25.2.1915 3e-f

6. Another recruiting cartoon. NDJ 4.2.1915 3c-d

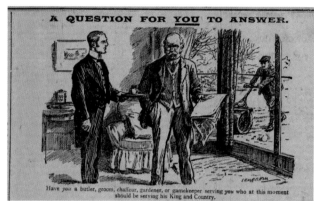

7. Send your servants to fight. BG 16.2.1915 7d-f

More cartoons designed to pressure men to enlist appeared in the local newspapers including one in the *Bideford Gazette* this month, though its clear class bias might strike us as odd today.

Bradworthy wasn't the only place where recruiting was slow. At Ashreigney where the 'majority of young men remained deaf to all entreaties' stating 'We bain't going till we be fetched.' The emphasis was still all on volunteering – with one letter, signed 'A Devonian', advocating the recruitment of North Devonians who had emigrated to the colonies. Not every man joined the Regular Forces, one alternative being the Volunteer Training Corps which had been established to allow men still employed locally to receive a basic military training. Another alternative was the National Reserve though even at this early stage of the war there were complaints about men not fulfilling pre-war promises, as a letter from a Parkham Reservist shows.

Casualties by now were a regular occurrence with men from across North Devon among the ever lengthening lists of those killed or wounded. One particularly sad death was of Pte. Walter Turner from Barnstaple who, aged just 19, was killed on his first day in the trenches. A condolence letter from his commanding officer Captain Pagan was published in the *Journal* which said Walter had been shot and 'died at once, and could have suffered no pain' – the usual form of words in letters sent to grieving parents. Not all casualties occurred on the battlefield – as with Frank Newcombe from Bideford who had been called up with the Royal North Devon Hussars but died at Exmouth probably from the kick of a horse.

Eye-witness accounts of fighting and military life were still appearing. Thus Pte. Frank Norman on sick leave at his parents' house in Barnstaple was interviewed by a journalist. He gave further details of the Christmas truce and how a German sniper had been captured trying to infiltrate the British lines. Most accounts came via letters home and varied from the celebratory to the heart rending. The former category sees that from Cpl. W.Ashton of Ilfracombe who told his aunt how he had obtained one 'of the Kaiser's famous Iron Crosses' from

LETTERS TO THE EDITOR

FARMERS SONS AND RECRUITING.

Sir,

We hear a lot of complaint about the slow way in which farmer's sons are coming forward to offer their service to their Country, and I am sure there is just cause for it. Allow me to state one case where a farmer's sons who is a National Reservist shirked his obligation made in time of peace. His father, I am informed, wrote to the Prime Minister and by this means got his son exempt from his duty. Is this fair to other National Reservists. In comparison may I state another case where a carpenter, also a National Reservist, who has a wife with seven children, has promptly been and passed the doctor for service, should he be called upon. This man may go away for a few months and come back to find his living gone, whereas the farmer, by paying a little extra wage, could keep the farm going until his son came back. This farmer has had neither man nor horse taken from him for the Army, and the only difference the war has made to him is that it has given him a higher price for the produce he has to sell. It is small wonder that we hear the working men's sons say "Let the farmer's sons go, then I will." Trusting you will find room in your valuable paper of to-morrow,

I am, sir,

ALSO A NATIONAL RESERVIST.

Parkham, February, 22, 1915.

8. A letter re farmers' sons. BG 23.2.1915 7d

a captured German officer. Another sent from G.Irwin serving on HMS *Canopus* to his relatives in Ashford gave an account of the Battle of the Falkland Islands and how his vessel now had sixty German prisoners on board.

Another letter, from Cpl. Herbert Eames of Barnstaple gave a less rosy view of the war with its clear description of the trenches.

Another from Sergt. Scobling of Braunton, who was in the Coldstream Guards, describes how he fought the enemy in hand-to-hand combat ending

9. HMS Canopus.

'The German cowards cried for mercy, but we gave them none because of their brutal treatment of harmless women and children.' Pte. J.B.Symons wrote to his parents in Barnstaple describing trench fighting commenting 'How peculiar that whereas I could not bear to witness an accident in civil life here I can pass lifeless bodies with scarce a glance.' More notices of PoWs appeared amongst them being one for Pte. Walter Bidder from Braunton who was in a prison camp in Germany. Such items were always of huge interest to anxious relatives who had only been told their men were 'Missing' and were desperately clinging to the hope they had been captured rather than killed.

Accommodation was still being sought for Belgian refugees and the offer of weekly payments attracted 200 applications to take them from Barnstaple alone.

Another 136 came from Lynton and 900 from Ilfracombe and one has to wonder how many of these were from guest house operators hit by a wartime downturn in bookings? At Torrington the town council discussed taking in between 40-50 refugees with even tiny Frithelstock taking in a family of five 'of the labouring class' as the *Bideford Gazette* report put it. In Bideford the Belgian Minister of State the Count d'Alviella came to

10. Trench warfare. NDJ 25.2.1915 5c

meet 60 out of the 175 of his fellow countrymen in the area who had gathered in the Town Hall. Whilst in Bideford he probably visited the Belgian Club set up in the Boy Scout HQ in Silver Street. The costs associated with supporting these refugees were being met from 'Relief Funds' set up in all the towns across the area with weekly subscriptions the commonest way of collecting money.

Also on the domestic front weekly egg collections were being held with the eggs being sent to war hospitals both here and in France. In Barnstaple the Mayoress sent 1000 eggs whilst an Appledore house-to-house collection saw 3-400 being gathered each week. Additionally a large number of knitted goods for the troops were sent from ladies in North Molton.

Such schemes would have allowed local people to feel they were 'doing their bit' – and their patriotism was bolstered by the showing of morale boosting films and drama in local venues. Thus the Barnstaple

11. Belgian refugees in Bideford.

13. Bath Terrace, Instow.

12. The Barnstaple Picture Palace in Silver Street.

Picturedrome staged the 'patriotic drama' film 'For the honour of Belgium' – followed a fortnight later by the films 'The Kaiser's Spy' and 'The Shirker's Nightmare' the latter directed at those who had yet to enlist. The Barnstaple Palace Electric Theatre had the film 'Apache or Hooligan Dance, as danced in the Low Parts of Paris' which probably alarmed wives and sweethearts of men in France – but might equally have encouraged young men to join the Forces!

At Petersmarland a 'Patriotic Concert' was held in the school featuring such songs as 'The Flag that never comes down' and 'Your King and Country want you' plus recitations in Devon dialect to raise funds. Of more lasting importance were three other occurrences this month. In Ilfracombe tourist charabancs were

14. Red Cross nurses working at the Instow Hospital.

15. Caroline Dark of Instow who was a nurse at the Instow Hospital.

commandeered by the military authorities and converted to motor wagons for the Army's use. At Instow the owner of Tapeley Park A.L.Christie finally opened a house in Bath Terrace as a Red Cross Hospital under Commandant Mrs.H.Miles and Quartermaster Miss M.Lock. The first wounded, from the Sherwood Foresters, immediately arriving by train.

At Bideford a small paragraph in the *Journal* announced that 'It is understood that negotiations have been taking place privately with a view to acquiring a site at East-the-Water, Bideford, for the establishment on a large scale of works by Messrs Kynock Ltd., ammunition manufacturers......The materialisation of the scheme would be a very fortunate happening for Bideford, where regular employment for male labour is needed.'

The First World War in North Devon

March 1915

March began with the usual lists of new recruits although it is clear that numbers were well down compared to earlier months. For example, only 7 men enlisted at Barnstaple in the second week of the month and at Ilfracombe only 13 had signed up over the preceding 6 weeks. To counter these low numbers a long 'Stirring Appeal' addressed to Devonians was published by the Devon Parliamentary Recruiting Committee. The final two paragraphs are reproduced here.

It is interesting that the only two places mentioned are Belgium and France, clearly the war had yet to be viewed as a World War. Also women were yet to be seen as war workers. Lord Fortescue who headed the Devon committee wrote to the local press suggesting that this lack of volunteers might lead to compulsory conscription – anathema to most at this early stage of the war.

The *Journal* published another appeal from Lt.Col.H.Ashton the Commanding Officer of the 6th Devon's depot in Castle Street, Barnstaple. After pointing out that the local battalions in India required another 150 men for their reserve company he wrote 'May I add that men who have been rejected on account of bad or deficient teeth can now be accepted, if they will please apply again.'

As a boost to enlistment publicity continued to be given to families with multiple sons in the Forces. Thus Mrs.Knill of 9 Hermitage Road, Ilfracombe was recorded as receiving a letter from the King congratulating her for having five sons in the Army and Navy. This was eclipsed only a few weeks later when Mr.& Mrs.John Smale of Hiscott in Tawstock received a similar letter as they had seven sons in the Army. Another morale-boosting report came this month when Signalman Frank Glover from Bideford who

> **MEN OF DEVON!**
> We appeal to you to strengthen our defence, to come forward now in such numbers and with such a spirit as to hasten the day of final victory, when the hateful yoke will be removed from the neck of Belgium, when the soil of France will be purified of the plague that now afflicts it, and when our beloved England will be no longer in danger of its very existence.
> **WOMEN OF DEVON!**
> We appeal to you to help the great and sacred cause by giving your consent and your blessing to the men who are willing to go, and to show in this vital matter the same patriotism and the same fine self-denial that you have shown in succouring the wounded and distressed.

1. A 'Stirring Appeal'. NDJ 11.3.1915 7c

2. HMS Cornwall.

Hartland Terriers in India.

A group of Hartland Territorials at Lahore. Back row: Lance-Corpl. Tom Newcombe, Ptes. G. H. Webber, Wm. H. Babb, James Colwill, Albert Hockin, Corpl. Morley Colwill. Second row: Ptes. Fred Thomas Walter, Leonard Deering, Frank Colwill (Military Police). Front row: Ptes. Ernest Prouse (Stackson), Sidney Jeffery, W. C. Nichol.

3. Hartland soldiers. Devon & Exeter Gazette 19.2.1915

had served on HMS *Cornwall* at the Battle of the Falkland Islands was awarded the Distinguished Service Medal. Additionally a photograph of Hartland men with the 6th Devons in India was published

If the Regular Forces were in need of more recruits the same wasn't true for the Volunteer Training Companies as, when the Barnstaple Corps held its first public parade this month, it had its full complement of 200 men although its captain was at pains to stress that membership shouldn't be seen as a way of enlisting yet avoid fighting. One reason for these moves to encourage more enlistment was the rising number of casualties. Amongst the dead were Pte.Robert Fordham from Ilfracombe who had only been married a year, Pte.William Avery of Barnstaple who left a wife and four young children and Pte.Walter Goodenough from Bishops Tawton who died 'fighting the Turk' (Turkey had allied herself with Germany at the start of the war). Such deaths would be notified to relatives by the War Office but often the first intimation would be by a letter from the dead man's friend. Thus in this month Drummer John Seery wrote to John Trace of Annery Kiln near Bideford telling how his son Harry had been killed by a shot through the heart. Rather bizarrely Seery included something in his envelope adding as a postscript to his letter 'This is also a piece of his writing paper which was in his breast pocket. The above show the hole where the bullet went through which caused his death.'

BARNSTAPLE RED CROSS HOSPITAL.

ARRIVAL OF FIFTEEN MORE SOLDIERS FROM THE FRONT.

Fifteen more soldiers from the Front arrived at the Red Cross (Miller Institute) Hospital at Barnstaple yesterday (Wednesday) afternoon, this bringing the total number at present under treatment at the Institution up to 43. The new-comers, who were conveyed in private motor cars from the Junction Station to the Hospital, are :—
Pte. G. Fauns, 2nd Batt. King's Own Royal Lancs. (frost-bitten feet);
Pte. J. Lafferty, 2nd Batt. Royal Irish Fusiliers (frost-bitten feet);
Lance-Corpl. E. Atkins, 2nd Batt. East Yorkshire Regt. (frost-bitten feet);
Pte. J. Burns, 2nd Batt. East Yorks Regt. (frost-bitten feet);
Pte. J. Smith, 2nd Batt. East Yorks Regt. (frost-bitten feet);
Pte. J. T. Black, 2nd Batt. Northumberland Fusiliers (frost-bitten feet);
Pte. J. Allman, 1st Batt. Royal Fusiliers (hip wound);
Pte. A. Roache, 1st Batt. Irish Guards (wound in shin);
Corpl. S. Fone, 2nd Batt. Cheshire Regt. (frost-bitten feet);
Pte. S. Marks, R.A.M.C. (wound in leg);
Corpl. F. Shufflebotham, 2nd Batt. Cheshires (frost-bitten feet);
Pte. H. Simmons, 1st Batt. East Surrey (rheumatism and frost-bitten feet);
Pte. J. Hartwell, 1st Batt. Welsh Regt. (frost-bitten feet);
Pte. H. Guy, 2nd Batt. Northumberland Fusiliers (frost-bitten feet);
Pte. E. Clarke, 2nd Batt. Gloucester Regt. (frost-bitten feet).

4. Arrivals at Barnstaple Red Cross Hospital. NDJ 11.3.1915 8d

THE GERMANS' RUTHLESS ACTS.

BARUMITE'S LETTER FROM THE FRONT.

Sergt. A. E. Lake, 3rd King's Own Hussars, second son of Mr. and Mrs. Edwin Lake, of Victoria-street, Barnstaple, in a letter from the Front, says :—
" We have had rotten weather—rain and snow the whole time, and knee deep in mud and water. But we were prepared for it. Before going in, we were stripped and rubbed all over with whale oil, and when we came out there were hot baths and Oxo. Then we went to sleep, and what a sleep— the first for six nights and five days. We were able to snatch a wink or two, but the German trenches were only seventy yards in front of us— so close that we were able to see their loop holes, and take snap-shots of them. Our casualties were very light—two killed and six wounded, but nearly everyone suffered more or less with frost-bite. In fact the order of the day is "Good hearts and bad feet." I am sending you a couple of postcards ; so you will be able to see what an awful mess they (the Germans) have made of the place, and they are still shelling it. In fact, it is safer in the trenches than in the towns. We spent four nights in a convent, and even there the shells have ruined half the rooms. Eight of the Guards were killed there just before we arrived. The enemy's idea is to hit the reinforcements ; but they do not do a lot of damage to the troops—it is the poor householders that suffer. I have a rosary that one of the nuns gave me as a keep-sake ; I will send it home later, with one or two other things that I have collected.'

5. A letter home. NDJ 18.3.1915 5b

Deaths on the battlefield were one thing but it seems that many deaths occurred through illness. Thus Pte. Darnell of Barnstaple succumbed to pneumonia, Pte.Shapland, also of Barnstaple (and a son of the founder of Shapland & Petter's) died of scarlet fever, Braunton's Cpl.Shambrook caught influenza and died whilst newly enlisted H.Britton, a Bideford Grammar School teacher, passed away due to 'fever' in London. That illness rather than enemy action was causing a high mortality rate is shown in the list of ailments of new arrivals at the Barnstaple Red Cross Hospital

Further eye-witness accounts of the fighting continued to appear. One from L/Cpl.C.Brown of Ilfracombe recounted how three shots from an anti-aircraft gun mounted on a Devon regiment's armoured car brought down a German aircraft. Another Ilfracombe soldier Pte.Sydney Macro had taken part in a charge against the Germans near Messines. During this he had 'bayoneted two Germans, smashed in the head of a third

The Hon. Treasurer of the Belgian Relief Fund desires to acknowledge, with thanks, the following donations and subscriptions:—Collection at Barnstaple Parish Church Infants' School, 12s.; Landkey parish (one week's subscription), £1; Ashleigh-road School (one month's subscription), £1; servants at Hawley (one month's subscription), 2s.; Mr. H. J. Hutchings (one month's subscription), 5s.; Miss Mew (one month's subscription), 10s.; Barnstaple Girls' Secondary School (one week's subscription), £1; Miss Marshall (four weeks' subscription), 4s.; Mrs. Brooks (four weeks' subscription), 4s.; Mr. F. W. Hunt (four weeks' subscription), 8s.; Mrs. Impey (four weeks' subscription), 4s.; Mrs. Symonds (five weeks' subscription), 5s.; Mrs. Martin (one month's subscription), £2; Barnstaple Grammar School (collection), 13s.; employés, Smyth and Sons, drapers (one month's subscription), 7s. 6d.; Mrs. Smyth (one month's subscription), 4s.; Mr. F. G. Smyth (one month's subscription), 10s.; Mr. T. Harkins (one month's subscription), 4s.; the Misses Yeo (two months' subscription), £1; Goodleigh parish (one week's subscription), £1; Mr. William Mules (proceeds of whist drive at Arlington), £1; employés, Alexandra Foundry (one week's subscription), 4s.; Mrs. Langdon (20 weeks' subscription), 10s.; Miss G. Ford (two weeks' subscription), 5s.

6. Helping the refugees. NDJ 11.3.1915 5d

7. 'Commons' Hospital at Northam with some wounded soldiers.

LUNDY ISLAND AS INTERNMENT CENTRE.

In the House of Commons on Tuesday afternoon,

Mr. WATTS asked the Under-Secretary for War whether his Department had considered the advisability of utilising the island of Lundy in the Bristol Channel for the internment of German prisoners; and whether he was aware that the present building thereon could accommodate as many as 1,600 prisoners, and that the old buildings, formerly used as houses for quarrymen, could in a few weeks be made suitable for several thousand prisoners.

Mr. TENNANT said the advisability of using Lundy Island as a place of detention for prisoners of war had been considered, and it was decided to be unsuitable.

8. Lundy as a PoW camp. NDJ 18.3.1915 5g

with the butt of his rifle after his bayonet was broken, and shot yet another.' Most accounts are not as bloodthirsty as this with many letters home harping on the wet conditions and the availability of food - though Pte.Mervyn Ninnies of Barnstaple reported on his trench work, 'Then there are wire entanglements to be put out in front, and that's a very trying job as the Germans are continually sending up what we call star shells, and they light the country for miles around, and then the men who are out have to duck even if it is water up to the waist.' Occasionally these letters home supply slightly unusual details of the men's lives – such as this one shown from Sergt,Lake of Barnstaple.

This military news would have taken up most people's attention but everyday life continued, albeit with unusual features, the major one of which was the continual arrival of Belgian refugees. Thus 100 came to Ilfracombe this month whilst other small numbers arrived at Hartland, Barnstaple and Bideford. In order to support them events such as a concert in Braunton were held and local subscribers to the Belgian Relief Fund were listed in local newspapers.

Eggs for the wounded continued to be collected and the men themselves arrived in local hospitals and convalescent homes including 7 at Court House, North Molton whilst wounded Belgian soldiers were being treated at Westwell Hall at Torrs Park in Ilfracombe – a temporary hospital which closed in April 1915. The Bideford branch of the Red Cross under Commandant Mrs.M.Bazeley prepared the large house 'Commons' at Northam as an auxiliary hospital for 36 men with the first 9 wounded soldiers arriving this month.

Bideford itself also saw definite news as to the establishment of a new munitions factory at East-the-Water in the town. This was to be built by Messrs.Kynock Ltd. 'ammunition manufacturers' to produce 'acetone or cordite' from wood. The 5-10 acre site was to have its own railway siding with the raw material being supplied by Messrs.Bartlett, Bayliss & Co. whose yard was adjacent.

Such a public description of a vital war factory might strike us as odd but this was before large scale Zeppelin bombing raids on this country and it is worth noting that apart from one or two cryptic references this is the last mention during the war of the factory in the local press.

Two examples of how the war itself was coming closer to North Devon occurred this month when, firstly, the ss *Bengrove* with a cargo of coal was sunk 'probably by a torpedo' 4-5 miles off of Ilfracombe. All 33 crew were saved and landed at Ilfracombe many having just a shirt and trousers to their name. Secondly, a letter was published in the *North Devon Journal* suggesting Lundy as a Prisoner of War camp for Germans – an idea the War Office did not take up.

The happiest piece of news this month was when Signalman Frank Glover DSM returned home to Bideford to be met at the station by a huge crowd. This was followed by a civic reception in the Town Hall where the Mayor presented him with an inscribed gold watch and chain (with his mother being given a plated jam dish) after which he was escorted to his house in Clifton Street by the town band.

The First World War in North Devon

April 1915

The decline in numbers of those enlisting continued this month with the Barnstaple recruiting officer who served both the town and a large surrounding area recording on average just one man per day during April. To encourage would-be recruits the local newspapers began publishing 'appeals' in the form of letters from serving soldiers some of which read suspiciously like War Office approved wording. Others like the second from Lt.J.Braddick of Northam sound rather more genuine.

BARUM SOLDIER'S APPEAL FOR RECRUITS.

Driver A. H. McLeod, of the Ammunition Column Royal Garrison Artillery, in a letter from the Front to his wife at Barnstaple, says:—
"Shrapnel shells are bursting overhead while I write, and the aeroplanes are a very fine sight to watch. We get a visit from a German taube nearly every night. One of these was brought down on Thursday. The guns are still banging away on their errand of destruction. The infantry—brave lads—are marching up to the trenches, some never to return again; but they go quite cheerful, never thinking about danger. When are the men at home coming out to replace these gallant soldiers? Tell them not to order their summer suits, but to accept the khaki, the only clothes worth wearing at the present time—and which will cost them nothing. No doubt they read about and see pictures of the War, but they ought to come out and actually realise what things are like. All that is necessary, in short, is for them to screw up their courage and to see the man with three stripes without further delay."

1. Serving soldiers appeal for recruits.
NDJ 29.4.1915 5g

GERMAN SNIPERS.
"Every fourth day I go up to the forward observation station, which is but 70 yards from the German infantry trenches, and they know you are there, but covered by our infantry, so they dare not rush out at you unless they charge our trenches. You bet your life I don't put up my head. They pot at my periscope when I put it up.
"Coming to the serious side, you people at home haven't the slightest idea what it is like, and I don't know how anyone who considers himself a man can stay there. It is a shame. I say, close theatres, pubs, and everything. I should like to have all unmarried fellows out here and shove them up in the first firing line. I believe conscription is our only remedy, but the cowards who are funking should have a different badge from us. If you could only see what I have seen it would kill you.

2. A letter from Lieut.J.Braddick BG
27.4.1915 5d

Additionally, jingoistic poetry was published including one from B.Reed of Fern Brook, Ilfracombe titled '*Wanted; Not Conscription – Volunteers*' A typical one of its eleven verses reads;

Sons of Devon, arise to service;

War is raging o'er the way.

Take your stand against the foeman –

Join the ranks without delay,

Help your brothers in the trenches,

Take your share of slush and mud.

Gird your sword against the legions

Though its price may be your blood.

Descriptions of the fighting in letters home which were then published in the local newspapers might well have given possible recruits second thoughts although such letters always stressed the nobility of the British as in to the bestiality of their enemies as in one from Pte.Endicott overleaf.

The bloody reality of war was sinking in with ever lengthening lists of those 'killed in action' or 'died of wounds'. Thus Pte.Alfred Giddy of Bideford, Pte.Harry Guard of Barnstaple, Pte.Gammon of Marwood and Pte.Crumb of Monkleigh all died in the trenches. One luckier soldier was Pte.William 'Curly' Matthews of Barnstaple who was reported as having died of his wounds in a letter from his 'bosom friend' Pte.J.Cornish – only for his widowed mother to receive notification a few days later from the Red Cross that her son was alive he having been taken to hospital in Norwich! This month saw the first public displays of photographs of men serving

BARUMITE'S LETTERS FROM THE FRONT.

Mr. and Mrs. Endicott, of King's Close Cottages, Barnstaple, have recently received several letters from their son, Pte. Bert Endicott, Royal Army Medical Corps, with the British Expeditionary Force.

Writing under date March 13th, Pte. Endicott says:—" We have just returned from four days in the trenches. We had two killed and about ten wounded. I was lucky; I was hit in the shoulder with a bit of shrapnel, but it didn't break the skin, and I am all right again now. Our troops succeeded in capturing a town; I expect you will see about it in the papers. We had a lot of German wounded and prisoners, and the poor chaps looked so bad that I could not help feeling sorry for them."

In the second letter (of March 15th) Pte. Endicott states :—" We went back to the trenches again on Sunday morning, and have just come out again this (Monday) afternoon. Everything was very quiet up there this time, and we only had two casualties. In the middle of last night we went out between our trenches and those of the enemy and brought in twenty wounded Germans. We wondered if their R.A.M.C. would risk their lives to save us, as we did to save their men. It was an awful journey, up to our knees in mud and water at times, and the dead were lying about the fields wholesale."

Under date March 20th, Pte. Endicott says :—" Have not been in the trenches since last Monday; we are having a rest now. Referring to the recent battle one German said ' Ze Eengleesh urteelery terrible.' We had a German aeroplane over us dropping bombs, and one piece dropped uncomfortably close to me—about 2ft. away. I now have it in my possession. Two bombs killed four people and wounded ten—all French civilians I think our guns brought the airman down at the finish."

3. Letter from Pte. Bert Endicott. NDJ 8.4.1915 6a

in the Forces with a frame containing 54 such shots of local men unveiled in Ilfracombe Town Hall whilst the Northam Boy Scouts placed a photograph of their former member Edward Currie in their meeting room he having gone down with HMS *Formidable*.

Another civic reception was held when Pte. George Wright of the Devonshire Regiment was welcomed home at South Molton. He had fought during the retreat from Mons and been wounded seventeen times. After five operations over six months he had been honourably discharged from the Army as medically unfit. The Mayor in his speech of welcome was remarkably obtuse when he noted 'Seventeen wounds, ladies and gentlemen. If the Germans use their ammunition on all occasions as they did on this Devon of ours it is little wonder that they are running short!'

EDWARD JOHN CURRIE.

Son of George and Rose Currie.
Able Seaman – R.N.
Killed on H.M.S. Formidable – Jan. 1st 1915.
Aged 17.

4. Edward Currie of HMS Formidable.

Whilst fierce fighting was going on in France and Belgium the men who had joined the 6th Devons and were in India were enjoying sightseeing and sports as shown by many cheery letters appearing in the local press. The Royal North Devon Hussars in Clacton passed their time in cross-country steeplechases, billiard matches and football games.

Another local military formation the Volunteer Training Corps continued to grow with the Bideford body reaching 70 men they carrying out drill in the town's Victoria Park and the Barnstaple Corps meeting near the Junction station.

5. RNDH men outside a pub in Clacton.

6 & 7. The Bideford VTC exercising in Victoria Park.

8. The Bideford VTC marching along the Quay.

9. The Barnstaple VTC by the station. (Copyright Beaford Arts)

10. The Torrington National Reserve.

In addition to the VTC there was also the National Reserve but as this photograph of the Torrington National Reserve shows they were rather old to be viewed as efficient troops.

On the domestic front more Belgian refugees arrived in North Devon with a Belgian Club being opened for them on the Strand in Barnstaple. In Ilfracombe the YMCA opened its premises to the 150 Belgians then in the town whilst in Fremington ten refugees were being housed and Braunton received its first family.

That they had settled in well was shown when two married in Barnstaple's Roman Catholic church this month. Some had even managed to arrive in Britain carrying some fine lace which was sold in Barnstaple to raise living expenses.

One odd event this month was when the Dutch steamer ss *Flora* ran ashore at Hartland. Luckily the crew were able to walk ashore and were then taken to Bideford – where they were placed

11. The Dutch steamer ss Flora ashore at Hartland/.

under military guard. An enterprising Ilfracombe photographer Ernest Lees cycled to Hartland to take shots of the stranded vessel but was only allowed to continue after close questioning by Naval officers and having promised to provide copies of the 17 photographs he took to the Flag Commandant of Plymouth.

The crew were viewed as 'aliens' hence their treatment – and this month saw the first court case under the Aliens Restriction Order which imposed movement limits on non-British nationals. Sabina Ham 'an English lady married to a German officer' was charged with travelling from Surrey to Instow 'without a permit from the registration officer'. The chair of the magistrates hearing her case in Barnstaple

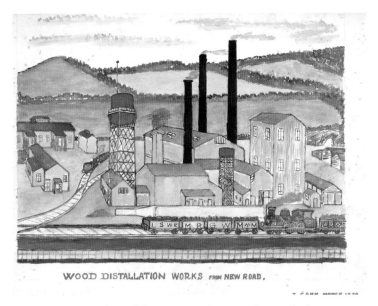

WOOD DISTALLATION WORKS FROM NEW ROAD.

12. A naïve watercolour of the Munitions factory with its rail siding.

dismissed the case on a technicality but did note 'As they all knew the country was flooded with spies – although they did not say that defendant was one of these.'

Two months after it was announced that a munitions factory based on wood distillation would be opening at East-the-Water in Bideford came news that 'The pre-prepared buildings will be quickly put together when the foundations are in, and it is expected when the works are in operation in June, about eighty men will be employed there.' This publicity about the new military factory might strike us as odd today but the first Zeppelin bombing raid on London only occurred in May 1915 – and as noted previously following this April article the works remain virtually unmentioned in press reports.

One other issue also surfaced this month. For many years the North Devon branch of the Preventive and Rescue Workers' Association (under various names) had been active in the area helping to keep young people on the moral 'straight and narrow' or 'rescuing many young lives from sin and misery' as they put it. At their April meeting in Barnstaple Parish Rooms their president, the Countess Fortescue, reckoned that owing to the war 'Great excitement and recklessness had come among young girls, and they were very difficult to deal with.' This theme was to be revisited often during the war.

On a happier note a Barnstaple soldier sent a captured German helmet, complete with a bullet hole, home to his grandparents – such relics were greatly prized and one wonders how he managed to send it back via the military postal service.

The First World War in North Devon

May 1915

The idea that the fighting would quickly be over had been long gone by this the tenth month of the war. Casualty numbers were spiralling upwards and the need for new recruits was becoming urgent. In North Devon 130 men of the local 6th Battalion of the Devonshire Regiment undertook route marches from Barnstaple to Bideford, Barnstaple to Ilfracombe and also Barnstaple to South Molton. Accompanied by a bugle band from Tavistock the aim was to secure 100 recruits who, after training, would be sent to the existing Battalions in India.

Arriving in Bideford the Mayor S.Chope speaking of recruitment said 'although Bideford had done so well there were still many young men there who could go if they would.' These sentiments were echoed by the Mayor of South Molton who, whilst welcoming the men in the Square before a large crowd, said 'If there were any slackers in the crowd he hoped they would feel ashamed and come forward' adding somewhat ominously 'If they did not do so voluntarily the Government ought to take the matter in hand and compel them to.' The marches do seem to have boosted numbers but only briefly.

One problem was that other units were attracting recruits at the same time. Thus the 2/7th Devon Cyclist Battalion visited Bideford early in May and secured ten recruits in a few days. Others enlisted into the Royal North Devon Hussars.

THE MAYOR OF BIDEFORD (MR. S. R. CHOPE.)

1. Mayor S.Chope

2. A section of the RNDH pictured in Barnstaple.

3. Some of the same men appear in this shot.

*4. Officers of the Barnstaple VTC.
NDJ 6.5.1915 6d*

In addition the various local Volunteer Training Corps were signing up men. Barnstaple, Bideford, Appledore, Northam, Westward Ho! and Ilfracombe all had VTC units and the *Journal* published a list of officers of the Barnstaple unit including, slightly unexpectedly, a clergyman.

By the end of May the first local, 'rural' VTC had been formed in Landkey.

Earl Fortescue, the Lord Lieutenant of Devon, visited Bideford to drum up recruits noting with admiration that the town had already provided 550 men for the Forces – around 1 in 7 of the entire male population of the town – including 8 shop assistants from Tattersill's Stores as shown in this advertisement.

This was heartening news but the local Recruiting Sergt.Greenway rather spoilt the atmosphere when he noted that the men left in the town were saying 'I will go when I am made and I shall not go before.' Another indication of problems with recruitment came this month when a 'Bantam Battalion' was initiated for the West of England. As their name suggests these units were for men initially rejected on account of their height they accepting men down to 5 feet in height. Concerns over the possible introduction of conscription were met with a Government denial, which saw a prolific Bideford poet, Edith Gerrard, pen an over-heated piece which was printed in the *Bideford Gazette* this month.

As mentioned, casualties continued to be reported, especially after the launching of the Gallipoli expedition. Local men were involved in this including Lt.Col.Robert Hume of Lynton who died of the wounds he received, having first joined the Army in 1885. Another Gallipoli casualty was Pte.R.Kendle of South Molton who was serving with the New Zealand Contingent. In addition to these were three local men; W.Tythcott of Bideford, S.Passmore of Combe Martin and E.Antell of Parracombe who, serving as Naval stokers, were killed when HMS *Goliath* was torpedoed by the Turks. They were among the 570 out of her complement of 750 who went down with the ship.

Such sanguine reports stand in contrast to the cheery, morale-boosting letters still being sent home by servicemen which were then published in local newspapers. Thus Pte.Herbert Eller wrote to his mother in

5. A Bideford shop's 'Roll of Honour'. BG 11.5.1915 5d-f

" NO CONSCRIPTION FOR BRITAIN," 22nd April, 1915

" No Conscription " ! This the news that joyfully we read to-day ;
So, with lightened heart and voice we shout Hurrah ! Thank God ! we say.
Ne'er shall Britain's jealous foes with truth cast on us with'ring shame,
" Britishers are cowards, shirkers ' ! that ' they're only men in name '.
Our fair Isles will rise EN MASSE, and shew them we are not afraid,—
Shew them well our grit and mettle ; and the stuff of which we're made.
Noble is our name in history ; noble were our deeds of yore ;
Noble are our deeds to-day—ay, noble as they were before !
Valiant men go forth to fight ! Why drag them ? none bend craven knee ;
If they fall, they fall in battle, fighting hard for victory !
Weigh the prowess of all Nations in the balance—England's Pride
Can compete and win with honour : she's not wrapped in coward's hide !
Motherland of lusty Sons ! just shew them truly you have need
Of their flesh and bone and sinews, in their love for you they'll bleed
With bright smiles upon their faces, with no quiver in their limbs
They will strive, and fight and conquer, till Death sight and senses dims.
They are noble—noble impulse finds a home in noble breast—
They go forth for noble causes ; come they back or meet they REST !
They will never shame their Colours, falter in the fiercest fight ;
Proud, aloft they'll raise their Standard for their Country, God and Right !
How the deeds of glorious valour, high resolve and brave renown
In the danger zone of ocean, on the battle-field, in town.
Fill our hearts with strong emotion, thrill the blood within our veins,
Seem to give us actual vision ; hear we martial sounds and strains ;
And we offer fervent praises to the Mighty God on high,
He has made our soldiers, sailors, sharers of His Majesty ;
He has made our brethren deathless, for their deeds will live for aye :
They may pass away from us, but love and sacrifice must stay
In mem'ry's depths enshrined, revered, sanctified by grateful love,
We yield what love has perfected to the Father up above !
                    EDITH C. GERRARD.

*6. Edith Gerrard's anti-conscription poem.
BG 4.5.1915 2e-f*

7. HMS Goliath.

Barnstaple saying 'If the Germans are not more careful how they fire their guns, I believe they will be hitting somebody before long.' Again L/Cpl.J.Winser of Brayford reckoned that the Germans 'detest our bayonets, and would sooner run miles than stand their ground with the British' whilst Cpl.Frank Colwill of Braunton, whilst home on sick leave, said 'The soldiers at the Front were extremely cheerful and were well looked after, especially with regard to tobacco etc.'

Other letters weren't quite so cheerful. Sergt.W.Scobling of Braunton wrote how 'A lot of our troops now refuse to take any prisoners' saying as they attacked the Germans 'Don't forget the Lusitania, boys.' This was a reference to a Cunard steamer that was torpedoed on 7 May with the loss of 1198 lives including 128 Americans – an act that swung US opinion against the Axis powers. North Devonian Pte.Frank Knill recorded how 'I am at present living in a cellar, and get into it by crawling through a hole in the wall' this being next to 'a big mound under which, we are told, lie 36 Germans.'

One particularly nasty aspect of the war is first referred to in letters home this month – the use of gas. Philip Slade-King of Ilfracombe noted that 'On the 22nd [April] the Germans sprayed the French trenches with tar, vitriol and asphyxiating gas, the troops fled in panic for two miles and the Germans broke through.'

8. Barnstaple Mayoress Mrs.F.Jewell.

Sapper R.Lang wrote to his brother in Barnstaple noting that when the Germans used 'their horrible gas…we cover our mouths with a wet cloth and fix a respirator over our noses, this takes off the worst of it.' The use of poison gas saw Lord Kitchener tell Parliament that the Allies would reply in kind.

One unusual letter came from R.Ridge of Ilfracombe who was in the forces that had entered German South West Africa. Notwithstanding that the retreating Germans had poisoned the wells with 'carbolic oil' and destroyed the railway lines the Allied troops were making steady progress and this German colony surrendered in early July.

Back in North Devon the Mayoress of Barnstaple Mrs.F.Jewell made known the military need for extra sandbags – and within a week she could announce that 500 were being sent to France. At the same time the Countess Fortescue appealed for bandages 'badly needed for our wounded soldiers and sailors in the Dardanelles.'

The sale of Belgian lace in Barnstaple had gone so well that Madame Vandeuelde Foiret who ran it repeated the exercise in Bideford. Other Belgians staged a fund raising concert in Barnstaple whilst another refugee couple married in that town's Catholic church. Clearly the refugees were settling in well but they were still 'foreigners' and as such subject to government suspicion as an advertisement from the end of the month proved.

One 'enemy alien' appeared in the Barnstaple court after he had been caught travelling more than the prescribed 5 miles from his registered accommodation in Lynton. Fritz Adler had actually been attending local hunts at the time and although he claimed to support Britain in the war rather than his country of birth he was still fined £10 plus £10 in costs – a very hefty sum at this date (about £1600 at current prices).

Local feelings were, of course, running high after the sinking of the *Lusitania* which had been denounced in sermons in local churches. Additionally the constant arrival of wounded men in North Devon hospitals would have heightened antagonism to any Germans. At Ilfracombe anti-German feeling would have

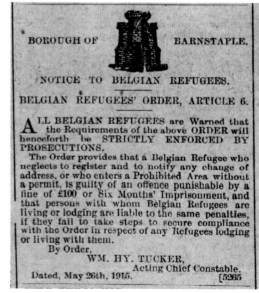

BOROUGH OF BARNSTAPLE.

NOTICE TO BELGIAN REFUGEES.

BELGIAN REFUGEES' ORDER, ARTICLE 6.

ALL BELGIAN REFUGEES are Warned that the Requirements of the above ORDER will henceforth be STRICTLY ENFORCED BY PROSECUTIONS.

The Order provides that a Belgian Refugee who neglects to register and to notify any change of address, or who enters a Prohibited Area without a permit, is guilty of an offence punishable by a fine of £100 or Six Months' Imprisonment, and that persons with whom Belgian Refugees are living or lodging are liable to the same penalties, if they fail to take steps to secure compliance with the Order in respect of any Refugees lodging or living with them.

By Order,

WM. HY. TUCKER,
Acting Chief Constable.

Dated, May 26th, 1915. [5265

9. An order concerning Belgian refugees.
NDJ 27.5.1915 1e

increased after the ss *Dumfries* was torpedoed off of the coast. Of the 53 crew all but 2 were brought ashore safely being accommodated at the Lyn Boarding House.

One event presaging more in the future was a strike by Barnstaple bakers who were demanding a 54 hour week with a minimum wage of 28/-. The strike was soon settled but as wartime inflation became rampant so such labour disputes became more common.

Also in this month warnings about a weakening of morality due to war-induced 'excitement' appeared to be true when it was reported how a 15 year old Barnstaple girl became infatuated with a wounded soldier in the town's war hospital. When he returned to his wife in Manchester she stole money from her mother and followed him. Brought back home she was found guilty of theft and was sent to a church-run girls' home – probably leaving many parents worrying about their own daughters.

Another woman making the news was Mrs.Perryman of Braunton whose husband had joined the Army. She then took over his cab business having 'undertaken the duties of grooming horses, washing carriages, as well as acting as driver' - a sign of things to come. If women were suddenly taking over positions previously occupied by men other aspects of normal life were also changing. John Christie, owner of the golf links at Saunton, gave permission to soldiers to play golf on Sundays – although he did write to the Rev.J.Davies of Braunton stressing 'he did not sanction its permanency.'

10. One of the Belgian refugees photographed in Bideford this month.

The First World War in North Devon

June 1915

As in previous months the need for more men to enlist was paramount and the Devon Parliamentary Recruiting Committee arranged for a 25 strong group of men from the 3rd Devons, known as the Special Reserve Battalion, including some wounded soldiers, to undertake a series of 'recruiting marches' through the area. They arrived from Plymouth at Mortehoe station at the end of May and marched behind their band to Woolacombe. Here various speeches were made with one speaker advising single women that 'the only sweethearts they ought to have today were those in khaki' adding 'the Germans were the most blackguardly, foulest, and most savage enemy this Empire had ever been up against.'

From here they marched to Lee where similar sentiments were expressed and then moved on to a flag-bedecked Ilfracombe where they were joined by 60 members of the Officers' Training Corps from West Buckland School. At this stop the speakers praised the 500+ men from the town who had enlisted –with some 300 photographs of them now being displayed in the Town Hall. Lieut.Larder who was in charge of the party remarked that on passing through the streets he had seen young men in some of the shops whose jobs could 'easily be taken by girls'.

Over the next few days the group marched to Lynton, returning to Barnstaple by train. From here the next day they marched to Bideford where 'recruit after recruit stepped forward in answer to the call, and

1,2,3 & 4. Men of the Devonshire Regiment on the recruiting march arrive in Ilfracombe.

were taken straight off to the doctor, passed and attested.' Some, however, 'were found to be under age or otherwise ineligible.' The following day they came back to Barnstaple and then marched to Landkey although the journalist covering the event noted that 'It was noticeable at all the villages that young men of military age were mainly conspicuous by their absence though at Chittlehampton four girls with relatives in the Forces joined the group and marched the 14 miles to Barnstaple where they 'marched through the streets….carrying rifles on their shoulders.'

The party's last day was spent in Barnstaple before returning to Exeter they being seen off at the station by a huge crowd singing patriotic songs. Whilst in Barnstaple Lieut.Larder did raise the complaint that many local farmers were refusing to allow their sons to enlist – a sore point and one which would be raised again over the next few years. Additionally it was later noted that 'of those who volunteered only a comparatively small number were really eligible' which rather detracted from the success of the proceeding. At many of the places the men stopped the local speaker proudly recorded how many men had enlisted in their parish – as shown in this set of figures.

Woolacombe – 54	Kentisbury – 20	Newton Tracey – 11
Lee – 40	Parracombe – 32	Westleigh – 50
Ilfracombe – 500+	Tawstock – 83	Bideford – 600
Lynton – 200	Lovacott – 4	Chittlehampton – 60
Combe Martin – 120	Horwood – 8	Barnstaple – c.1000

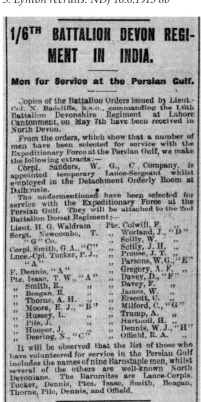

THE visit of the Recruiting detatchment of the 3rd Devons to Lynton last week resulted in 13 recruits (inclusive of those who volunteered at Tuesday's meeting) successfully passing the medical test, and being sent on to Exeter. Their names are:—Messrs. G. P. Crocombe, Harold Reed, W. Copp, D. W. Hoyles, Albert Ash, John Bulger, E. Sedgebeer, Horace Davey, T. Essery, A. Wigmore B. Crick, P. Murley, Samuel Sloley. Several of the recruits left on Thursday, and on the station, prior to their departure, they were presented by the Rev. Gordon Baillie and Mrs. Baillie, with half-a-crown each, and by Mr. T. Trevenen with cigarettes.

5. Lynton recruits. NDJ 10.6.1915 8b

1/6TH BATTALION DEVON REGIMENT IN INDIA.

Men for Service at the Persian Gulf.

Copies of the Battalion Orders issued by Lieut.-Col. N. Radcliffe, D.S.O., commanding the 1/6th Battalion Devonshire Regiment at Lahore Cantonment, on May 7th have been received in North Devon.

From the orders, which show that a number of men have been selected for service with the Expeditionary Force at the Persian Gulf, we make the following extracts:—

Corpl. Sanders, W. G., C Company, is appointed temporary Lance-Sergeant whilst employed in the Detachment Orderly Room at Dalhousie.

The undermentioned have been selected for service with the Expeditionary Force in the Persian Gulf. They will be attached to the 2nd Battalion Dorset Regiment:—

Lieut. H. G. Waldram	Pte. Colwill, F.
Sergt. Newcombe, T.	„ Worland, J., "D "
"G " Co.	„ Scilly, W. „
Corpl. Smith, G.A. "C"	„ Scilly, J. H, „
Lnce.-Cpl. Tucker, P.J.,	„ Prouse, J. T. „
"A "	„ Parsons, W.G. "E"
F. Dennis, "A "	„ Gregory, A. F. „
Pte. Isaac, T. W., "A "	„ Davey, D., "F "
„ Smith, E., „	„ Davey, F. „
„ Beagan, R. „	„ James, W. „
„ Thorne, A. H. „	„ Erscott, C. „
„ Moore, E. J., "B "	„ Milford, C., "G "
„ Hussey, L. „	„ Trump, A. „
„ Pile, J. „	„ Hartnoll, H., „
„ Hooper, J. „	„ Dennis, W. J., ."H "
„ Deering, N., "C"	„ Offield, R. A. „

It will be observed that the list of those who have volunteered for service in the Persian Gulf includes the names of nine Barnstaple men, whilst several of the others are well-known North Devonians. The Barumites are Lance-Corpls. Tucker, Dennis, Ptes. Isaac, Smith, Beagan, Thorne, Pile, Dennis, and Offield.

Names of the men continued to be published in the local newspapers as with these men from Lynton.

Amongst the men from Bideford were 2 'Bantams' – John Edwards and John Shortridge.

The various Volunteer Training Corps continued to sign up men with new groups being set up in Fremington, Braunton and Lynton. The Barnstaple Corps was photographed by R.L. Knight with copies being displayed in his High Street shop. The Bideford Corps on one occasion marched to Northam Burrows where they met contingents from Northam, Appledore and Westward Ho! Here they carried out various drills – none of which seemed to have much to do with trench warfare.

Whilst all this was going on in North Devon a selection of those local men already serving in India were being selected to join an 'Expeditionary Force' going to the Persian Gulf to attack the Turks. It should be noted that they volunteered for this almost certainly hazardous undertaking.

They wouldn't just be fighting the enemy but would also have to deal with the debilitating temperatures. Indeed in the same week as this report about the Expedition arrived in North Devon another news

TORRINGTONIAN KILLED IN ACTION

Great sympathy was expressed for Mr. and Mrs. T. Nicholls, of Calf-street, Torrington, when it became known, on Monday that they had received an intimation from the War Office that their son Harry had been severely wounded in France on May 9th and died the same day. The deceased upon leaving School became an errand boy for Messrs. Snow and Co., and so completely won the confidence of the firm that he was made storeman at an early age. He held the position at the time of his enlistment in September. He was a steady and well-conducted young fellow, greatly liked, and his death so soon after passing out of his teens is deeply lamented by a large circle of friends.

Private Nicholls was one of ten Torringtonians who crossed to France together early in April, five of whom were wounded in the same battle in which young Nicholls lost his life. The other four are making good progress.

7. The death of Pte.H.Nicholls of Torrington. NDJ 10.6.1915 5e

6. Volunteers from the 1/6th Devons off to fight in Mesopotamia. NDJ 17.6.1915 6b

item concerned William Hammett from Appledore, a member of the Royal Naval Reserve, who had died of sunstroke in the Persian Gulf.

Other casualties were recorded in Gallipoli including Major J.Bruce of Barnstaple and Pte.William Crang of Ilfracombe. Often the newspaper reports of these deaths were accompanied by small obituaries – usually brief given the young age and limited life experience of so many – as with Pte.Nicholls of Torrington..

Letters home continued to be printed in the newspapers. One from Pte.Symons to his parents in Barnstaple detailed the semi-domestic arrangements he had found in some German trenches – 'Dug outs made of wood entirely, and the walls papered or covered with printed linen. Shelves too, openings for windows, and in some furnished stuff too. Their trenches beat ours altogether.' Such correspondence was usually censored by the men's officers but one from Pte.C.Wood to his brother in Ilfracombe must have somehow escaped their attention he writing about a British sally 'by some very mysterious means they knew everything about the attack, and were waiting for our lads four deep.'

Not all were so negative, however. Thus when Driver Albert McLeod wrote from Flanders he mentioned the still novel Royal Flying Corps 'Aeroplanes continue to be very active. We often see a dozen up at once scouting around ….All our airmen are heroes and not until the war is over shall we know the great part they have played in this the greatest of all wars.'

One letter described the fighting in West Africa where the Germans had some small colonies. Seaman R.Cann of Bradiford had been serving on HMS *Challenger* when they shelled various German garrisons and Cann landed with other sailors, Marines and British native troops to capture them. Another theatre of war in Africa featured in a letter from Vincent Attree of Lynmouth who was in the force that had invaded German South West Africa. Here 'The country is fifty times harder to fight than the Germans' there being a severe lack of fresh water and food.

Letters also appeared written from Gallipoli and these were particularly harrowing. Mr and Mrs.Handford of Torrington heard from their son serving as a dentist on a hospital ship in the Dardanelles who wrote about the boats coming to his vessel 'one after the other with dead, dying and wounded.' The most terrible letter, however, came from Pte.P.Tresise of Barnstaple who recorded how 'Some of our men that we treated had their noses cut off and some had the tendons in their legs severed, and one officer was found crucified with four bayonets through him.'

Doubtless horror stories like this spurred those at home to ever greater efforts to support the fighting men. Thus in Ilfracombe Miss Ellis Winsham sold 'gun models' and raised £19 for the French Red Cross Society. Also in Ilfracombe the town's Girl Guides began sending monthly parcels of food and cigarettes to the Devon Regiment in France. In Barnstaple Italian street musicians collected £9 for wounded soldiers. The Mayoress of Barnstaple sent another 1700 sandbags to help the war effort whilst Mrs.Johnson of Ilfracombe Vicarage sent 167 'respirators' to the Belgian Army – presumably home-made fabric ones. One report this month came from the Ilfracombe Patriotic Fund which had been established at the outbreak of the war to help those in the town, especially the families of men in the Forces, experiencing

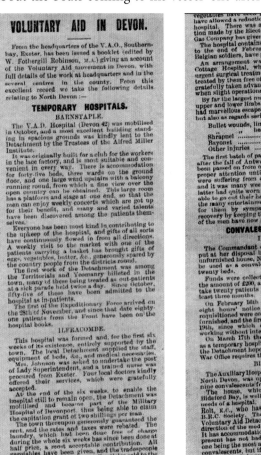

8a & b. Wartime hospitals in North Devon. NDJ 10.6.1915 3c

hardship. Out of 204 claims some 121 were granted with recipients being given food and coal. Whilst this was occurring weekly subscriptions to help Belgian refugees were still being collected – and publicised.

This month saw the publication of a booklet giving an account of the Voluntary Aid Detachments in Devon. These were groups of volunteers, both male and female, with some medical training, who were to operate auxiliary hospitals in time of war. Set up in 1909 they did extremely valuable work during the First World War. The *North Devon Journal* carried details of local hospitals from this booklet.

Women continued to take over jobs of men who had joined the Forces. Thus at Torrington Miss Lily Snell replaced her father on his postal round whilst in Barnstaple Miss Florence Richards took on a meat delivery round. It was also noted how the two daughters of Captain Kelsall of Westward Ho! had gone to Serbia to work as nurses. At the same time pre-war Suffragettes in Bideford raised £37 for these Serbian hospitals as well as others in France.

It wasn't just women who were joining the war effort as nine South Molton Boy Scouts offered to help patrol the North Devon coast. Apparently 'The formal consent of parents and employers is required before lads are accepted for this duty, and this is being obtained by the Scoutmaster.' The idea that Germans might land along North Devon's coastline saw the first case under the Defence of the Realm Act for not obeying the blackout. John Parsons of the Bath Hotel in Lynmouth was fined £2 for not obscuring lights so they were 'invisible from the sea' the magistrates warning that 'in the case of any future offenders undoubtedly greater severity would be shown.'

Perhaps the oddest story this month was when councillor Pollard of Bideford town council proposed that all 'Harmsworth daily papers' (e.g. the *Daily Mirror* and the *Daily Mail*) be banned from the town's library after they had attacked Lord Kitchener over the lack of artillery shells for the guns in France. After discussion Pollard withdrew his motion.

The First World War in North Devon

July 1915

After the strenuous efforts to attract new recruits in June then July saw a steep decline in enlistments with one report reckoning 'The slump in recruiting is attributed to hay-making operations' though it was 'confidently expected that when these are completed many more men will come forward.' Indeed to ensure the harvest was gathered in, the Army has arranged to give furlough to a limited number of soldiers'. The highest number of recruits this month came from Bideford when seven men joined the 'New Army' in one week – the being a name for the newly trained battalions rather than existing Regiments. Doggerel poems were still being published to spur young men to enlist including one by a serving soldier.

Around this time local organisations began preparing what was termed a 'Roll of Honour' listing all the men from their parish or group who was serving in the Army or Navy. Thus Torrington School produced theirs whilst the one at Westleigh was displayed in the church porch. Presumably the idea was to both honour the servicemen and let parishioners know who wasn't on the list.

If recruitment to the Regular Forces was low the local Volunteer Training Corps continued to attract men with both the Northam and Lynton bodies reaching a strength of 50 whilst Ilfracombe had 80 members.

That the decline in recruitment was more serious than was realised saw the government introduce the National Registration Act. This was the compilation of a list of all adults between the ages of 16 and 65 by volunteer enumerators, with special 'pink forms' being reserved for men of military age. That this was pretty comprehensive is shown from Bideford where the town was split into nine areas with forty-seven enumerators carrying out the work. An editorial in the *Journal* on the completion of the list reckoned 'There are many who regard the National Register as the inevitable fore-runner of Conscription. We believe the result will prove that they are mistaken. The information collected will prove of immense value, especially in the direction of organising the productive powers of the nation. But compulsory service is another thing. Miracles have been accomplished by virtue of the spirit of voluntaryism so inherent in English character, and there will be no Conscription until the resources of voluntary service have been exhausted. But if Conscription is found to be really necessary, the nation will acquiesce. For the needs of the State

ENLIST !

A VOICE FROM THE TRENCHES.

There's a lull in the fighting now, mother, and
    I've time to drop you a line,
For I'm always thinking about you, mother, and
    the dear old days lang syne.
I sometimes doze in the trench, mother, for one
    gets used to the noise,
And when I do I dream, mother, that I'm back
    with you and the boys.
And we sit by the fire once more, mother, and I
    may tell you tales of the War—
Things you would hardly believe, mother, some of
    the sights I saw.
Some think it is paper talk, mother, but alas ! 'tis
    all too true,
And Jack, and Tom, and Harry, and Dick would
    come if they only knew.
At other times I have dreamt, mother, that I was
    back in the dear old home,
Where we used to sit of an evening, and play
    games, and yarn.
And I may be telling a tale, mother, of some brave
    deed I saw,
Or the saddened fate of a Belgain girl who died
    from the shame she bore,
Or of others driven mad, mother, by the cruel,
    lustful Huns,
Till I see the lads around me reach out as if for
    their guns ;
And I know by the look on their faces the foe
    would get his due,
And Jack, and Tom, and Harry, and Dick would
    come if they only knew.
And then I wake in the trench, mother, as the
    shells go shrieking by,
But I do not fear to die, mother—I do not fear to
    die ;
For I'm proud to be a soldier—I'm glad to be in
    the fight,
When I think of the wrongs committed, when I
    know we are in the right ;
When I think of somebody's sister, when I think
    of somebody's child,
When I think of somebody's mother, and I think
    of them all defiled ;
And then I think of the lads out there, and wish
    it were only true
That Jack, and Tom, and Harry, and Dick were
    joining the Colours too.

[The foregoing lines were forwarded from a trench
in Gallipoli by Corpl. G. H. Bridger to his
mother (Mrs. Bridger, of Burland Cottage,
Marwood), who has another son fighting in the
Dardanelles.]

1. A doggerel poem advocating enlistment. NDJ 1.7.1915 6e

TORRINGTON COUNCIL SCHOOL ROLL OF HONOUR.

TEACHERS.
Territorials.—Alfred Sharland and Harold J. Richards.

OLD BOYS.
Aeroplane Machinist.—Herbert Elsworthy.
R.A.M.C.— Percy Capell, William Dyer, and Augustus Page (driver).
Colonials.—Arthur Pyke, Edward Green, and Walter Selby.
Telegraphists.—Cyril Hooper, Ernest Edwards.
Cyclists and Motorists.—Thomas Weeks (despatch rider), Claude Leate, and Fred Allen.
Royal Navy.—Robert Sandford, Ernest Ware, Walter Hutchings, Fred Bangham, Charles Jones, William Sillifant, Robert Palmer, Harry Allen, Walter Baker, Stanley Hancock, and Ernest Stapleton.
Royal North Devon Hussars.—Llewellyn Lloyd, Arthur Heard, George Stapleton, Frederick Sing, Ernest Hooper, William Fishleigh, Arthur Eastmond, John Elliott, Frederick Hobbs, James Martin, Charles Martin, Wallace Lake, Harry Frayne, Fred Hutchings, John Short, Frank Weeks, John Hoyle, Fred Stacey, Thomas Reddaway, George Moxworthy, Frank Parnacott, Thomas Hockin, and Thomas Hutchings.
Territorials. — Michael Hearn, Ernest Guard, Arthur Jones, Percy J. Lile, Sydney Davey, Richard Gist, William J. Bowden, Joseph Parkhouse, Fred Parkhouse, Ernest Parkhouse, Archie Guard, James Baker, Balmond Fursman, Stanley Fursman, James Gent, Lawrence Parnacott, John Green, Albert Norman, Joseph Jenkins, William Baker, Thomas Green, Emmanuel Davey, Thomas Slee, and Cyril French.
Army.—Alfred H. Davey, John Downman, Thomas Matthews, William Bowden, John Davey, Arthur White, Charles Stapleton, Cecil Matters, Harry Colwill, Charles Colwill, Thomas Bidgway,

2. Part of the Torrington Council School 'Roll of Honour'. NDJ 8.7.1915 2c-d

WESTLEIGH'S ROLL OF HONOUR.

Practically every eligible young man in the parish of Westleigh has now enlisted. The latest recruit is Mr. A. Baulkwill, who "signed on" last week. Westleigh's Roll of Honour has been placed in the porch of the Parish Church. The names of the men on service are as follows :—Navy—Messrs. Wm. Dark, Henry Farthing, Ernest Gard, Wm. Harris, Alfred Jeffery, F. Percy Lee, William Mountjoy, Charles Parker, F. Parkin, and A. Baulkwill. Army—Messrs. John Allen, Edward Badcock, Arthur Beer, James Buse, Alan Butt, John Christie, Charles Dark, Thomas E. Farthing, William Ford, Thomas Fulford, Joseph Gard, Edward Harris, George Harris, Reuben Harris, R. Philip Hearson, G. Neville Hearson, Geo. Hill, Geo. Holman, William May, Alfred W. Molland, Archibald Oliver, Frederick J. Parker, John Parker, Wm. Parker, Samuel Parker, Richard Parker, Henry Pedlar, Joseph Pike, Henry Saunders, John Tithecott, James Berry Torr, Frederick Samuel Week, and Walter Wills.

3. Westleigh's 'Roll of Honour'. NDJ 29.7.1915 6b

4. An inspection of the Ilfracombe VTC.

are paramount. The Allies mean to win, and they must win.'

Agricultural needs may have restricted the flow of recruits but the ever lengthening casualty lists probably acted as a deterrent as well. These included 21 year old Royal Marine William Cann of Ilfracombe, 20 year old Pte.Frank Chard of Chulmleigh, 18 year old Trooper Frank Hunt of Braunton and Pte.George Stuckey of Combe Martin who left a widow and seven children. One particularly unlucky man was Pte.Alfred Batley of Bideford who was a pre-war Regular. He had been in the trenches at Flanders and suffering frostbite was sent home and on recovery posted to guard duty on Scilly where he developed pneumonia and died. He was given a full military funeral at Penzance. All military deaths, however, were still seen as noble by those at home with a vicar at Mortehoe speaking, during a memorial service, of the dead soldier as 'fighting manfully for his King and Country and dying a glorious death on the field of battle.'

CHAPTER 60.

An Act for the compilation of a National Register. A.D. 1915.
[15th July 1915.]

BE it enacted by the King's most Excellent Majesty, by and with the advice and consent of the Lords Spiritual and Temporal, and Commons, in this present Parliament assembled, and by the authority of the same, as follows :

1. A register shall be formed of all persons, male and female, between the ages of fifteen and sixty-five (not being members of any of His Majesty's naval forces or of His Majesty's regular or territorial forces), subject to the exceptions mentioned in this Act.

Register of persons between the ages of fifteen and sixty-five.

5. National Registration is brought in.

It is odd that such sentiments were still being voiced given the rather more objective accounts in the many letters being sent home by servicemen which then saw publication in local newspapers. Thus Cpl.Bridger of Marwood said of being in Gallipoli that 'death has been all around me' whilst Pte.H.Gomer of Georgenympton wrote of the fighting around Ypres where he had passed 'a huge crater, caused by the explosion of a mine, 20 foot deep and 25 yards wide, containing a large number of dead bodies of Germans as well as French and

English.' Cpl.Frank Knill of Barnstaple recorded how he was chatting to a friend in a dug-out who then walked about 30 yards away - and was 'blown to pieces' by a shell.

Several letters expressed concern about continuing shell shortages whilst many emphasised the need for more men to sign up and fight the 'frightful Hun' though most were fairly cheery in tone with the occasional one painting war as a big game. An advertisement for 'War Munition Volunteers' appeared in local newspapers this month – presumably linked to the shortages referred to.

One unusual casualty was a Belgian soldier, Camiel Kirckvoorde, had been shot in the head in France and was brought to Westwell Hall Hospital in Ilfracombe where he died with the bullet still in his brain. He was given an impressive funeral with all his countrymen and women then in Ilfracombe attending.

6. An advertisement for munition workers. NDJ 1.7.1915 4f

8. The funeral of Camiel Kirckvoorde.

7. Westwell Hall Hospital, Ilfracombe.

Positive notes were always struck in reports on the awarding of medals – none more so than when 18 year old 2nd Lieut. George Moor won the VC in the Dardanelles fighting by rallying his retreating men and recapturing a trench. Admittedly his link to North Devon was tenuous he having been born in Ceylon and

2nd-Lieut. GEORGE R. D. MOOR, V.C.
Photo, Central Press

9. A cigarette card showing the Braunton VC.

was serving in the Hampshire Regiment when he won the decoration – but his mother lived at 'St.Berwyn's' in Braunton and was 'very well known in the Braunton district'. This was enough for North Devon to claim him as their 'Hero'.

That such morale boosting news was needed is shown when one considers the on-going problem of shell shortages and the divisive attacks on Lord Kitchener who was then the Secretary of State for War and ultimately responsible for munitions. Barnstaple town council received a letter from Kitchener urging them to obtain as many men as they could for the Forces and after reading it the Mayor called for a vote of confidence in him as 'They all remembered the very scurrilous attacks made upon Lord Kitchener a few weeks ago by some leading London newspapers, these attacks being undoubtedly most unjustifiable and uncalled for.' Torrington town council passed a similar motion in the same week.

10. F.Jewell, Mayor of Barnstaple.

At the same time as the Barnstaple Mayor was proposing this motion his wife was continuing to collect sandbags and was pleased to accept 500 from Holsworthy whilst at Northam three women had organised a group to make 1300 sandbags. The pressing need for these was explained in a letter published in the *Journal* this month.

Correspondence.

[To the Editor of the *North Devon Journal.*

SANDBAGS WANTED.

Sir,—"It is doubtful whether anyone, not actually in the field, at all realises what the word 'Sandbag' means to the soldier in the firing line, or how urgently millions, and yet more millions, of sandbags are needed to stem the casualty lists." Miss Tyler, from whom I am quoting, gets many appeals from the front. An R.F.A. officer complains of "the shortage" of sandbags. The wife of another R.F.A. officer remarks on the urgent need of the artillery for sandbags, as they have "the huge guns to cover," and are not so well dug in as those in the trenches, while an infantry Lieutenant writes:—"We want a tremendous lot of sandbags. Our division alone has been using 1,000,000 a month. For our battalion alone we usually require 2,000 a day." "If," he adds, "you saw a shell burst upon a parapet with sandbags, and on one without, you would soon see how many lives they save." A Colonel of the R.F.A. appeals to the kind people who have helped them so greatly with warm things in the Winter to make sandbags for them now. "A mile of trenches," he says, "will require 100,000 sandbags, not counting the many that are wanted to protect the number of places within two or three miles behind. And they have not time to empty their bags to carry them on, but want new ones." An R.F.A. Captain describes the advance of the infantry:—"Each man takes ten bags under his arm as he runs out. When fired at he drops, and fills a bag as he lies for cover. Then he dashes on again with his remaining nine bags, to repeat the manœuvre again and again, always leaving the filled bag to cover some man behind him. In this way the whole line advances, with temporary cover, until they can dig themselves in." We are told :—"The men will do almost anything if only they have enough sandbags."

The supply of sandbags required is endless. They should be 14 inches by 33 inches when quite finished ; stout strings tied on fully three inches from the mouth. Applications for further directions can be made to Miss Tyler, Linden House, Highgate-road, London, N.W., who is glad to receive few or many bags, to be sent direct to the Front.

E. M.

July 6th.

11. An appeal for sandbags.
NDJ 15.7.1915 3f

Other war related work was reported on when Messrs. Ellis and Sons of Marlborough Road in Ilfracombe built and sent off another six 'motor waggons' to the Army – having already sent twelve.

Given that the war had been going on for nearly a year it seems odd that one piece of news, with its chilling wording, appeared this month. It read 'Several Germans of military age were sent by the Chief Constable (Mr.R.S.Eddy) from Barnstaple on Friday morning for internment in concentration camps in compliance with the Government's regulations.' They were joined a few days later by three more Germans and an Austrian from Ilfracombe.

In sharp contrast to their treatment North Devonians continued to support Belgian refugees living in the area via their weekly subscriptions. Sadly not everyone welcomed them as in Bideford John Squire, a labourer, got drunk and 'shouted to some women who were foreigners, 'Clear out of this country you____. What business have you over here?' He was arrested and fined 12/-. The women were almost certainly Belgian and were probably amongst those being employed in the new munitions factory.

The following Barnstaple Boy Scouts have volunteered, and have been accepted, for coast-guard duty on the South Coast of Devon:—P. Short, D. Tuckett, G. Ackland (1st Devon Troop), W. McLeod (Newport Wesleyan Troop), and J. Delve (Boutport-street Wesleyan). These Scouts, accompanied by District Commissioner Lloyd, left Barnstaple for Kingsbridge on Saturday morning last, being given a hearty send-off by their fellow Scouts.

13. Boy Scouts as Coast Watchers. NDJ 22.7.1915 4e

12. The Shapland & Petter factory – the large buildings to the left.

This unfortunate case came at the same time as another strike broke out in Barnstaple where cabinet makers asked their employers for a 'War Bonus' of an extra 2/6 per week. The dispute was referred to the Board of Trade for arbitration with the men agreeing to work until a decision was reached. During the war the main cabinet making firm in Barnstaple was Shapland & Petters and it is known they produced aircraft propellers, and possibly wings, for the Royal Flying Corps so settlement of this dispute was important.

Also in this month a second case of having 'unobscured lights' on the coast came before the Barnstaple magistrates. Rather unexpectedly the culprit was Commander Bernard Prichard of the Royal Navy who lived at Woolacombe. After being reported a policeman delivered the court summons - only for Prichard to assault him! In court Prichard claimed that being continually on duty in the North Sea for the previous 10 months 'had considerably affected his temper and made him very irritable.' The bench wasn't convinced and fined him £2.

One wonders if such aggressive offenders were encountered by the local Boy Scouts who were now on coastal patrol duty? A 5-strong group from Barnstaple left for South Devon this month where they worked under the supervision of the Coastguards. One hopes they didn't have to haul bodies up a cliff as happened at Hartland where three badly decomposed corpses were dragged up from the beach by Coastguards. A subsequent inquest found they came from the *Scottish Monarch* torpedoed off of Southern Ireland some time before.

More cheerful news came from the Instow Red Cross Hospital where a Miss Harding married Commander C.C.Johnson with wounded soldiers and nurses as guests.

Women were also the main people behind a street collection for the French Relief Fund in Barnstaple – as shown in this contemporary postcard.

14. *The wedding at Instow Hospital.*

15. *Collecting in Barnstaple for the French Relief Fund.*

The First World War in North Devon

August 1915

After a year of war Britain was facing a severe and possibly disastrous shortage of fighting men but this August saw a sudden increase in local enlistments with some 86 men joining various Regiments with numbers enrolling in Pioneer Battalions and the Royal Flying Corps. Additionally more joined the Volunteer Training Corps with the newly formed Torrington one quickly attracting 40 members. This appears to have been down to the widespread belief that the National Registration Act was a precursor to conscription – but if men enlisted before this was introduced they could still select which service or regiment they wanted whereas conscription would remove this - hence the sudden influx of recruits.

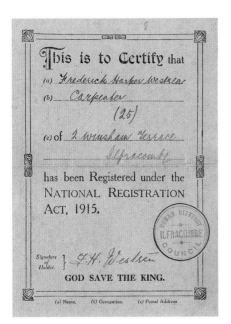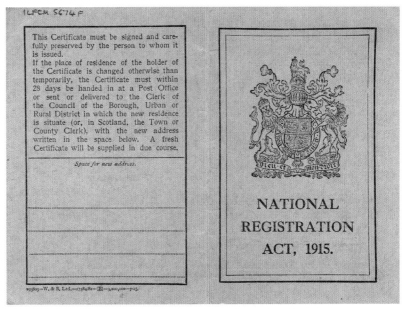

1a & b. A National Registration card.

The operation of the Act itself was being undertaken throughout North Devon all this month with the Registrar General sending explanatory directives to all district and borough councils. This came with a request that they be displayed on church and chapel doors so people could see what was expected of them – and be made aware that failure to complete the return would see an initial fine of £5 with a continuing penalty of £1 a day for every day in default.

At Torrington the town was divided into 8 areas and 16 enumerators appointed whilst Barnstaple had 25 divisions with 43 enumerators 21 of whom were women. In Combe Martin the 10 enumerators were all local councillors whilst Fremington had 12 enumerators. Once the forms were delivered and then collected a few days later they were sent to either Barnstaple or Bideford where the results were tabulated by large numbers of volunteers. Interestingly there seems to have been no cases of people refusing to complete the forms in North Devon. Summing up the effort involved an editorial in the *North Devon Journal* reckoned 'the work was accomplished smoothly and smartly' with the results allowing the government to organise 'the productive powers of the nation.' Whilst the tabulation was going on Lord Kitchener was forced to say that registration was not the forerunner to conscription – which wasn't actually true.

ARTHUR SANDERS VANRENNEN.

Son of General D.C. and Mrs Vanrennen. Lieut Colonel ~ Lincolnshire Regiment. Killed at Gallipoli ~ August 15ᵗʰ 1915. Aged 55.

2. Lt.Col.Verennen.

3. Sergt.Alexander Green.

All this work at home didn't conceal the fact that local casualties continued to mount inexorably. Thus Pte.George Westcott of Dolton died of his wounds in France. He had been wounded before and whilst home on leave said 'he was sure he should not see Dolton again.' Major Harold Colston of Buckleigh House in Westward Ho! had been recorded as 'Missing' at Ypres in April – with his body only being found this month. Other deaths were reported from the Dardanelles including Major J.Bruce of the Royal Artillery whose father lived in Barnstaple, Pte.William Prouse of Hartland, 2nd Lieut.Rowland Raw of Umberleigh House killed 'in his first engagement' and Lt.Col. Vanrennen of Northam.

Even when servicemen had been captured they were still at risk. Captain Archie Sutcliff of Torrington was in the Medical Corps when taken prisoner during the retreat from Mons in the first months of the war. Sent to a Prisoner of War camp in Germany where the conditions were very poor he died of typhus along with many others.

The publication of letters sent home from the Fronts saw noticeably fewer appearing though whether this was due to tighter censorship or problems with the postal service is unclear. One that did appear came from Cpl.Hayes of Exford who noted 'We – the bomb-throwers – went up to the trench 32 strong, and when we came back there were only six of us left.' L/Cpl.O.Greenslade in France writing to his parents in Barnstaple recorded 'The five days in the trenches meant five days of hard work on fatigues etc, but we didn't suffer much loss of men like the two of our Companies who were holding the first line; they lost something like 100 men killed and wounded.'

Rather more cheerful letters came from the local men in India with Quartermaster Edward Snow from Braunton reckoning 'I don't think we have much to grumble about.' Snow included photographs of his fellow soldiers and scenes in India which were 'passed around the village to all who have relatives in India.' Other letters spoke of

4. The Devonshire Regiment crest in India.

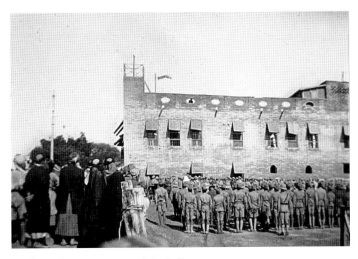

5. The 1/6ᵗʰ Devons on parade in India.

billiard games, athletics meetings and bowling matches. One of the soldiers there was Sergt. Alex Green who is shown here wearing his tropical uniform in a photograph taken in Bombay. He was a keen photographer and took these pictures; the first showing the crest of the Devonshire Regiment worked in stones, the second a military parade in at their base in India.

Another photograph was published in the *Journal* this month, a very rare occurrence. It showed local men who were serving on HMS *Colossus* with all being identified – an unusual acknowledgement of the Royal Navy at a time when news from the Army dominated the paper's columns.

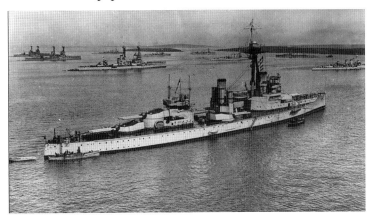

7. HMS Colossus.

6. North Devon men serving on HMS Colossus. NDJ 5. 8.1915 2d-e

INSTOW V.A.D. HOSPITAL.

The Instow V.A.D. Hospital has done much good work since the War started in the way of caring for wounded soldiers. Over fifty men have stayed there for various periods, and a large batch who recently left were all enthusiastic in their appreciation of the kindness extended to them during their stay at Instow. The accommodation is for 20, but there are only eleven soldiers under treatment at present, others being expected daily. Sister Norrish, late of St. Bartholomew's Hospital, London, is now in charge during the temporary absence of the Commandant (Mrs. Miles). There are eleven nurses in the Detachment, and many other ladies in the locality render valuable assistance. Dr. Ellis Pearson, of Bideford, is the visiting medical officer. The men much appreciate the motor drives given them in the magnificent car which is lent weekly by the Misses Houldsworth, of Westward Ho. Periodicals and newspapers are regularly sent for the use of the men. The following are the names of the soldiers now on the books :—

Staff-Sergt. Bovey, R.A.M.C.
Sergt. Stevens, 3rd Sherwood Foresters.
Sergt. Regin, 1st Hampshires (from the Dardanelles).
Lance-Corpl. Davies, South Wales Borderers (from the Dardanelles).
Pte. Ranger. 2nd Devons.
Pte. Miers, 1st Devons (Crediton).
Pte. Hingston, 1st Devons.
Pte. Fielding, East Lancs.
Pte. Howarth, East Lancs.
Pte. Roche, 1st Royal Munster Fusiliers.

Also featured in the newspaper were accounts of the ongoing local production of sandbags with the Mayoress of Barnstaple receiving 99 from Bulkworthy School and 250 from Barnstaple Methodists. At Torrington the Mayor and Mayoress staged a concert in their garden which raised £18 which was spent on material for making sandbags. Lessons on how to make them were held at Lynton whilst at Bishops Tawton a 'Working party' was producing socks, mufflers, mittens etc for soldiers they having started in August 1914. Belgian refugees continued to be helped with a house-to-house collection for funds at Tawstock and a Flag Day in Mortehoe which raised £11. One rather bizarre story concerned a Belgian baby baptized in the Barnstaple Catholic church who was 'named after the reigning monarchs of the Allies.'

Further reports came in of women taking over enlisted men's jobs with a Miss Hill of Lee doing her brother's postal round whilst in South Molton 'Owing to a shortage of harvest workers, six ladies assisted in hay-making on a farm.' Female nurses continued to care for the never ending arrival of wounded

8. The work of the Instow Hospital. NDJ 19.8.1915 5b

soldiers. The Instow VAD Hospital saw a change in Commandant when 'Nurse Winifred' from Bideford took over – with a small report appearing in the *Journal* which gave some idea of its work.

North Devon hospitals seem to have dealt with men with relatively light wounds for the most part given that 19 wounded soldiers were invited to play at the Barnstaple Bowling Club. Most nurses were women but in South Molton there were two VAD units – one all-male and the other all-female.

The cabinet maker's strike in Barnstaple ended with the strikers not getting the 'War Bonus' they had asked for. Nothing daunted the Barnstaple branch of the Workers' Union met in town where a Miss Varley recounted

9. Wounded men on a day out at Instow. (Copyright Beaford Arts)

how women members were getting better wages elsewhere in England – 'and the Union was going to bring about this state of things in Barnstaple.'

On a lighter note the month ended with a report on a fete at Westward Ho! held to raise funds for the local Volunteer Training Corps which featured 'Kaiser Bill skittles' – one can probably guess what this involved.

The First World War in North Devon

September 1915

September saw the final tabulation of the results of the National Registration drive. At Bideford the town council appealed for extra volunteers to carry out the work as those doing it, including teachers on holiday, were working 5-6 hours a day. Both Braunton parish council and the South Molton Rural District council thanked their enumerators with the chairman of the latter pointing out that over 6000 forms had been distributed which had to be analysed into 75 different occupational classes followed by further sub-division and finally being put in alphabetical order. Most councils sent letters of thanks to the volunteers for all their hard work.

Whilst this clerical work was carried out new recruits to the Forces continued to dribble in. At an inspection of the Bideford VTC Lt.Col.Kirkwood who commanded the Devon Depot at Exeter baldly stated 'Recruiting was going very badly now.' New ways of encouraging men to come forward included a fascinating letter from Sergt.Maj.W.Wicketts who had won the Victoria Cross and came from Alwington near Bideford. He wrote to the vicar of Alwington and included this plea; 'Now sir, are there any more young men about your parish who have not yet joined. If so, tell them to come along, we want them. There are none better able to crush the murderer of dear little children and women than the boys of Devon, who if they only knew what I know, would soon be with us.' L/Cpl.Leo Pulkinghorne from Lynton, who was back in North Devon recovering from his wounds 'spent three days at Barnstaple Fair as a recruiter. He tackled large numbers of young fellows, and as a result of his patriotic appeals he secured 13 recruits.'

1. Barnstaple Fair

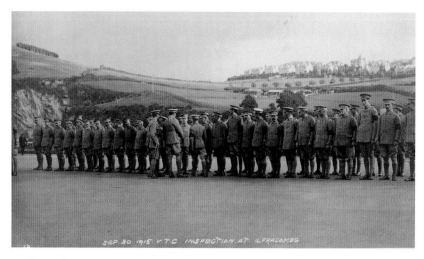

2. Ilfracombe VTC being inspected this month.

3. The Cross Tree, Braunton.

Pressure was also being put on men in the VTC to join the Regular or Territorial forces with some success as when twelve men from the Ilfracombe Corps signed up.

At Braunton J. Yeo Tucker held an open-air meeting at the Cross Tree where he spoke on 'The War and the shirkers'. He claimed that 270 Braunton men were already serving but more were needed – especially those whose jobs could be done by women, he adding 'In Braunton there were lady cab drivers, and young ladies who delivered meat from door to door. Women were even ploughing in the fields, and assisting in all kinds of agricultural and other labour.' At another meeting two weeks later Tucker announced that there were 151 men in Braunton between the ages of 18 and 38 who were not in the Forces he presumably having obtained these figures from the National Registration returns.

The rector of Ashreigney preached a sermon comparing the 'selfish, soulless and cowardly action' of men who refused to enlist with the 'heroic, devoted and truly splendid fighting men' who had signed up. Surprisingly he also said that 'politicians had so fed our people with lies upon lies, and newspapers had so befogged them with yet other lies, that men whose natural impulse would have been to respond at once to any clear and solemn call, were utterly bewildered as to what to believe or whom to trust' – a rather outspoken view at this time. As already mentioned another way of encouraging recruits was to publicise families where multiple members had enlisted – with the *Bideford Gazette* going one better this month by publishing a set of photographs of the five sons of Mr & Mrs.Galliford of Westward Ho! who were all serving.

Women were becoming more visible doing what had previously been men's jobs with it being reported that 'The first lady booking clerk to act on the railway at Barnstaple is Miss Phyllis Hayward of Gloster Road.' Additionally Mrs.Newman, wife of the railway gatekeeper at Castle Quay in Barnstaple took over his job, albeit temporarily.

That these replacements were necessary can

4. Gallifords in the Services. BG 21.9.1915 2c-e

be seen in this month's list of casualties. More men were dying in the Dardanelles including 21 year old Drummer Frank Sanders of Barnstaple, Pte.John Tucker of Fremington and Pte.G.Litson who was the first from Lynton to die he being aged 44 and officially over the 'military limit'. Another older fatality was that of Pte.Frederick Rice of Barnstaple who was 36 whilst Pte.Albert Ward who succumbed to fever with the local regiment in India was aged just 18. When Pte.Wallace Lees of Ilfracombe was killed in France his officer wrote to his parents saying 'your son died doing his duty, and will be remembered as always having done his duty with a light heart' which may or may not have been a consolation to them.

Most letters home were rather more cheerful than this of course, indeed a selection of letters from his ex-pupils in France sent to F.Lord, headmaster of 'Sts.Philip & James' School in Ilfracombe have been published by Ilfracombe Museum in a book by Jane Dendle entitled 'For those that come after us'. Most were full of cheery news though Herbert Huxtable denounced 'people in England who are issuing pamphlets to men telling them not to join the Army.' He also included 'a few views of some of the ruins of places out here'. Produced in large numbers by French and Belgian postcard publishers they served to give relatives at home some idea about the scale of destruction at the Front.

5 & 6. Postcards showing ruins sent home to Barnstaple.

One letter from a Barnstaple member of the Royal Engineers who only signed himself 'Sapper' gives a very long and detailed account of trench warfare including the construction of dug-outs and erection of barbed wire entanglements – as described in this extract opposite.

One wonders if he ever got to use any of the sandbags that continued to be sent out from North Devon? This month saw 300 coming from South Molton, 300 from Lynton and 400 from Torrington. At Barnstaple it was recorded how Miss Elsie Heayel of 37 South Street had collected around 100 walking sticks and sent them to Boulogne for the use of wounded soldiers in the hospitals there. Also this month 8 year old Ruby Toms of Combe Martin dressed as a Red Cross nurse and collected £3.7.6 for sick and wounded servicemen. Other citizens and groups continued to subscribe weekly sums to support Belgian refugees living in the area. One Torrington Boy Scout Reginald Rendle was presented with a medal by the town Mayor this month for saving the life of Jean Schoeters a young refugee who had fallen into the River Torridge.

The biggest news in North Devon, however, was what the *Journal* headlined as 'Serious Strike at Barnstaple – Whole of the cabinet makers out'. The long simmering dispute which had seen the men continue working until the result of arbitration was announced came to a head when some 250 men employed at the Raleigh Cabinet Works of Shapland & Petter and the Barnstaple Cabinet Works came out on strike and paraded the streets following the refusal of the companies to pay a 'War Bonus'. Both had been engaged on government contracts hence the men's claim for a war-related wage increase. The men struck 'with dramatic suddenness'

Well, I have just one more incident I would like to relate. If I spoke the truth I have others, but I think I have already taken up too much of the valuable space in your paper—so now for my last.

We had just returned from night work, and a very risky job it was too. There was a certain part of the line that had no barbed wire out in front of the trenches; so we were called upon to get some put there. Our Captain (in whom we have great faith) hit upon a good scheme by which we could carry the barbed wire fence already made, and by "jumping" a stake into the ground it held the wire up, so we all got our fence laid out on the parapet of the trench, ready to dash out and fix it up when the signal was given. At last the signal was given, and I can assure you it was no longer than possible before we dived headlong into our trenches. Our luck was dead in, for not one single "star-shell" went up, to which some of us owe our lives. We had just returned, and some of us had gone to sleep, when we heard the awful word, "Gas!" Most of us were undressed, and by the time we managed to put on our respirators, boots, and coats, and gather up our arms, it was stifling. All the time our gunners were sending their shells at them as fast as they could. The Germans were doing the same, and splinters were flying all over the place. We stood there awaiting orders from our Captain. We received orders to march off and get on to as high ground as possible. By the time this had been done the wind had freshened considerably, and was proving a good friend to us. I can assure you we felt proud of the drivers, and also of the drivers of the ammunition columns, who sometimes went up with three men and six horses and came back with one man and two horses and half a limber—the rest having been hit by a shell. But they had died a soldier's death, and no praise can be too high for their conduct. Needless to say we did not all come out Scot free on that eventful day, but I don't wish to mention our number of casualties, for it brings back some old times (that will never come again) with men who have done their best.

Well, Sir, I would like to thank all those kind people who sent my comrades and myself gifts of various descriptions, for I can assure you they are thought a lot of by those who are fortunate enough to receive them.

Believe me, yours truly,
"SAPPER."

7. 'Sapper's' letter. NDJ 9.9.1915 2b

8. Barnstaple Bowling Club with wounded soldiers.

with picket lines quickly being set up outside both factories. An offer from Shaplands was turned down with the workmen unanimously passing a demand for an increase in their wages of 1d an hour.

For their part Shapland's claimed that 'we have been so adversely affected by the War (owing to the fact of losing over one hundred men who have joined the Forces) that it has greatly restricted our output.' A.N.Oliver of the Barnstaple Cabinet Works added that owing to the lack of orders it was 'impossible to meet the men's demands.' The next week the workers held a public meeting at the Forester's Hall to put their case with the chairman being C.Peters 'President of the local Trades' and Labour Council'. Various speakers explained how the price of food had increased due to the war and how woodworkers in other parts of the country had all received pay increases – comments that were met with loud applause. Over the next few weeks little happened though the strikers were heartened that many of the 150 branches of the Furnishing Trades Association were willing to supplement strike payments to the families of the Barnstaple men. A tea was held for the wives and children of the strikers at the town's Forester's Hall which was followed by a speaker stressing the need for families to support their menfolk.

Given the importance of the government contracts Sir George Askwith summoned the employers and Union representatives to London. Here a new offer was hammered out for an immediate rise of 2/- per week plus ½d an hour with another ½d increase coming in January 1916. Returning to Barnstaple the Union officers presented the offer to the men who accepted it – news which 'was received with the greatest satisfaction' in North Devon.

A rather happier event was Barnstaple Fair which this year saw an amazing innovation when the ceremony of 'Proclaiming the Fair' was filmed and then shown at the Palace Picturedrome in Silver Street. The film was advertised with these teasing lines 'Don't miss seeing the Barum Fair pictures. See if you can spot yourself. You may be surprised what you are doing, and who you are snapped with.' The programme also included 'All latest War news in Pathe's Animated Gazette'. Wounded soldiers were seen at the Fair with another 45 being invited to play at the Barnstaple Bowling Club.

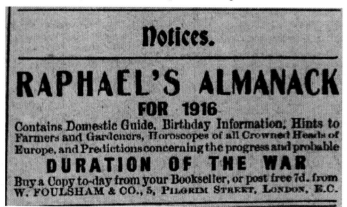

9. 'Raphael's Almanack' foretells the end of the war. NDJ 30.9.1915 6e

One peculiar court case came before the Ilfracombe magistrates. The report on it appeared in the *Journal* under the heading 'Charge of flashing cycle lamp' it being sandwiched between 'School Attendance Cases' and 'Charge of Fortune Telling'. The journalist recounted how Samuel Thomas had been arrested at Combe Martin after lighting his bicycle lamp. Told to extinguish it by a 'coast-watcher' he did so but even so he was fined 10/- the magistrate noting 'There were young men who made a practice of annoying the coast watchers by showing lights.'

Given that the 'fortune teller' case saw a woman fined £1 an advertisement in local newspapers the next week seems rather odd.

The First World War in North Devon

October 1915

Recruitment this month seems to have increased with one group of 15 men for Mortehoe trying to enlist en bloc. Two were rejected on medical grounds and one appears to have been only old enough to serve as a drummer boy. Why this group presented themselves as a body is unclear. At Challacombe a new Roll of Honour listing those village men who were fighting was posted on the church door, presumably embarrassing those who had not yet joined up.

This was all very well and by now 2½ million men had voluntarily enlisted but more were needed and thus the Derby scheme was launched. Named after its organiser Lord Derby it saw all men aged between 18 and 41, apart from those in essential occupations, asked to 'attest' their willingness to serve and who would only be called-up when actually required. Fears that the NRA would be used to get men to enlist were proved when each eligible man's National Registry card was copied onto another card which was sent to his local constituency's Parliamentary recruiting committee. The North Devon committee then split the area into three divisions – Barnstaple, Bideford and Ilfracombe and at the three towns (plus Combe Martin and Braunton) public meetings were arranged where councillors and clergy would be invited to hear details of the scheme.

CHALLACOMBE.

A NEW Roll of Honour for this parish has been affixed to the Church door:—Royal Regiment of Artillery, Gunners Charles and Henry Antell, Expeditionary Force; Corps of Royal Engineers, Major F. R. H. Eustace, Corpl. W. B. Dallyn, Sapper E. G. Davy, Expeditionary Force; Royal North Devon Hussars, Sergt.-Major F. J. Leworthy, Trooper C. H. Ridd, Trooper T. J. Webber, Trooper A. Antell, Trooper W. H. Webber; Army Service Corps, Herbert Edwin Ridd.

1. Challacombe's 'Roll of Honour'. NDJ 14.10.1915 5e

The first of the meetings was held in Barnstaple's Albert Hall where the Mayor F.Jewell began by saying that on his way to the Hall he had counted 80 young men who he considered should be in khaki. He added 'He thought it nothing less than a disgrace and a blot upon their little town that men should be walking about the streets in this way at such a time.' He then quoted figures from the National Registration showing that there were 1200 eligible young men in Barnstaple alone – and before anyone could point a finger he added that two of his three sons were serving. He went on to claim that 'If he were a girl he should be ashamed to be seen lolling about with a fellow dressed up in civilian clothes.' All this met with loud applause.

He was followed by W.Wilson who explained the scheme which would see volunteer 'canvassers' visit the men in their homes over the next six weeks to try and pressure them into voluntarily enlisting before they had to attest and probably, and inevitably, be called up. Apparently many of these canvassers were local councillors, discharged veterans or the fathers of serving soldiers. Women were not allowed to canvas but they did contribute by locating eligible men who had moved address. Another 'characteristically racy' speech came from Bryan O'Donnell who was attending his 604th recruiting meeting in 13 months. The meeting concluded with twenty young men stepping forward to enlist – again to applause.

2. The area in front of the New Inn, Bideford.

A similar meeting in the Alexandra Hall in Ilfracombe saw W.Wilson again speaking, he noting that voluntary enlistment wasn't enough to supply the Forces with their weekly need for 30,000 men to, in his cold-blooded phrase 'replace the wastage'. The meeting at Bideford was held outside the New Inn and again featured Wilson along with S.Chope the Mayor who announced that there were still 700 men of military age in Bideford who had yet to join the 7-800 who had already gone. Oddly 'He trusted that the day was far distant when compulsion would have to be resorted to.' At a recruiting meeting in the Pannier Market the next day 14 recruits came forward.

Given these moves it isn't surprising that a wave of volunteers enlisted over the next few weeks – and especially so following the execution of Nurse Edith Cavell on the 12th of October which created an up-welling of fervent hatred against the Germans after it was reported throughout the world. As if to prove the need for the Derby scheme the death toll this month was larger than usual with at least twenty one local men listed as 'killed in action'. Most of these deaths were notified to the men's families in the much dreaded telegrams from the War Office but not all as this sad report shows.

The family of CSM George Glasson from Barnstaple heard from a fellow soldier in the 8th Devons how Glasson had been recorded as 'Missing' but then 'His pay book and papers have been returned to the Brigade headquarters by the salvage men, who take them down from anybody they find on the field dead.' The community at Landkey was hit with three deaths this month – Ptes.Herbert Woollacott and Charlie Cornish and Rifleman Ernest Ridd who were all killed within days of each other. Also killed in France this month were Ptes.Sidney Kelly and Thomas Curtis, both of Northam.

BRAUNTONIAN SOLDIER KILLED IN ACTION.

Mr. and Mrs. W. Leeman, of Hapsleigh-terrace, have received the news that their son, Pte. W. Leeman, Devons, has been killed on active service in France. The sad news was received on Tuesday in a letter from a member of the Field Telegraph Company, who, whilst out discharging his duties, found the body of the young Brauntonian. On searching Pte. Leeman's pockets to ascertain his name, he found several letters and photographs from his mother, and also a portrait of his fiancée, Miss Nancis. He then wrote to Mrs. Leeman, enclosing the letters and portraits, and also stating that they had given him the most decent burial they could, the same evening and expressing his deepest sympathy with the parents. On receiving the distressing news Mrs. Leeman fainted. Mr. Leeman has written to the War Office to get official news of his son's death, but so far no answer has been received. The deceased, prior to joining the Army, was a gardener at Umberleigh, where he was held in the highest esteem both by his employer and friends. His father is a retired member of the Metropolitan Police Force. Mr. and Mrs. Leeman have the sympathy of Brauntonians generally in their bereavement.

THOMAS CURTIS.
Son of Ellen Curtis.
Private ~ 8ᵗʰ Devons.
Killed at Loos ~ Sept.25ᵗʰ 1915.
Aged 19.

SIDNEY KELLY.
Son of Thomas William and Ellen Kelly.
Lance Corporal ~ 8ᵗʰ Devonshire Regiment.
Killed at Loos ~ September 25ᵗʰ 1915.
Aged 19.

3. The death of Pte.W.Leeman. NDJ 7.10.1915 5b   *4. Pte.Thomas Curtis.*   *5. Pte.Sidney Kelly.*

So many deaths in so short a time must have hit these villages hard. When Cpl.George Dalling died his parents in Barnstaple received notification from the Australian High Commissioner. Their son had emigrated to South Africa where he had fought in the Boer War before moving on to Australia where, on the outbreak of war, he joined the Australian Light Horse before being posted to the Dardanelles in which place he met his death. He was one among the many such North Devon men who had gone to the Colonies, returned to fight - and die in their mother country's war. The death of a man in Mesopotamia was recorded this month. Pte.Frank Colwill from Hartland had been among those posted to India who later volunteered to serve in the Persian Gulf. Sadly he fell ill with enteric fever and died, the first of many to die in this theatre of war.

With all the emphasis on persuading more men to fight what was termed the 'hateful Hun' it is slightly unexpected to read in a letter from Pte.William Huxtable to his sister in Berrynarbor that 'it was quite a common experience for conversation to take place between occupants of the opposing trenches. One day a German soldier shouted 'We hope to have our Christmas dinner in London' the prompt rejoinder being 'We hope to have ours in Berlin.'

A rather more serious account of the war came from Trooper T.Foster from Ilfracombe whose letter describing the battlefield provides a vivid sense of what ordinary soldiers were experiencing. 'Half way along this road is a farmhouse, where apparently a band of Germans made a stand, as they are lying around in all directions….After you pass this house the stench of dead becomes quite pronounced, and seems to point to the fact that the Germans could noy bury their dead during the heavy bombardment that preceded the attack.'

With Christmas coming moves were set on foot to send treats to the troops. T.Knill of Barnstaple organised a series of concerts to raise money to send a Christmas pudding to every North Devon man on active service whilst Mrs.Baillie of Lynton was sending gifts of chocolate and soap to men in Mesopotamia. A more organised effort occurred at Braunton where a Soldier's Comfort Shop was opened to receive Christmas gifts for British PoWs in Germany. By the end of the first day it was already filled with 'parcels, food, cigarettes, warm socks and other comforts'.

Other morale raising efforts saw the Lynton Cinema Pavilion give an evening's takings to the Russian Flag Day fund. Such events were common right through the war and Ilfracombe Museum possesses a book containing many versions of the various emblems sold on these days.

At Bideford half of a legacy left to the Church Lad's Brigade by Arthur White an old member who died at Ypres was spent on buying the boys khaki uniforms and puttees.

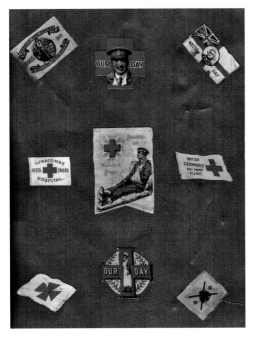

6. A page from the Ilfracombe Museum book.

7. 2nd Lt.Arthur White

Money continued to be donated to support Belgian refugees with a report noting that in Bideford there were 113 such refugees living in 38 houses in the borough. One thing exercising minds in Ilfracombe this month was whether the council could persuade Lord Fortescue the Lord Lieutenant of Devon to billet soldiers in the town over Winter. Although Summer tourism numbers were still healthy it was thought that having troops in town would ensure the local economy stayed buoyant. Fortescue wrote back saying there would be no billeting of troops over Winter as it was 'bad for discipline, bad for training and very expensive' although by the end of the month the Army Service Corps was sounding out the Ilfracombe Police as to how many soldiers might be billeted in unoccupied houses in the town.

Cinemas were regularly showing war newsreels but this month Poole's Myriorama arrived in Barnstaple. This rather old-fashioned variety show included painted scenes of the Dardanelles battles and 'sensational' illustrations of the Zeppelin raids on London mounted on rollers to give a semblance of movement. The Electric Palace Cinema in Bideford was rather more modern when it showed a whole series of films with titles like 'Lord Kitchener at the Front', 'The Greek Army in Action', 'Portuguese Cavalry' and 'The Allied Fleets in the Dardanelles'.

AN APOLOGY.

WEST PUTFORD.
18th September, 1915.

WHEREAS since the outbreak of War I have on several occasions in the presence of different persons made statements to the effect that Major Scott-Browne of Buckland Filleigh, Highampton now serving in His Majesty's Army was interested or had shares in Krupp's Works in Germany and that it was therefore in his (Major Scott-Browne's) interest that the War should be prolonged as much as possible and this was the reason of his taking such an active interest in recruiting.

Now I hereby admit that the whole of these statements are absolutely untrue and without any foundation and I tender to Major Scott-Browne my sincere apology for having made use of such statements and I undertake not to repeat them.

I also agree that Major Scott-Browne may make what use he thinks proper of this apology.

Signed by me Thomas Lewis of West Putford, Blacksmith, this Eighteenth day of September 1915 in the presence of Wm. B. Seldon, Solicitor, Bideford.

THOMAS LEWIS.

8. 'An Apology'. BG 5.10.1915 4d

A flurry of letters appeared this month about the hooter or 'siren' on the new munitions factory at Bideford. The first came from 'A Workman' who reckoned that 'Messrs Kynock's syren [sic]' was 'a great help to keeping regular hours at work' but this was accompanied by another protesting about the hooter 'which disturbs the whole neighbourhood at 5.30 a.m and at 6 o'clock a.m.' These two letters gave rise to another twelve over the next few weeks arguing on both sides – including one from 'A Field Gunner' in France and another in Devon dialect. One signed 'Early Bird' read 'Awake resident! Are you aware that our country is at war and that it is essential to get as much munition work as possible out of the few capable men who are left.' In actual fact the noise and frequency of the hooter seems to have been reduced and the complaints ceased.

A more 'serious' item was announced when a Miss Clara Codd gave three lectures on Theosophy in Barnstaple. This esoteric belief system had been around for many years but it received a fillip during and after the war as it claimed to tackle 'Life, Death and Destiny. Re-incarnation and its answer to Life's Problems'. Chaired by George Doe, the town clerk of Torrington, Miss Codd expounded on the thinking behind Theosophy explaining 'there is no death' – a message desperately seized on by relatives of dead soldiers.

A rather bizarre notice termed 'An Apology' appeared in the *Bideford Gazette* this month following some very slanderous comments to which the Major in the case clearly took grave exception.

The First World War in North Devon

November 1915

This month's news was dominated by the large wave of recruits as a direct result of the Derby scheme – what was termed 'a splendid response'. At Barnstaple in the first week 44 men enlisted 'the highest number of recruits secured in any one week since the outbreak of war'. At Braunton 10 recruits came forward though several were under age and thus disqualified. Bideford recorded 15 recruits and Ilfracombe 21 though at Combe Martin following a recruiting meeting 'there was no immediate response.'

The 'recruiting boom' as the *Journal* described it continued through the month with another 26 men enlisting into the Regular Army at Barnstaple in the next week followed by 21 in the week after that – although these figures were dwarfed by the 86 who joined in the last week of the month.

A similar spike was reported at Lynton where 11 new recruits were obtained and at Bideford where 25 enlisted in the final week. At this latter place wounded soldiers from the 'Commons' Hospital at Northam were given 'A post of honour' at a recruiting meeting in the Pannier Market though it was noted of the large crowd attracted to the event 'the proportion of those eligible for enlistment was comparatively small.'

1. Some of the new recruits.
NDJ 4.11.1915 5f

2. New recruits at Bideford.
25.11.1915 5b

This list includes William Lyle from Littleham whose medals including those for the Boer War are pictured on p.167.

In addition some 50 men enlisted into the Royal North Devon Hussars most of which regiment were still serving in England. Healthy numbers also enrolled into the local VTC units with the Lynton Corps rising to a membership of 62. The VTC were now called on to provide training for men who had attested but had yet to be called up – which might explain why there was a sudden inspection of these bodies in North Devon by the County Commandant Sir Richard Harrison.

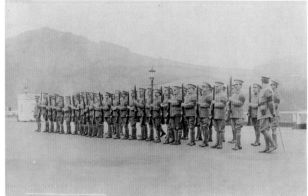

3,4,5. The Ilfracombe VTC on parade this month.

Public pressure on men to join the Forces became intense and to stop constant hectoring of willing men the government issued khaki armlets bearing the Royal Crown to three special groups;

a.   Attested men awaiting call-up.

b.   Men who had tried to enlist but were rejected on medical grounds.

c.   Men invalided from the Forces.

In several places the council set up a 'Tribunal' to decide which local men should be 'starred' this indicating which men could be most easily spared from their current occupation - though men so identified did have the right of appeal. At the same time the teams of canvassers appointed by local councils to visit eligible men and demand to know why they hadn't enlisted were briefed as to their work. At Bishops Nympton for example 11 such canvassers were employed whilst Combe Martin had 5, Lynton 6 and Ilfracombe 24. The canvas was rapidly carried out with the first results coming before the end of the month. Thus in the 83 parishes in the South Molton area where there were still some 3400 men of military age, 1500 had been canvassed and 275 had promised to enlist. In the Barnstaple area of the 5194 eligible men 2159 had been approached and 808 had 'expressed willingness to enlist'. Canvassers in the Torrington area were similarly successful but had been met with demands from married men that single men should be called up first – and there was some rancour over local farmers encouraging their labourers to join the Forces yet keeping their own sons at home claiming they were indispensable to the running of the farm. The threat of conscription was now being publicly voiced by the Prime Minister as this news item shows.

The only dissenting voice to this gradual slide towards conscription came from the Barnstaple & District Trades and Labour Council who announced their opposition to 'compulsory service, military or industrial, being forced upon the workers of this country' though they did support 'the continuance of the voluntary system'.

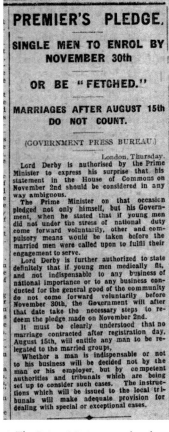

PREMIER'S PLEDGE.

SINGLE MEN TO ENROL BY NOVEMBER 30th

OR BE " FETCHED."

MARRIAGES AFTER AUGUST 15th DO NOT COUNT.

(GOVERNMENT PRESS BUREAU.)

London, Thursday.
Lord Derby is authorised by the Prime Minister to express his surprise that his statement in the House of Commons on November 2nd should be considered in any way ambiguous.

The Prime Minister on that occasion pledged not only himself, but his Government, when he stated that if young men did not under the stress of national duty come forward voluntarily, other and compulsory means would be taken before the married men were called upon to fulfil their engagement to serve.

Lord Derby is further authorized to state definitely that if young men medically fit, and not indispensable to any business of national importance or to any business conducted for the general good of the community do not come forward voluntarily before November 30th, the Government will after that date take the necessary steps to redeem the pledge made on November 2nd.

It must be clearly understood that no marriage contracted after registration day, August 15th, will entitle any man to be relegated to the married groups.

Whether a man is indispensable or not to his business will be decided not by the man or his employer, but by competent authorities and tribunals which are being set up to consider such cases. The instructions which will be issued to the local tribunals will make adequate provision for dealing with special or exceptional cases.

6. The Prime Minister speaks of conscription. BG 16.11.1915 3d

One wonders how keen the attested men were – especially if they read the stream of casualty reports published weekly in the local press. Amongst these were Ptes.Dick Parker and William May of Westleigh, Pte.Ernest Blackmore of Combe Martin, Pte.Ernest Keating of Ilfracombe and Trooper John Robins of West Down who was wounded in the Dardanelles and then brought back to Southampton where he died - leaving a widow and nine children. As if these deaths on the battlefield weren't concerning enough the North Devon casualty lists this month included seven men who had died of dysentery either in Gallipoli or Mesopotamia.

Eye-witness accounts of the fighting appearing in the local press must have added to their concerns although it is noticeable that the letter writers this month only offer generalisations about their experiences without the detail seen in earlier months. One letter came from Mech.S.Sergt.Wilfred Matthews writing to his uncle in Ilfracombe who described the completely devastated state of Ypres after fighting earlier in the year. A Cpl.R.Watkinson writing to Miss James of Hallsannery near Bideford described one attack in France by the 7th and 8th Devons where 'You would not think any living soul could live through the noise, to say nothing of the shells.' One wonders about the truth of the story in a letter from Pte.W.Gibbs of Ilfracombe who stated 'when his Company captured four German guns at Loos they found the gunners chained to them.'

At home Mrs.Jewell, the Mayoress of Barnstaple, convened a meeting of women to set up a 'War Supply Depot' in the town. The depot opened only weeks later at the Golden Lion Hotel where Jewell was able to announce that both Tawstock and Arlington working groups had affiliated to the depot with many more parishes expressing an interest.

7. The Golden Lion Tap, Barnstaple.

While his wife was establishing this depot her husband issued an appeal for money and clothing to help the 75 Belgian refugees in Barnstaple. Numbers of Belgians in North Devon were, however, decreasing at this time with the *Journal* noting at the start of the month that at South Molton 'the last company of Belgian refugees left…for a refugee camp' whilst the original ten refugees in Bickington had now fallen to just three.

Mrs.Jewell's involvement in this work was mirrored in many other spheres as when the local War Agricultural Committee staged meetings in Barnstaple 'to consider questions of male and female labour' with local farmers being urged to employ women – especially the wives of soldiers. A meeting of the Barnstaple Education Committee in the same week heard one speaker conclude that 'Young women would require to be trained to take the places of the men in shops, and not only to serve behind the counter but to keep accounts in order to maintain the organisation of businesses.' Such classes as the speaker advocated began almost immediately in the town such was the urgency of the situation. At Bideford the Grammar School was already employing female teachers owing to the shortage of males many such having enlisted, whilst the Barnstaple Rural district council agreed to replace eligible men with women wherever possible. Councillors themselves were affected by the war as though elections were due this month they were cancelled by a special Act of Parliament leaving sitting councillors in place until the war was over.

A rare photograph was published in the *Daily Graphic* and reproduced in the *Bideford Gazette* showing a Mrs.Daw of Yeolden in Northam, the Honorary Secretary of the 'Vegetable Products Committee' and the stall she had set up in Bideford Pannier Market. Here she collected produce to send to the Navy.

Events aimed at maintaining civilian morale continued to be held, one of the most notable being the visit of Lieut.G.Moor, the youngest VC winner in the British Army, to his mother's home in Braunton.

8. *Mrs.Daw's market stall. BG 2.11.1915 8e-f*

She met him at the village station along with a civic party, the local vicar and a large crowd. Here he was presented with an illuminated address and although 'looking pale and....evidently very weak' briefly replied and was then driven through streets bedecked with flags of the Allies.

The First World War in North Devon

December 1915

The impact of the Derby scheme continued to be felt this month with a 'rush' to attest. Over the weekend of 10th-12th December so many men turned up at the attestation centres that 'special arrangements' had to be made to cope with the numbers who presented themselves. At Barnstaple the Albert Hall was used and it saw 622 men pass through on Friday 10th and 710 on the Saturday. A similar 'rush' was experienced at Bideford where 500 attested on Friday and 600 on Saturday – with even another 60 on Sunday. South Molton saw 120 on Saturday and 71 on Sunday. Torrington's centre was 'besieged' with some 486 men attesting. The only problem with this huge influx of men willing to serve was that 'Nearly a thousand of those who presented themselves for attestation in North Devon were rejected on medical grounds.' Even with these numbers there was still acrimony over farmers' sons not coming forward, as this letter shows.

1. A letter re the sons of farmers. BG 7.12.1915 8a

As noted previously local VTCs were asked to train these attested men and J.Brewe, the Commandant of the Barnstaple Corps, wrote a letter to the *Journal* offering training to any man who desired it he pointing out 'it will enable men to get over the irksome recruit stage with a minimum of inconvenience' – and help their prospects of promotion in the Army – which probably wasn't the most important thing on the minds of these men.

They would have read the various letters home being published in the papers such as one from Cpl.William Ackland

2a & b. Cyril Ireland writes to his old headmaster. NDJ 16.12.1915 3c-d

of Barnstaple. He wrote it to his mother as his father and brother were serving in the Forces whilst a younger brother in the Boy Scouts was a 'coast watcher'. He described how the trenches in his area were so full of mud and water that the men were 'not allowed to stop in them' as long as previously and whilst there he was exposed to 'deadly fire'. Another letter from Cyril Ireland to his old headmaster in Ilfracombe gives a vivid picture of the perils of trench warfare.

Along with these eyewitness accounts came the reports of casualties including Trooper George Huxtable from Barnstaple, the fourth member of the Royal North Devon Hussars to die in Gallipoli. Two more members of the regiment were killed there this month. One was Trooper William Ley of Ilfracombe who after being wounded was taken to a hospital ship. Here he died – 'The cause of death was compound fracture of the right leg, amputation and frost bite.' The second was Sergt.William Loosemore of Barnstaple who was killed by a Turkish sniper, he leaving a widow and six children.

3. The human reality of the war. NDJ 30.12.1915 3d

4. A female butcher in Barnstaple

These were all personal tragedies of course but they were overshadowed by Britain's total casualties up to December 9th, details of which were released this month.

Horrifying as these figures are the number of 'Missing' men is surprising and probably is mute testimony to the ferocity of artillery where bodies could literally be obliterated.

Given this level of casualties and enlistments male labour was becoming scarce and more women were taking over men's jobs and here in North Devon a woman at North Molton was recorded as doing a postal round of 9 miles every day. Additionally the Local War Agricultural Committee received resolutions from the Torrington, Bideford and South Molton districts suggesting that boys and girls aged 12 and above be released from school to work on local farms.

Women by now were also helping the Forces and not just as nurses as this month saw a room in the Lion Buildings, Silver Street, Barnstaple made available to the local branch of the Women's Territorial Signallers Corps. This was a semi-military body whose members learnt morse code in order to take over from male signallers in the UK and free them up for service overseas. Women working in the Barnstaple War Supply Depot consigned anther 200 scarves and 400 pairs of mittens to the Army whilst an appeal by the Mayor and Mayoress of Barnstaple saw enough money raised to send a Christmas present and a special card to local men serving abroad. Similar presents were sent to local PoWs from the Braunton shop. At Clovelly and Bideford a Miss Deane from the Board of Trade held public meetings to identify 'work which women may do during this war' she acknowledging 'there was much prejudice against the idea of women working and doing what they had never done before.' This presumably included Miss Lee of Barnstaple who was acting as a butcher.

Nurses at the Barnstaple Red Cross hospital in the Derby lace factory's Miller Institute all received presents as did their patients – with the celebrations being especially joyous given the 'instinctive feeling that victory and peace will be proclaimed' before the end of 1916.

5. The Miller Institute, Barnstaple.

This might have been the hope but at Ilfracombe 'Craigmore' was taken over as another convalescent home for wounded soldiers although it didn't open until August 1916.

By this date groups of Red Cross nurses were spread across North Devon – with one particular group being photographed in the Rectory grounds at North Tawton.

Children were also helping the war effort by subscribing their pocket money to buy Christmas presents for the soldiers and sailors via 'The Overseas Club' – for which they received a colourful card recording their gift.

Not only did children help Servicemen but some dressed up as their fathers including this unnamed boy who is wearing a miniature uniform, complete with puttees, with a Devonshire Regiment badge on his hat.

One unexpected death due to the war occurred in Appledore where 73 year old Captain Thomas Fishwick, a local shipowner, was found drowned next to the Quay. At the inquest he was said to have 'had a little drop of drink' and then fallen over the Quay in the pitch black which was itself due to the 'blackout regulations'. Not every place was observing these rules as stringently as Appledore as when Alice Lovering was fined 5/- for having 'unobscured' lights in her windows at Combe Martin the local 'coast watcher', Mr.Vincent,

6. A distant view of 'Craigmore', Ilfracombe – to the left.

7. Red Cross nurses at North Tawton. (Copyright Beaford Arts)

reckoned that if he 'really did his duty he would have to summon half of Combe Martin.'

As 1915 came to an end the *Journal* noted how a brass tablet to the memory of George Skinner, killed in action in France, was placed in Chittlehampton church – the first war memorial of so many more to be erected in North Devon.

8. The Overseas Club 'thank you' card presented to a Bideford boy.

9. A boy dressed in the Devonshire Regiment uniform.

The First World War in North Devon

January 1916

The year began with the publication of national figures resulting from Lord Derby's scheme. Of just over 5 million eligible men some 2.8 million had presented themselves for attestation – of whom 428,000 were rejected on medical grounds. Derby himself noted the success this represented but pointed out that some 651,000 'starred' single men had not 'offered themselves' and this was unfair to those married men who had. Men were allocated into a Class based on the year of their birth. Class 1 was for those born in 1897 i.e. 18 year olds but they were not to be called up until they were aged 19. Class 2 was for those born in 1896, Class 3 for 1895 and so on up to Class 23 for those born in 1875.

These national figures came out in the same week as Prime Minister Asquith introduced the Military Service Act. Simply put this specified that single men 'with no grounds whatever for exemptions or excuse' who had not attested would 'be treated as if they had attested.' This, of course, was compulsory conscription by any other name. Asquith went on to say there would be a right of appeal to local 'Tribunals' on various grounds i.e.

1. men were employed on vital war work
2. men were the sole support of others
3. men were ill
4. men had a conscientious objection to war

It was this last concession that would cause much trouble in months to come.

Results from Derby's scheme in North Devon were actually very good – with Lynton recording the best response as only 6 eligible men in the parish had not attested. Pressure to finally attest came from two directions. Firstly the armlets or 'badges' worn 'proudly' by attested men would have singled out those without them and secondly, the Rolls of Honour that were becoming ever commoner. At Lynton the Roll displayed the names of 275 recruits to the Army and 55 to the Navy from the nine parishes centred on Lynton. At Loxhore a Roll which was hung on the church door had 18 names on it. Such Rolls made it clear to everyone who had and who hadn't come forward.

The first Tribunals were set up a week after the Prime Minister's speech and they appear to have been modelled on those earlier bodies looking at the 'starring' of men. In Barnstaple the members were the Mayor F.Jewell, Alderman H.Barrett, W.Cooke, A.Hopper and T.Hodge and at their first meeting they heard 17 claims 'to be put back in later groups' (i.e. to defer their 'call up') with 'several' applications being allowed. At Bideford 3 appeals were heard and only 1 granted this being due to 'special circumstances'; at Northam 5 appeals were considered with 3 'put back several classes' and the other 2 dismissed. Whilst these Tribunals were sitting Lord Derby sent telegrams to local councils asking them to make yet another approach to unattested, single men and ask them to voluntarily attest – the last gasp of 'voluntaryism' in the war. Postcards issued around this time stressed the patriotic duty of men to enlist.

STAND UP FOR JESUS (1)

STAND up!—stand up for Jesus! Ye soldiers of the Cross;
Lift high His royal banner, it must not suffer loss.
From victory unto victory His army He shall lead,
Till every foe is vanquish'd, and Christ is Lord indeed.

BAMFORTH COPYRIGHT.

1. A postcard issued early in the war highlighting patriotic feelings.

That every man would be needed was brought home to North Devonians when it was announced that the 1/6th Devons, the local Territorials in India, were 'to mobilise for service with the Indian Expeditionary Force at the Persian Gulf.' They were to join the volunteers from the regiment who had already gone there and suffered casualties. Another of these men died of his wounds this month he being L/Cpl.Charles Copp of Ilfracombe who had been one of the first to enlist in August 1914. He was joined a few days later by 19 year old Pte.Henry Thorne from Barnstaple who also died of his wounds.

More casualties were recorded in France including 24 year old L/Cpl.Mervyn Roach from West Down his death being the first to be marked in the *Journal* with his photograph.

Other casualties in the Dardanelles included 19 year old Pte. Charles Slack from Landkey and Captain Clemson of Stevenstone. One Royal Navy sailor Frank Goman from Barnstaple died when ammunition exploded on his ship HMS *Natal* while it was at anchor whilst Arthur Gayton from Bickington went down with his merchant steamer in the Mediterranean.

The war was becoming even more bitter if a letter from Pte.Frank Norman of Bradiford is anything to go by. Fighting in France he noted 'It's nothing but mud and water out here, even worse than last year' adding 'We had a very quiet Christmas; no talking with the Germans this Christmas like we did the last.' Bert Reed of Braunton in a letter to his sister reckoned 'The Huns will find that their next gas attack will have a very different effect to what I witnessed last Whitsun, when so many of our brave troops were practically murdered.' A letter from Trooper W.Watts of Goodleigh to his old schoolteacher Miss Boon stressed the monotony of life in the trenches at Gallipoli saying 'You feel very shut in as you see little, except earth walls and sandbags except when looking through a loophole.'

THE LATE LANCE-CORPL. MERVYN ROACH (WESTDOWN).

2. L/Cpl.Mervyn Roach. NDJ 20.1.1916 6a

3 & 4. Sentimental postcards sent to Servicemen away from home.

Letter writing was a two-way exchange but very few letters sent to men in the Forces seem to have survived. Two very sentimental cards sent from a Bideford family to their soldier father are probably typical of the morale-boosting messages sent.

Gifts weren't confined to Christmas and various working groups were producing goods that would be sent to servicemen through the rest of the year. Thus the Lynton War Hospital Supply Depot had thirty women turning out various requisites every day. Westleigh's Women's War Working Party was making pillows, towels, hot water bottle covers and socks using material purchased by well-wishers. A group meeting in Lynton three days a week was making dozens of crutches for wounded soldiers.

The Bideford & District War Supply Depot sent felt slippers and pyjamas to military hospitals and 'two bales of mufflers and mittens' to France.

Rather more negative news came from

5. Crutch making at Lynton

Barnstaple where bakery workers were in dispute with their employers over Christmas pay. The Mayor offered to arbitrate, he coming down in favour of the employers – whereupon the bakers said they would be submitting a new working contract. Such labour disputes were to flare up many times in the course of the war.

The First World War in North Devon

February 1916

The month began when the MP for Barnstaple, Sir Godfrey Baring, explained, via articles in the local press, the workings of the Military Service Act which he explicitly admitted introduced compulsory military service. In an attempt to find a historical precedent he went as far back as the Anglo-Saxon militia and, in order to make the Bill more palatable, pointed out it would only be in force for the duration of the war though that of course was a rather open-ended commitment. A week after his article appeared 'Groups 10, 11, 12 and 13' were ordered to report for induction into the Army on February 29th. At this time posters were placed in prominent spots, giving the date on which each Class would be called up with each man receiving an individual notice. It was up to each man to report himself for duty and there were penalties for failing to report and for inducing or helping a man to absent himself.

Appeals against the Act continued to be heard by the new Tribunals. In North Devon some 11 local Tribunals were established – at Barnstaple, Bideford, Torrington, Ilfracombe, South Molton, Northam and Lynton along with four rural based ones covering country areas – with one Appeals panel covering them all. In addition there was a County Appeal Tribunal and a Central one in London which heard important 'test' cases. Most of these were staffed, as in the case of Barnstaple, with Mayors, councillors and gentry though in Ilfracombe F.Rigsby, who was a shop assistant, was chosen to represent 'the working classes'. The Barnstaple body this month heard 14 applications granting 7 and rejecting 7. Ilfracombe's Tribunal, sitting for the first time, processed 3 applications with 2 rejected and 1 adjourned.

As can be seen these cases were reported in some detail in the local newspapers with full names usually quoted thus providing a valuable and unique archive given that in 1921 the government ordered that all files, other than a few 'specimen' ones, be destroyed, probably on the grounds of sensitivity especially with regard to conscientious objectors whose wartime stance was seen as bordering on traitorous by many.

ILFRACOMBE LOCAL TRIBUNAL.

A public meeting of the Ilfracombe Local Tribunal was held at the Town Hall on Tuesday evening, to consider claims for postponement and exemption. This was the first meeting of the enlarged body, and there were present Messrs. W. H. Andrew, J.P., R. Fry, E. Mitchell, H. J. H. Cope, W. R. Foster, J. Richards, and R. M. Rowe, with Mr. R. H. Stevens (secretary), and Colonel Maxwell (military representative). Mr. Andrew was voted to the chair.

Mr. J. H. Blackmore (Winsham) applied on behalf of a son for postponement until the tillage had been completed, which would be about the end of April or the beginning of May. The application was not granted.

Mr. E. J. Bolam, photographer, applied for exemption on the ground that he was the sole support of a father aged 63, and a sister, besides having business liabilities that could not be met if he had to give up his business. He said he had three brothers at present in the Army, and another just joining. The case was adjourned to this evening (Thursday).

A claim for exemption was put forward on behalf of Frederick Charles Hancock, 10, Broad-street, on the ground that he was necessary in the business of haulier carried on by his mother, a widow. It was stated that there were three married brothers also connected with the business. The claim had been made irregularly in the first instance, and applicant sent a letter, but did not attend the meeting, having had due notice. The Committee was informed that Hancock had already received his railway warrant. The claim was dismissed.

The Committee afterwards considered a number of claims, which were all ordered to be sent forward.

1. The Ilfracombe Tribunal.
NDJ 24.2.1916 8e

With both the Derby scheme and the Act in place the massive pressure to obtain recruits abated somewhat though there were still news items appearing designed to encourage 'shirkers'. Thus it was reported how a Miss Williams of St.James' Place, Ilfracombe had received a letter from the King congratulating her family as her nine brothers were all in the Forces along with 9 other relatives including cousins, nephews and brothers-in-law.

That recruitment had almost been too successful was discussed at Braunton parish council where councillor Frankpitt recounted how local tradesmen were concerned that with all the young men away their income would drop. To counter this he suggested the council contact the War Office requesting that soldiers be sent to the village where they could be trained – and help the local economy. On a more positive note it was reported how Bidefordian Sergt.Vernon Boyle of the 2/6th Devons in India had been awarded a BSc 'honorary war degree' by the University of London. Again the council at Lynton applied to the War Office for a captured German gun to honour their 'splendid response' to the call for men there being not a single unattested man in the village by this date. They had to wait some time for this war trophy – and when it did arrive it became a very contentious issue.

Winter had seen few major attacks in France and Belgium so casualties were comparatively few this month though one man was especially unlucky. Lieut.Thomas Llewellyn was a 22 year old clerk in the Borough Accounts office in Barnstaple who enlisted into the 3rd Devons, travelled to Devonport where he developed pneumonia and died – all in just two weeks. A second local soldier to die of pneumonia was Sergt.Sam White of the 2nd Devons who was given compassionate leave to return to Braunton for the funeral of his grandmother and then developed his fatal illness on his return to the Front. Trooper Richard West also of Braunton was invalided home from Gallipoli with dysentery and sent to Sheffield Hospital where he died aged 24. One Naval Reservist who died as a result of enemy action was Dennis Williams of Bideford who was serving on a minesweeper in the Mediterranean when it struck a mine and sank.

Sapper R.Long of Barnstaple was allowed home on leave from France and a journalist interviewed him at length. Amongst his long account of erecting barbed wire entanglements, tunnelling mines under the German lines and the need to avoid snipers he noted that when the British captured a trench he and his fellow engineers immediately worked 'to reverse the parapets to enable our men to withstand the vigorous and repeated attacks of the Germans.' After paying tribute to the French and Belgian troops he went on to say that the Germans 'were a finely built race' they being 'one of the finest military nations in the world' which statement would probably not have got past the Army censor if he had written it in a letter home.

A common thread in many letters was the pleasure in receiving gifts from home and this month saw a list of goods sent from the Barnstaple War Supply Depot which included 1000 pairs of mittens and 60 scarves. At Torrington a group of women under the direction of the Mayoress Mrs.G.Copp had sent 100 mufflers and 200 pairs of mittens whilst the Appledore Working Party dispatched 100 pairs of mittens, 55 mufflers, socks and pyjamas. 'Comforts' could also be purchased as this advertisement from G.Boyle of Bideford shows.

Other women continued to replace men in various fields thus at Ilfracombe the Post Office

Comforts for our Brave Soldiers at the Front.

Kee-Pu-Warm Lambskin Waistcoats

With or Without Sleeves, with Natural Wool Fleece.

Also GLOVES, Same Material.

WOOL SLEEPING BAGS & WATERPROOF VALISES.

Wool Gloves, Mitts, Socks, Scarves, Sleeping Caps, Spencers, Cardigan Jackets, Golf Jackets, Jerseys, Underclothing.

LARGE STOCK TO SELECT FROM.

G. BOYLE, Outfitting Department, 4, HIGH STREET, BIDEFORD.

2. 'Comforts' for the troops. BG 8.2.1915 1e-f

employed its first female telegraph messenger and Parkham saw a woman carting turnips whilst at Clovelly a group of village women worked to remove boulders blocking the entrance to the harbour. Meetings at Barnstaple and South Molton led to the compilation of a register of women willing to undertake agricultural and other work – though as a letter from Mrs.L.Morgan of Bishops Tawton pointed out when local farmers paid just 3d an hour to female farm workers most women would choose better paid jobs as domestic servants.

One woman made the news not for her work but rather as an 'alien' suspected of espionage. Bettina Von Hutten was charged with travelling more than 5 miles from her registered residence at Woody Bay Hotel. She was actually an American who had married a German baron though they were now divorced. Her solicitor said that as an American she wasn't an 'enemy alien' and although the magistrates said she had committed an offence she was only bound over in the sum of £5.

A rather more serious case of possible espionage came when Ernest Lees a photographer of Ilfracombe was charged with taking pictures of a wrecked ship at Mortehoe contrary to the regulations banning sketching of

3. The wreck at Mortehoe – possibly the photograph taken by Lees.

photographing of the coastline. This was Lees' second charge on these grounds he having been similarly arrested in April 1915. In this instance his clever solicitor got the case dismissed on a technicality but the fact that Lees was charged showed the continuing paranoia over spies.

This fear was heightened when a Zeppelin raid on various places in England saw 54 civilians killed and 67 injured. One enterprising Barnstaple shopkeeper saw a commercial opportunity and began advertising 'Anti-Zep Blinds'.

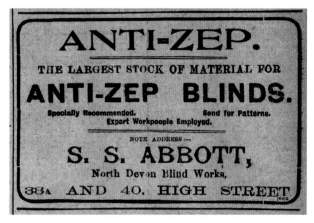

4. Black-out blinds. NDJ 24.2.1916 1f-f

The First World War in North Devon

March 1916

Men who wished to avoid or delay being conscripted under the Derby scheme had to apply for a hearing before their call-up papers arrived and this saw ever increasing work for the local Tribunals and lengthening coverage in local newspapers. The first sitting of the Barnstaple Rural District body heard 45 cases with the Tribunal clerk noting he had received 103 claims from conscripted men and 40 from those who had voluntarily attested. Exemptions were given in many cases especially where the applicant was a farmer or the sole breadwinner in a family. Other applicants weren't so lucky having their requests rejected and being ordered to serve – often after feeble attempts at humour by the Tribunal members as shown in this instance.

Very soon after they were set up each Tribunal had a 'Military Representative' assigned to its numbers who argued against those seeking exemptions – often in much stronger terms than the civilian members.

The Barnstaple Rural body was the first to hear cases of Conscientious Objectors (COs). Thus Alexander Grey of Knowle, Braunton a market gardener said 'he

Amos Gammon, of Morte-Hoe, who applied for his son (Walter Philip Gammon) engaged on mail cart work, admitted he had another son, who had been rejected.—The Chairman : What does he do ? Applicant : He suffers from indigestion.—The Chairman : Indigestion ?—Applicant : Yes, and he is crippled in his feet.—The Chairman : He must be careful what he eats. (Laughter.)—The application was refused.

1. A Tribunal member attempts humour. NDJ 2.3.1916 5g

strongly objected to all forms of military service on ethical grounds'. He was then asked if his land had been in France would he have defended it from the Germans? – to which he replied 'Perhaps I may under a stress of emotion have resisted them.' Evidently his answers angered the Tribunal members as its chair the Rev.J.Dane at one point said 'Send him to mend barbed wire in front of the trenches'. On hearing his application was rejected Grey announced he would appeal. Henry Bedford of Atherington, a horseman on his father's farm and another CO, stated 'I am a follower of the Prince of Peace, a preacher of the Gospel, and am ambassador of Christ. My mission is the reconciliation of men to God, and not their destruction.' He was exempted on the condition he stayed working on the family farm.

The Ilfracombe Tribunal meeting on the 3rd March was the first to pose the famous CO question when Sydney Watts was asked 'what he would do if a German soldier assaulted his mother?' to which he replied 'it was a question of supposition, and he declined to answer'. He was granted exemption but only from 'combatant service' being expected to enter the Medical Corps. The first South Molton Rural Tribunal hearing this month interviewed many agricultural workers but no COs – but they did hear how John Perryman a wheelwright from Bishops Nympton was no longer available he having gone to work in a Taunton munitions factory. Tribunal members clearly believed he had done this just to avoid conscription and on questioning his father as to when he had decided to go to Taunton got the answer 'When Lord Derby's letter came for volunteers.' In the event Perryman was given 2 month's exemption after which he was ordered to come before them.

The Barnstaple Borough Tribunal sat weekly and 'at their first meeting this month they heard 19 cases including that of 19 year old Leonard Parker an apprentice who was ordered to join the Army as 'his small experience' of work didn't make him 'indispensable'. Two COs appeared including William Parker the driver of a 'motor bread van' who at one point during his questioning made the reasonable observation 'The Lord Jesus Christ has distinctly told us we are to love our enemies. You cannot love them by shooting them.' Both applications were refused. At the Tribunal's second meeting 15 applications were heard with exemption only being granted in one case. Among those rejected were 4 from COs including that from William Chilcott who appeared holding a Bible in his hand. Even though he offered to serve in the Medical Corps the chairman, Mayor F.Jewell, wasn't satisfied asking him at one point if he really believed in not defending himself and his country. When Chilcott said yes Jewell replied 'that is the attitude of a fool'. This was the first case where a CO announced he was a member of the Plymouth Brethren

Exemption was asked for in respect of Horace Stanley Youings (25, married), manager of the Bideford branch of Dornat and Co.—Mr. C. A. Youings made the application in respect of his son, who he said was in sole charge of the mineral water factory at Bideford. Owing to the enlistment of the former staff, his son did all the work, including bottling, being only assisted by a boy. He also made the syrups used in the business by a secret process, known only to one other man, who was often ill. Unless exemption was granted it would mean closing the business, with consequent loss to his son after the War. Owing to ill-health, he (Mr. Youings) had for a long time been unable to attend to his business, and another son (who might have helped) was serving with the Royal North Devon Hussars.—The Military authorities did not assent, it being thought a woman could do the work.—Mr. Youings characterised this as simply ridiculous. The firm had already sent every available man, and if his son were taken it would mean the shutting up of the factory.—Mr. Hodge asked what was the actual number of employées before the War.—Mr. Youings: Eight or nine; and we have let every man go. My son does the repairs to machinery, and everything. It would be impossible for a woman to do the work.—Mr. Horace Youings also further explained the position.—In answer to Rev. T. F. Daffen, Mr. C. A. Youings said the factory was working all the year round. Among other things, institutions were supplied with syphons for invalids.—Exemption was granted for six months.

2. Horace Youings appeals. NDJ 23.3.1916 8b

sect they, unusually, not recognizing George V as their King, that position being filled by God. He was refused exemption as was his brother Reginald and another CO Robert Cowle. One CO Frederick Reeves was ordered to be medically examined before a decision on his case was reached. The third meeting saw another 14 cases heard, with another member of the Chilcott family, Arthur, announcing he was a CO. He had been a preacher for 8 years and at his hearing he embarked on a long exposition of his beliefs – only for the Mayor to interrupt with 'Cut it as short as you can.' Chilcott began again only for the Mayor to lose his temper saying 'What! Call yourself an Englishman. It makes one's blood boil. I am surprised to think we have such a man in the town.' Needless to say he wasn't exempted – and indicated he would be appealing. The last meeting of the month saw another 10 cases including one fascinating case involving Horace Youings.

Whilst Barnstaple was the busiest Tribunal other ones were busy processing their many applicants. Thus Torrington Rural deliberated on 16 cases including one CO whilst the Ilfracombe panel heard 18 cases –

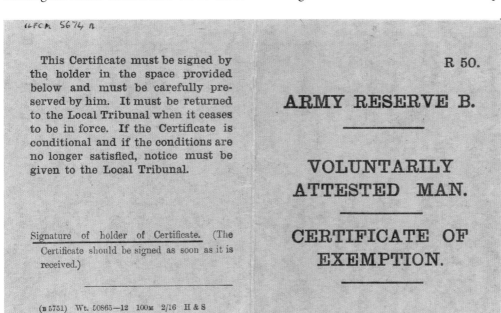

3a. An exemption form for an Ilfracombe man.

Local Tribunal: Name *Ilfracombe*

Address *Town Hall*

Certificate No. *8.*

This is to certify that:—

Name (*in full*) *Fred Harper Western*

Address (*in full*) *2 Winsham Terrace Ilfracombe*

Age *36* Where attested *Barnstaple*

Group *19* Number on Group Card *28*

Occupation, profession or business *Carpenter*

is exempted from being called up for Military Service.

The exemption is*

Temporary expiring on the 11th April 1916

The ground on which the exemption is granted is

that serious hardship would ensue owing to domestic obligations. (a)

Signature *R. H. Stevens*

Date *14/3/16.* for the Tribunal.

* State whether the exemption is absolute, conditional (in which case the conditions should be stated) or temporary (in which case the period of time should be stated).

3b. An exemption form for an Ilfracombe man.

with one seeing an unusual disagreement between a civilian member and the 'Military Representative'. S.Balment, a married dairyman, applied for exemption but the Army man present reckoned 'a woman could do the work' - to which W.Foster replied 'the Military Authorities talked in a very airy and irresponsible fashion about women taking the places of men, in cases where it was not all practicable.'

The Bideford Tribunal heard 17 cases but while they were going through these a public meeting in the Town Hall attended by over 400 attested married men recorded the men's anger at what they saw as the government reneging on their pledge to conscript single men first. They passed a resolution demanding the suspension of the call-up for married men until all single men had gone plus 'adequate provision' for the families where the father had already been conscripted.

It will be remembered that North Devon had an Appeals Tribunal hearing appeals from the district Tribunals and this was first convened in the last week of March at the Barnstaple Forester's Hall. This was held in public with five panel members including a woman, Miss Chichester of Arlington Court. Sixteen appeals were heard including one by the 'Military Representative' against a decision by the Barnstaple Rural Tribunal. Seven COs appeared and 6 were ordered to join the Forces to carry out non-combatant roles whilst 1 was refused any exemption – though this wasn't to be the last that was heard of them. Some COs did agree to serve as medical orderlies or stretcher bearers and this photograph show the 'Barnstaple Seven' – seven COs who fell into this category.

4. The 'Barnstaple Seven' – COs who enlisted in the Medical service.

Reading through these reports one cannot but think that some of the refusals by Tribunals seen harsh. For example the Northam Tribunal heard from William Kemp(e) of Westward Ho! as to how he looked after his father and that two of his brothers had already been killed in action whilst another had lost a leg in the fighting – and one other was still serving. He was given just 3 month's exemption in order to make arrangements for the care of his father. He was later recorded as 'Missing' and was presumed dead.

The reason for this harshness might be seen in the local casualty lists which saw a large increase this month mainly amongst those killed in Mesopotamia where North Devon men were heavily involved in what came to be called the Battle of Kut. The 40 men from the 6th Devons who had volunteered for early deployment in Mesopotamia had been attached to a force pushing Northwards towards Baghdad.

WILLIAM KEMPE.

Son of Samuel and Ann Kempe.
Private – 2nd Devon Regiment.
Missing – Presumed Killed.
Aged 33.

5. Pte.William Kempe

"OVER THE SWEDES AND TURNIPS."

6 & 7. Photographs of the 6th Devons on the march to Kut.

6TH DEVONS ON THE "ROAD" TO KUT.

Faced with an overwhelming Turkish army the 8000 strong British/Indian Army under Major General Charles Townshend retreated following the Tigris river but decided to make a stand at the small town of Kut. Here they were besieged – with the Turks constructing defensive positions further down the Tigris, including the Dujailah Redoubt, to stop any relief force. This tied down the Turkish army which was seen as useful to the overall British strategy in the region but when Townshend reported (inaccurately) that he only had one month's food supply a relief force of 19,000 men (later increased to 30,000) including the rest of the 6th Devons was hastily organised and marched North from Basra to help their comrades.

They first met the enemy at the Battle of Sheikh Sa'ad and after a bloody fight the Turks fell back. Further engagements followed with large losses but the Turks were then reinforced with 20-30,000 men. The British then attacked the Dujailah Redoubt on March 8 but this proved a costly mistake with some 4000 men being killed. Colonel G.Oerton who commanded the 6th Devons published a small pamphlet in 1948 which described the attack as a 'blunder' with its 'suicidal frontal attacks' with the element of surprise 'completely thrown away' by the Generals present.

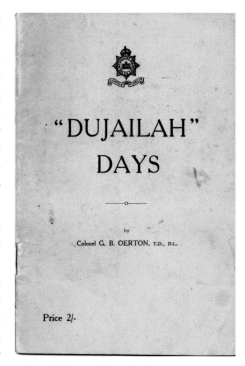

"DUJAILAH" DAYS

by
Colonel G. B. OERTON, T.D., D.L.

Price 2/-

8. *'Dujailah Days' by Colonel G.Oerton.*

Following this failure the Kut garrison surrendered – a move described as 'the worst defeat of the Allies in World War One' by historian Christopher Catherwood.

The first local death from this battle to be recorded in the *Journal* was that of Lieut.H.Baillie who was the youngest son of the vicar of Lynton. Further details of the fighting came the next week with the shocking news that eight more officers from the 6th Devons had been killed with others being wounded. The dead officers were Major R.Fox from Horrabridge, Captain R.Dunn-Pattison of Braunton, Captain E.Bowhay of Torrington, Captain J.Stranger of Holsworthy, Lieut.G.Tizzard of Barnstaple, Lieut.W.Vicary of Ilfracombe, Lieut.A.Heriz-Smith of Bideford and Captain G.Watson of Crediton. A report on the battle where they died then appeared along with the first notices of deaths amongst the rank and file.

A week later the *Journal* carried news of three Barnstaple and two Bideford men killed whilst a very long list of 'Casualties in the Devon Regiment' was published though which theatre of the war they had been fighting in is not specified. Further deaths in France and Gallipoli were reported along with a rare one of a woman. Nurse Lilly Prideaux from Lynton died of pneumonia whilst caring for wounded soldiers at Woolwich Hospital – the first female casualty from North Devon.

1/6th DEVONS IN ACTION.

Death of Another Officer.

Since the publication last week of the list of officers of the 1/6th Devons killed and wounded in the action in Mesopotamia on March 8th further news has been awaited with intense anxiety throughout North Devon, for every town and village is represented in the affected Regiment. As there are so many families in the district directly affected, the Mayor of Barnstaple (Councillor F. A. Jewell) communicated with the War Office authorities asking that, in view of the aggravation of anxiety by suspense, the details of casualties shall be notified as soon as possible.

On Monday news was received at Bideford in regard to three men—Private Percy Braund, 22, of Annery Kiln, seriously wounded, and Private Fred Beer (eldest son of Mr. and Mrs. Fred Beer, Wimborne Terrace, Bideford), and Private (Drummer) Wm. Arnold, 22, eldest son of Mr. and Mrs. Thomas Arnold, Newport Terrace, East-the-Water, dangerously ill from gunshot wounds. Before joining the Army Braund was a gardener at Northam. Both Beer and Arnold were members of the Church Lads' Brigade, and Arnold was also a successful member of the Bideford Amateur Athletic Club. He is an excellent shot, and for two years won the Heriz-Smith Shield offered to the Church Lads' Brigade, of which he was a sergeant. A sturdy lad and good athlete, two years ago he ran second in the Marathon race promoted by the B.A.A.C.

On Monday a cablegram was received by Mrs. Bishop, of Newport-road, Barnstaple, wife of Lieut. and Quartermaster Bishop, of Barnstaple, stating that her husband and Regimental-Sergeant-Major Hudson were all right. Both Lieut. Bishop and R.-S.-M. (formerly Sergt.-Major) Hudson were associated with the 6th Devons' Headquarters at Barnstaple before the War.

Mr. and Mrs. W. H. Reed, of Thornlea, Exeter, were notified by the War Office on Monday that their son, Lieut. Douglas Reed, previously reported wounded, is very dangerously wounded.

9. *Local casualties from the Battle of Kut.*
NDJ 23.3.1916 5f

Additionally further eyewitness accounts of the war were published including the first about Salonika in Northern Greece where a multinational force of Allies had landed to meet an army made up of Austro-Hungarians, Bulgarians and Germans. A letter from Percy Burgess to F.Lord the Ilfracombe headmaster, who received so many letters like this from his former pupils, described conditions this force faced.

Another letter from an Ilfracombe soldier, Jonah Evans, in Belgium showed a rather touching belief that the war was soon to finish when he wrote 'My word what a last show the Germans are making. I really think it is their last hope, but they will never do much now their back is broken, and I am hopeful of the War finishing before another winter.'

At home working parties continued to produce 'comforts' for servicemen with the Barnstaple War Supply Depot supplying not just mufflers, mittens and socks but also '16 helpless coats, 16 nightingales and 10 dressing gowns'. A new group was based in Georgeham they producing 32 mufflers, 38 pairs of mittens and 6 pairs of socks. One unusual letter published this month requested 'the collection and drying of many wild plants' used by pharmacists that were formerly imported from Germany. This letter came from Maud Wainwright and Florence Gould of Barnstaple and was yet another example of the involvement of women in the war. During one Tribunal case it came out that a Chulmleigh school employed three female teachers who had replaced enlisted men, whilst in Bideford the local Women's War Work Committee run by Mrs.Dow had organised the movement of six young women to work in a Birmingham munitions factory. At the same time the county council agreed to children of both sexes leaving education at 12 years of old to work on the land. The oddest news this month was the report that Ilfracombe churches were being insured against 'air raids and bombardment' – the parish church for £10,000 and St.Peter's for £7000.

10. A letter from Percy Burgess.
NDJ 23.3.1916 5b

The First World War in North Devon

April 1916

The month began with an unusual court case in Torrington. Ernest Phillips of Dolton was charged as 'an absentee under the Military Service Act' he having been summoned to the Army but not going. P.c.Bastin who arrested him said 'the prisoner scarcely did any work, and his chief object in life was to lie in bed.' He was fined £2 and handed over to the military authorities. Several other such cases were reported from Bideford and Ilfracombe - with similar outcomes.

Ignoring the call-up was rare though appeals against conscription were becoming ever commoner, thus the first sitting this month of the Bideford Tribunal saw 22 appeals with South Molton Rural having 19 and Ilfracombe 14. At the latter Henry Hale was directed to 'non-combatant service' due to his 'mental health' – a very rare acknowledgement of mental illness at this date. In the same week 9 cases were heard by the North Devon Appeals Tribunal. At the hearing for CO Charles Williams it was recorded how he had joined 'the Society of Reconciliation', a pacifist group, only in February after conscription came into force. He was ordered to enlist 'the statement being received by the public with applause.'

To the Editor of the *North Devon Journal*,

CONSCIENTIOUS OBJECTORS: A SOLDIER'S VIEW.

DEAR SIR,—The excuses made by conscientious objectors before the tribunals at home are causing no end of amusement among the troops here, and not a little disgust, especially that section—and I am glad to find they are in the minority—who base their objection to taking up arms against an unscrupulous enemy on the ground of Christianity. As a North Devonian, I am sorry to observe, in the perusal of your valuable paper, that my own native county is not absolutely free from this class. Were it possible for some of these people to travel —as I have done—through some of the towns and villages of Northern France, and witness for themselves the wholesale destruction of some of the most beautiful cathedrals and churches in Christendom ; the thousands of once happy homes laid desolate, the furnishing of which must have cost the occupants years of anxious toil and care, the pity of it, the utter misery of it, must surely appeal to any man—particularly an Englishman— who has an ounce of Christianity in him. Does not the brutal murder of Nurse Cavell, the wholesale slaughter of hundreds of women and young children, the violation of pure young girls in public squares by these beasts of Germans before the very eyes of their parents, the latter, because they rightly objected to such savagery, being shot down like carrion—do none of these things, I say, appeal to their better nature, and call out for vengeance ? No ; they emphatically declare—I would not so much as lift my hand against the perpetrators of these atrocious crimes—it is un-Christian ; it is not in accordance with the teachings of Holy Writ ! Now, sir, I have no time for arguing this question, but I am bound to say I am sorry for the religion which does not permit a man to take part in punishing such crimes to the uttermost. The question arises : Is it *conscience* or *cowardice* which keeps these individuals from wanting to fight the Germans ? My own humble opinion is, sir, and the same opinion is held by every individual man who is doing his bit here, that these standbacks are simply using religion as a cloak, behind which to hide. What would the late Sir Henry Havelock, General Gordon, or Lord Roberts, three of our greatest Christian heroes, have thought of them ? I am, sir,

Yours faithfully,

FRED J. MITCHELL (Sergeant), Salonica (late of Westdown), March 25th, 1916.

Given the religious basis for CO's appeals it was doubtless heartening for Tribunal members to read an article published in the parish magazine of Barnstaple's St.Mary Magdalene church. In it the writer quoted the 37th 'Article of Religion' of the Church of England viz; 'it is lawful for Christian men, at the commandment of the Magistrate, to wear weapons, and serve in the wars' – though given that most COs quoted the Bible rather than church rules this probably didn't alter their views. This interpretation of religious rules seems to have been used to overcome Asquith's promise about moral beliefs being respected. It is worth noting that clergymen were granted automatic exemption as happened when the Rev.O.Evans, a Methodist minister at Torrington, appeared before that borough's Tribunal this month.

In the same issue of the *North Devon Journal* that saw his case reported there was a letter from a serving soldier denouncing CO's religious objections.

As the month progressed it became clear that exemptions were only being given in very few cases – generally where the men were farmers or could prove that, if called up, food production would suffer. Occasionally, however, men were exempted if they had other family members in the

1. Denouncing COs. NDJ 13.4.1916 2g

Forces. Thus the Barnstaple Rural Tribunal granted exemptions to William Rooke, a farm labourer of Wrafton, who had four brothers serving, and William Crocombe of Combe Martin four of whose brothers were in the Forces whilst a fifth had been killed in action. Some men who claimed they were the only support of aged or infirm relatives were told that as the Government paid an allowance to these relatives when a man joined the Forces no exemption would be granted – which seemed to negate another of Asquith's original promises regarding conscription.

When the North Devon Appeals Tribunal met for the second time this month CO Arthur Chilcott appeared and stated he 'would not do anything to help the military machine'. Unfortunately for his case evidence was produced that he had been working locally on the production of munition boxes – he was ordered to enlist as a non-combatant. At the same meeting three other COs were refused exemption, with E.Worth being another who had been making munition boxes although he made the point 'If onc strikes a match in the street now there is a heavy tax upon them, the people say one is helping the war.'

At the Lynton Tribunal two applicants were told women could their job but Sidney Jones, a house furnisher and ironmonger, disputed this arguing 'women were not fit to lift about heavy furniture and ironmongery'. H.Cooper a photographer appearing on behalf of his employee A.Tothill reckoned that it would take a year at least to train a woman in photography to replace him. Both lost their cases. At the Barnstaple Tribunal a week later when a master baker was asked if he could get a woman to take an employee's place replied 'No, bread baking is too hard work for women.' In this case the applicant was given exemption as bakers were seen as vital to maintaining food supplies. Again at a Torrington Rural Tribunal a farmer blankly stated 'he did not think women were much good for farm work.'

2a, b & c. Eye witness accounts.
NDJ 20.4.1916 5c

It was this month that saw the Government order Workhouse officers to detain any vagrants of military age until 'the arrival of a military escort.' The government also ordered that conscription apply to men from their 18th birthday – and removed exemptions from horsemen, ploughmen and cattlemen under the age of 25. That conscription was now the main way of raising new troops was shown when the Recruiting Office at Ilfracombe was closed on 21st April.

These new conscripts would have taken the place of the dead and wounded who this month included 3 men dying of their wounds and 2 who died of disease – with only 2 being killed on the battlefield – an indication of the still relatively basic state of medicine at this date. Thus L/Cpl.Lambden of Bideford died of pneumonia, Lieut.J.Platt of Youlston died of his wounds and Pte.A.Manning of Marwood was killed in action.

Letters from survivors of the Dujailah battle began to appear in local newspapers and they are so graphic that a few are reproduced here.

3. Torrington Boy Scouts.

Whilst their menfolk were away fighting more and more women were being drafted in to do what had previously been men's jobs. Women carters were seen in Barnstaple and a female drover turned up at the town's Cattle Market, with a Bideford hotel employing a female porter. At South Molton three women were working on allotments while in Ilfracombe a list was drawn up of women willing to undertake agricultural work. Some 100 people attended a meeting of the Women's War Agriculture Committee at Arlington Court to hear the group's Secretary Miss Chichester say 'It would be very difficult during the next year to cultivate

4. Boys 'drilling' at Kings Nympton. (Copyright Beaford Arts)

the land unless the women were properly organised in order to take the place of men.' Another speaker referred to creches 'started in many parishes' which freed up women for farm work. In addition to women local Boy Scouts were helping the war effort by organising the collection of waste paper for recycling and younger boys were 'drilling' with wooden rifles – as shown in this shot from Kings Nympton.

In times of national exigency we suppose natural beauty must give place to practical utility, and so one finds many lovely spots, whose chief glory was the magnificent woods of larch firs, quite denuded of trees and only resembling the Canadian clearings, the white stumps showing too clearly what has happened. This is the case right through the West Lyn Valley and at Woody Bay, while pretty much the same is going on in the extensive Bonsidecott Wood, at the foot and on the side of mighty "Summerhouse," the mountain sentinel and pride of both townships.

5. The destruction of the countryside. NDJ 27.4.1916 3e

One aspect of the 'war effort' led to complaints, this being the felling of large numbers of trees for use as trench supports by the military. A Lynton journalist expressed these concerns succinctly this month.

Another correspondent, J.Lucas, wrote to the *Western Morning News* suggesting that German PoWs be employed on building a breakwater and harbour at Lundy Island. He noted that 'we are keeping and feeding thousands of them in absolute idleness, while necessary undertakings such as I have indicated are standing still for want of labour.' Perhaps he did not realise that prisoners had been used (illegally) by a previous owner of Lundy in the eighteenth century? The oddest complaint, however, was probably one from the Combe Martin Jam & Preserve Company who, at their AGM, heard the chairman R.Clogg point out that because their glass jars came from France and Belgium there had been a major shortage at the start of the war – leading them to replace them with 'Barum ware jars' [Barnstaple pottery] which enabled them to increase their output.

The First World War in North Devon

May 1916

May began with the news that some 5 million men were now serving in the Forces – but that even more were required if the Allies were to win. It is perhaps surprising therefore that at the first meeting of the North Devon Appeals Tribunal this month out of the 26 cases that came before them only 9 were refused with exemptions or adjournments granted to the rest. Some of these were men who had already been granted a short exemption who were now reapplying at the end of that time – only to be granted another as their grounds for the appeal had not changed. As before the many difficult cases were sometimes leavened with attempts at humour as when Frank Rawle of High Bickington, the local slaughterer, appeared and claimed 'I kill for everybody from the cottager to the clergyman' – only for Captain Vosper, the military representative on the panel, to ask 'You would not mind killing Germans?' to laughter. He was ordered to enlist.

Whilst these cases were being heard the Torrington Rural Tribunal were listening to H.Holwill, manager of the North Devon Clay Company, argue on behalf of 24 of his employees. He pointed out that before the war the company employed 145 men but 47 had left for the Forces and several others had gone into reserved occupations – with output falling from 30,000 to 20,000 tons a year. Of the 24 he applied for 5 were ordered to enlist immediately while the rest were given 2 or 4 month exemptions. Tribunal decisions could still be fairly harsh as shown in this one opposite by the Appeals Tribunal.

At the same Appeals Tribunal one case was heard where the members 'did not like the facts of it at all' it seeming to them 'that it was an attempt to keep the son from serving in the Army'. W.Muxworthy, aged 22, was farming 59 acres at Parracombe – but his tenancy was very recent and seemingly only taken to allow him to claim exemption as a farmer. He was actually allowed to stay until October but was told he would then have to enlist. Such 'artificial' tenancies were to come before the Tribunals quite often. In another case the Lynton Cliff Railway applied for 3 men on the grounds that the company was 'incorporated under Special Act of Parliament' which designated them as 'a carrying company' which gave their employees protection from conscription to a certain extent. The Lynton Tribunal ordered one man to enlist and gave exemptions to the other two for 4 months.

On being unstarred by the local Tribunal on April 18th, Sydney Bament, an attested man, aged 18, a horseman and ploughman in the employ of Mr. Smyth-Richards, at Kentisbury, was appealed for by his employer, being represented at the Tribunal by the bailiff, Mr. Bament. — The bailiff said that the farm was 230 acres, 100 acres being arable. Two pairs of horses were worked, and unless these were worked there would not be sufficient work for the manual labourers—four men, a boy, and the bailiff. Two of the horses were colts, and the boy of 16 could not manage the horses.—By the Bench: One colt had to be worked with one of the older horses, so that in any case the boy, if taught to drive, would have to deal with a colt which he was unable to do. If the appellant was taken no horse work could possibly be done, as the other men were suffering from various infirmities, thus being incapable of managing the horses. If no horse work could be done no manual labour would be needed, and the other men would be dismissed.—Capt. Vosper: I attended a conference of agricultural and military representatives on Appeal Tribunals, on Saturday, and we arrived at a substantial agreement that for the present, at any rate, we would allow, if possible, and if the Tribunal thought fit, one man to each team of horses that are at work, provided the horses are not worked as a luxury, but are really necessary for the land. I suggest that a young man of 18 should not get absolute exemption—it is still up to the farmer to get somebody older. One does not press to take into immediate service a man of this description. Another part of the agreement we arrived at on Saturday was to the amount of labour to be left on the land. It was distinctly laid down that the farmer himself should take up one of the certified occupations as well; he should either be the shepherd or the cattleman.—Mr. Metherell urged that the horsework must be considered. There were plenty of men but scarcity of capable horsemen on this farm.—The Chairman said that the boy of 16 should be trained to drive horses; and the Tribunal gave two months to get him trained. —Mr. Bament: I shall not attempt it; I shall only get the boy killed.—The Clerk: You can appeal at the end of two months.—Mr. Bament: I shall not attempt to teach him to drive those colts. —The Clerk: Get some older horses. The military authorities appealed against the

1. A harsh decision. NDJ 18.5.1916 5f

Half way through the month a new power was given to the Tribunals. Where men were given exemptions they could now be directed to join their local Voluntary Training Corps. In the event the vague wording behind this power meant that it was up to the man whether they joined or not – and as was pointed out at a meeting of the Barnstaple Borough Tribunal it was asking a lot of men who began work at 6.30 a.m. to attend evening drills of the VTC.

By this stage in the war COs appearing before Tribunals were becoming a rarity so it was unusual when Walter Trebble of South Molton appeared before the North Devon Appeals Tribunal. He claimed to be an 'auxiliary postman, cycle agent and clock jobber' and although passed for non-combatant service by his local Tribunal refused to enlist; his application was rejected. An earlier CO made headlines this month. It will be recalled that Arthur Chilcott on his appearance before the Tribunal had refused to help the war effort in any way. Ordered to enlist he had been taken to Exeter Barracks where, refusing to either work or be medically examined, he was sentenced to '28 days' field punishment'. He then refused to accept this punishment and was sent for Court Martial it being noted that he was 'courteous and respectful' all through the process and indeed 'expressed appreciation of the kindness and consideration shown by the military authorities.' Notwithstanding this the court sentenced him to 112 days detention in a military prison – though this was appreciably lower than five other COs who were also court martialled at the same time and sentenced to 6 months in prison, they including S.Pethick from Holsworthy.

Another local CO Charles Williams of Braunton was arrested after failing to report for enlistment and as usual in such cases he was fined £2 and handed over to the military. In a similar case concerning J.Whitham, an 'author' of Parracombe, he refused to pay the fine but the police said they had found £1.18.0 on him when arrested – and this was taken by the magistrates to cover the fine before he was taken away by the Army.

As in every month casualties were being recorded in the local newspapers with 11 deaths from fighting in May including Pte.J.Edward of Bideford, Cpl.Gerald Milton of Braunton and Pte.Fred Greenslade of Rackenford. Three more soldiers succumbed to illness whilst Pte.Robert Stoneman of Bideford, after initially being reported as being killed at the Battle of Kut, was then found to have been sent to Baghdad as a prisoner of the Turks where he died – the fate of many Turkish prisoners – indeed a figure as high as 50% has been suggested. Further eyewitness accounts of the battle were printed including one by a *Western Morning News* journalist serving with the 'Kut Relief Force' which was probably pored over by relatives of the local men engaged in the fighting.

This disaster had spurred North Devonians to greater efforts to aid their men and following a special appeal by the Mayor of Barnstaple some 20,000 cigarettes, 10,000 tea tablets, 480 Oxo cubes and 'miscellaneous parcels' were sent to Mesopotamia – with more coming from all the surrounding towns and rural areas. This was in addition to the large quantity of 'comforts' sent to British troops in Serbia and East Africa at this date. Such gifts were paid for in various ways as shown by the accounts of the Barnstaple War Supply Depot published this month.

BALANCE SHEET OF THE BARNSTAPLE WAR SUPPLY DEPOT, from November 3rd, 1915, to May 23rd, 1916.

	£	s.	d.
Collected at Preliminary Meeting	2	6	4
Proceeds of Picturedrome (per Mr. W. J. Cooke)	20	8	0
Municipal Charities	5	0	0
Organ Recital at Baptist Chapel	4	1	0
Proceeds of Bridge Drive	6	3	0
Pilton Contribution	8	0	0
Newport Contribution	3	0	0
Cage Bird Show	3	10	6
Women's Unionist Association Tea	3	0	0
House-to-house Collection (per Mrs. Dennis)	21	11	6
Concert arranged by Miss Pile	17	10	6
Proceeds of Billiard Match (per Mr. W. L. Croot)	2	4	0
Part surplus from Mayoress's Tea to Soldiers' and Sailors' wives)	9	0	0
Performance at Theatre (per Miss Jenkin)	30	0	0
Part proceeds of Sale of Work (per Mrs. Dennis and Mrs. James)	5	0	0
Part Collection English Flag Day (per the Mayoress)	5	0	0
Sale of Waste Paper (per Mrs. Dennis)	2	17	2
Tea money at Depôt	28	14	0
Mr. Guard	4	0	0
Dr. Jonas	3	0	0
Mrs. J. Harper	1	1	0
W. Richards and Co.	1	1	0
Miss D.	1	1	0
Mr. and Mrs. Richards	1	0	0
Mr. Richards	1	0	0
Mrs. Faviell	1	0	0
Mrs. Incledon-Webber	1	0	0
Mrs. Hinchliffe	9	5	6
Sums under £1			
	£201	15	3
Expenses	186	5	1
Balance in hand	15	10	2

Hon. Treasurer: Mrs. JAMES.

2. The Barnstaple War Supply Depot accounts. NDJ 25.5.1916 4g

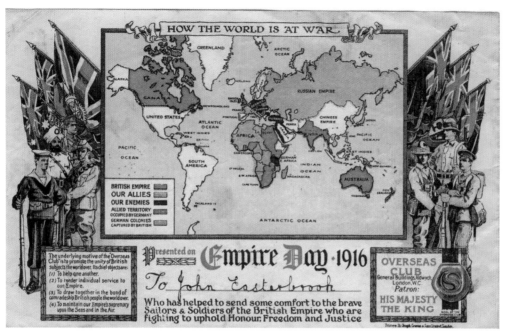

3. An Empire Day card.

Another source were children as this 'Empire Day' card records – Jack Easterbrook was a local boy who as an adult became the man in charge of Bideford railway goods yard.

It will be noticed how many women were involved in the Depot's work and it is clear from many reports that many more were being employed on the land. This month saw South Molton MP George Lambert write an article for the *Sunday Herald* in which he forecast a 'coming food crisis' owing to the enlistment of so many farm workers. At one point he wrote 'We are told that women can take the place of men. No doubt women can, if they wish, do a considerable amount of light work at harvest time, weeding, looking after cattle to some extent, and so on….Woman cannot drive horses, plough or harrow like skilled men.' In fact the 'food crisis' didn't really materialise until 1918 when the Government was forced to introduce rationing for many foodstuffs.

Lambert apparently hadn't seen a report produced for the Devon County Agricultural War Committee this month which showed that across 200 Devon parishes some 2000 women had indicated they were willing to work part-time on farms. As to training them

4. George Lambert MP.

in the necessary skills Seale-Hayne College near Newton Abbot was to allow women to attend classes and the County Dairy School would continue to teach milking and dairy hygiene to women. At the same time moves by the county council allowing children to leave school and work on the land hadn't been very successful it being reported that only 67 pupils over 13 were actually being employed.

Of rather more interest to the Barnstaple Education Committee was the question of children going to local cinemas and seeing 'unsuitable films' – with one member F.Hunt asserting that a rise in juvenile crime locally was attributable to these films and as such censorship should be introduced immediately. In fact cinemas at this time were helping the war effort with, for example, the Palace in Ilfracombe donating one night's takings to help wounded French soldiers whilst all cinemas were paying a special 'War Tax' on ticket sales. They also showed the only moving pictures of the war and these were immensely popular with the people - also being seen by the Government as morale boosters.

Audiences clearly weren't put off by the possibility of air raids though Bideford and Northam councils did issue a notice telling people what to do in the event of a raid.

Although private cars were still a rarity their owners had to obscure their lights at night in order to foil bombardment from German warships. Unfortunately William Jones of Barnstaple was charged with driving with 'unobscured' lights but luckily the magistrates dismissed him with a caution. Another oddity came when Barnstaple council ordered that the striking of all public clocks in town be stopped – no reason was given but presumably this was to allow tired war workers to get an uninterrupted night's sleep. The authorities did, however, bring in one innovation that affected everyone when 'Summer Daylight Saving' was introduced thus giving workers an extra 130 hours of daylight and allowing a major saving in the use of coal gas for lighting, The motion in Parliament passed by 170 votes to 2.

AIR RAIDS.

THE TOWN COUNCIL OF BIDEFORD and the NORTHAM URBAN DISTRICT COUNCIL deem it advisable in the interest of public safety to issue the following precautionary notice in view of a possible Air Raid on the Town and Neighbourhood

1. —Warning of the approach of hostile air craft will be given by three long blasts on a Hooter or Syren Whistle, with Six Seconds interval between each.

2. —Immediately on such alarm Householders should see that **all lights in their houses are extinguished, and in particular that all gas taps are turned off, and that the gas is turned off at the meter,** and also that any Public Lights outside their respective houses are extinguished.

3. Inhabitants are particularly requested (except where otherwise directed) to remain in their houses during the continuance of any raid, as crowding in the streets is most dangerous and obstructs the work of the police and other officials.

4.—Directly all danger is over a prolonged blast will be sounded on the Hooter or Syren Whistle.

It is quite possible that warning may be given and no raid follow, but these instructions are given to the Public by way of precaution.

By order of the Councils,

S. R. CHOPE, Mayor.
W. T. CHARLEWOOD,
Chairman Northam U.D.C.

Dated 1st May, 1916.

5. An air raid warning. BG 2.5.1916 2e

The First World War in North Devon

June 1916

This month saw further bad news for North Devon families. A first list of those taken prisoner by the Turks at the Battle of Kut was published naming 17 men – many of whom were to die in the notoriously bad Turkish prison camps.

A national disaster also had local impacts. On 5 June 1916 HMS *Hampshire* hit a mine and sank whilst carrying Lord Kitchener, the Secretary for War, on a secret visit to Russia to discuss the war. Of the 749 persons on board only 12 survived and amongst the officers who went down with the ship was Lt.Cdr.Richard Skynner of Bideford who had only been recently married. Only days before Britain's Grand Fleet had met the German fleet in the North Sea and a massive fight ensued which

The list of West-countrymen supposed to have been taken prisoners by the Turks at Kut include the following, of the Devon Regiment (attached to the Dorsets) : — W. R. Colley, Bideford ; F. Davey, Winkleigh ; Lance-Corpl. F. P. Dennis, Barnstaple ; W. Dennis, Barnstaple ; A. Norman, Barnstaple ; W. Parkhouse, Appledore ; J. H. Scilly, Appledore ; W. Scilly, Bideford ; E. Smith, Barnstaple ; Corpl. G. Smith, Bideford ; A. Trump, Ilfracombe ; and F. Turner, Winkleigh. The supplementary list (published on Monday) of men believed to have been taken at Kut include the following of the Devons (attached to the Royal West Kent Regiment) :—W. Gooding, Chittlehampton ; T. Harvey, Barnstaple ; G. Lugg, Dulverton ; P. Smale, Landkey ; and S. J. White, Beaworthy.

1. Prisoners of the Turks. NDJ 29.6.1916 5d

became known as the Battle of Jutland. Two eyewitness accounts were published in the *Journal* both from Ilfracombe men – R.Gumm on HMS *Tiger* and Stoker Eric Kipling – see next page.

The idea of a 'Brilliant Victory' has not been accepted by historians as the Germans sunk 14 British ships losing 11 themselves although the German surface fleet didn't put to sea again during the war concentrating rather on submarine warfare. Gumm's reference to 'carnage' was true with a combined death toll of nearly 10,000 sailors. North Devonians who died included Lieut.Robert Chichester of HMS *Black Prince* the son of Rear Admiral Sir Edward Chichester of Youlston. Others were Gunner W.Beer of Bishops Tawton on HMS *Lion* and Stokers Wesley Cann and William Short on HMS *Defence* both from Barnstaple. Unusually the *Journal* published quite a few reports saying how sons and husbands serving on ships involved in this battle had sent messages home saying they were safe. One Torrington man who died in this sea battle is commemorated in the town cemetery. Robert Palmer was serving on HMS *Black Prince* when he too went down with the ship – which is represented in a naïve carving on his family gravestone – with the vessel's name picked out in lead letters.

In addition to these two major reverses further North Devonians were dying in various theatres of war. Thus Sapper Ulysses Harris from Woolacombe died in Salonica aged 22, Captain Hugh O'Brien of Instow, the commander of an anti-aircraft battery, was killed in France and L/Cpl.Stanbury from Barnstaple died of his wounds in Mesopotamia. Others succumbed to illness including 26 years old Pte.W.Hearn from Buckland Brewer who, whilst undergoing initial training at Wareham, died of heart failure. Local people could still

86

'COMBEITE'S STORY OF NAVAL BATTLE.

A "Brilliant Victory" For The British.

Mr. E. J. Gumm, a 'Combeite, who was on H.M.S. "Tiger" during the great naval battle off Jutland on May 31st, writes the following interesting letter to Mr. H. J. Macey, Headmaster of Holy Trinity Boys' School, Ilfracombe:—

Dear Mr. Macey,—In fulfilment of my promise to write when the "day" again arrived, I pen you a few lines. I can well imagine yours and the state of mind of the public in general when you heard the official announcement last Friday. I can begin in no better way than by assuring you that Admiral Beatty, in his address this morning, describes the battle as a "brilliant victory" for us. One will have to admit that it was dearly won, but if you consider that the brunt of the battle fell on nine battle cruisers, then you will see that ours was no mean achievement. Again, outside the gallant lives that have gone, only one really capital ship has gone, viz., the "Queen Mary," whilst on the German side, five of their best ships, including the "Hinderburg" (14 2in. guns), have gone. Men in the "Invincible" who were in a position to see, state that at one time we were firing at five ships; a haze then came over them, and when it c'eared, only three were seen; so probably they went down. We, in addition to fighting a numerically superior force, were also fighting the conditions, as the Huns held the Eastern side, which, with the sun making for the West, silhouetted our ships against the horizon. I cannot see how their losses can be under 10,000 —a terrible death roll, for such a few hours. We waited 16 months for them this time; I think they will keep us another twelve waiting again. They will come again! I am confident on that point, and my sincerest wish is that I may, for my third occasion, occupy my position in this magnificent ship. We are, I believe, credited with sinking (by ramming) one submarine—I well remember the time. The ship seemed to lift out of the water and drop again. I thought we had gone to our Maker, as we thought we had been torpedoed.

Before finishing, I should like to tell you that a naval battle is a gruesome affair—only those who have taken part in one will ever realise the carnage, &c., which goes on. But rest assured that when the next 'day' arrives, the British Navy will not be found wanting. Man and boy—they were magnificent!

COMBE SAILOR'S EXPERIENCES IN NORTH SEA BATTLE.

Amongst the crew of one of the light cruisers attached to Admiral Beatty's Fleet was Stoker Eric Kipling, a son of Mrs. Kipling, 5, Springfield-road, Ilfracombe, who was home for a couple of days leave last week and told to a Press representative his experiences of the great fight off Jutland.

Kipling is a native of the town, and was at one time in the employ of Messrs. Smith and Son. He was at sea three years in the merchant service, and joined the Royal Navy in January 29th.

In common with all who took part in the battle whose experiences have been published, Kipling says that the licking given to the Germans was a very much bigger one than one would appear from a mere comparison of losses so far as they can be substantiated. As soon as our big ships appeared the Germans' one idea seemed to be to get away as fast as they could.

When they were facing our cruiser squadron they had the advantage of numbers, and they made the most of it. Their shooting was good, but later on when they saw the only alternatives were flight or annihilation, it was not so good.

The cruiser on which Kipling was a stoker went into action between 4 and 5 in the afternoon. The weather was beautiful and the sea as calm as a mill pond. Later on the sea got up and the weather became bad. Kipling was employed passing ammunition, and from his position close to the top deck had a good view of what was happening. He said that while daylight lasted it was not so bad, but after dark the scene was terrible—nothing but smoke and flame all round, and the din was appalling. He saw the "Queen Mary" go down. It was all over very quickly— one moment a sheet of flame and the next nothing to be seen of her. Kipling's vessel did not sustain much damage, though she was amongst those that chased the flying foe to the last possible moment. She then returned to the scene of the fight to search for possible survivors. They only found one man alive. He was one of the crew of the destroyer "Tipperary," and had been in the water from 11.30 p.m. until 6 the next morning. In spite of his long night immersion he only complained of feeling cold and hungry, and after a good meal and a warm up, was none the worse.

Kipling showed no sign of the ordeal he had been through. It was his first experience of a big fight. His vessel was only a few miles away when the Zeppelin L20 was brought down.

2 & 3. Two eye-witness accounts of the Battle of Jutland. NDJ 15.6.1916 3a + 29.6.1916 7a

4. Robert Palmer's memorial in Torrington cemetery.

read a variety of eyewitness accounts of the war including one unusual one from E.Northey a naval man who had been serving in West Africa and taken part in the capture of German Kamerun (today's Cameroon). He noted 'The climate out here is very unhealthy and the heat is almost unbearable' he having had two bouts of malaria.

Whilst these various battles went on the Tribunals in the area continued to hear from those not willing to be conscripted – with the Barnstaple Rural one hearing 45 cases in one day. The meeting started with J.Gaydon from the Board of Agriculture pointing out that

TORRINGTON RURAL TRIBUNAL.

Torrington Rural Tribunal sat on Saturday. There was no particularly interesting feature about any of the cases, in most of which temporary exemption was granted. The following decisions were given:—Wm. Pett, horseman, Shebbear, two weeks; J. Tythcott, horseman, Alverdiscott, six months; Chas. Jeffery, market gardener and farm hand, Weare Gifford, six months; R. Nethercott, boat and shoe maker, Winkleigh, six months; Thos. Phear, cowman, &c., Webbery, adjourned for a fortnight; P. W. Carter, wheelwright, &c., Ashreigney, refused; Percy Copp, horseman, Torrington, four months; W. E. Heard, horseman, Moor Park, two weeks; J. Folland, farmer, Sheepwash, six months; N. Budd, farmer and contractor, Dolton, six months; H. J. Ley, farm bailiff, Shebbear, four months; Chas. Dunn, small holder, Dolton, four months; Richard Stacey, horseman, Petrockstow, six months; G. B. Bond, farmer, Frithelstock, six months; H. Parkhouse, horseman, Chulmleigh, four months; Wm. Madge, horseman, Dolton, six months; Wm. Dare, horseman, Dolton, six months; H. Down, cattleman, &c., Petrockstow, four months; J. Moore, labourer, St. Giles, six months; H. Manning, horseman, Winkleigh, six months; A. Woolacott, farmer, Dolton, six months; A. G. Hunkin, tenant farmer, Petrockstow, six months; H. G. Reed, butcher and farmer, Dolton, six months; J. T. Lane, head teacher, Winkleigh, six months; W. J. Keatt, miller, &c., Shebbear, four months; R. Gilbert, cattleman, St. Giles, six months; A. Lake, farmer, Weare Gifford, six months; G. Short, farmer, Winkleigh, six months; A. Cole, cattle, Winkleigh, six months.

5. Torrington Rural Tribunal decisions. NDJ 15.6.1916 3e

food production 'was one of growing importance and intense interest' – the clear implication being that panel members needed to exempt more farmers and their workers. This appears to have had an impact as of the 45 (mainly agricultural) cases only 5 were not given exemptions. At a Torrington Rural Tribunal a few weeks later a similar pattern was seen with men being given exemptions for varying lengths of time.

A number of applicants asked for exemptions until after the harvest had been gathered in but at one meeting of the North Devon Appeals Tribunal Lieut.Stirling, the military representative, said 'I have distinct instructions that farmers can get soldiers, skilled men, to help at harvest times, and ten per cent of the Home Service men in the country are at liberty to go.' This sounded straightforward but at a later meeting of the Barnstaple Rural Tribunal when J.Reed of Eastacombe was told to obtain soldiers to get the harvest in he said 'There is a tremendous lot of red tape to get men.' One case, however, indicated how social pressure might be brought to bear on those seeking exemption when Robert Petherick of Kentisbury applied on behalf of his 20 year old son, also called Robert, one of the panel members noted 'there was a very strong feeling in the parish in regard to this case' as 'Not a single man had gone from this farm for service – and Mr.Petherick had also three strong daughters.' He was told his son had to enlist

Several unusual cases were heard at the Barnstaple Borough Tribunal one being when the RSPCA applied on behalf of their North Devon Inspector Edgar Spary. The charity put up a strong case but the fact that Spary had served 10 years in the Royal Marine Artillery and 5 years in the Reserves meant he had to go. This was unlike Francis Dobbs who 'had the direct management of some 200 women' at the Derby Lace Factory. The fact that the firm was making camouflage and mosquito nets for the Army saw him left in place.

6. The Derby Lace Factory.

Given the nature of their work it is surprising that not more incidents such as one recorded at South Molton occurred. Here the chair of the town's Tribunal reported how a member had been 'publicly abused' by a man whose application for exemption failed.

By this time the men being called up were amongst the oldest identified under the Derby scheme. At one meeting of the Barnstaple Borough Tribunal this month 17 men were examined with all being over 34 with five aged 40 or 41. In fact only one man, aged 39, was ordered to enlist. Another man, 40 year old Henry Taylor, was exempted as he was a widower with nine children – 'the Town Clerk remarking, amid laughter, that there was thus an advantage of having a large family.' Albert Brewer, a 36 year old Barnstaple man, was given exemption as he was the only man, apart from the Captain, 'capable of driving the steam fire engine' used by the town's Fire Brigade. Another unusual case concerned James Smart who managed a 'fat and bone factory at Brinworthy'. His employers stressed that he was the only skilled man they had for the production of tallow 'used in the manufacture of high explosives, for which there is a constant demand'. He was granted an exemption.

It was this month that men in the Volunteer Training Corps took a new oath of allegiance to the King and were sworn in as members of the new Devon Volunteer Regiment. This meant they were 'liable to be mobilised at any time in the event of invasion – actual or imminent' just like the Home Guard in the Second World War. One man who wasn't helping was Pte.Albert Stone of Barnstaple who appeared in court charged with being 'an absentee' from the 3rd Battalion of the Devonshire Regiment. He was remanded to await a military escort though whether he merely overstayed his leave or was the first local deserter is unclear.

The recent consignment of goods to the Devons in Mesopotamia, in connection with the Comforts Fund organised by the Mayor of Barnstaple, was accompanied by the following letter:—"Mayor's Parlour, Barnstaple, June 22nd, 1916. Dear Col. Ratcliffe,—On behalf of the inhabitants of Barnstaple, Bideford, Okehampton, Southmolton, Holsworthy, Braunton, and district, I have much pleasure in informing you we have sent for your brave and gallant Devons the following :—20,000 cigarettes, 6 tins matches, 1,152 handkerchiefs, 1,152 pairs socks, 432 clip buttons, 2 footballs, 2 cricket sets, 576 pairs boot laces, 1,152 packets stationery and pencils, 144 bottles sterilising tablets, 432 shaving sticks, 72 safety razors, 500 mosquito net squares, and a box containing towels and soap. We hope to forward you a further consignment of goods in a few days, particulars of which I will forward. I trust that the goods will safely arrive, and feel sure you will appreciate the gifts as much as the previous parcel of cigarettes, matches, boot laces, and stationery which were forwarded. Our Committee, composed of representatives of the places before-mentioned, join me in wishing you every success and blessing, with the fervent hope that ere long we may welcome you home.—Yours sincerely, F. A. Jewell, Mayor of Barnstaple."

7. Comforts sent to the troops. NDJ 29.6.1916 5e

Even though many men were being given exemptions those in

the field still needed help from people at home. More goods were sent to local men in Mesopotamia following the Battle of Kut with the *Journal* publishing a list of the various items sent.

These were 'comforts' but military items were still being sent with 'Mrs.Kearney's sandbag party' at Combe Martin making around 1000 sandbags with the women intending to hold a fete at the Rectory in August to raise cash to buy more materials. More women were helping farmers, as at Chittlehampton where a number were 'seen weeding the corn, pulling plants, picking up loose stones from the meadows, while in some places they have followed the plough'. At Ilfracombe three women were working a market garden and Devon county council went as far as to employ female School Attendance Officers – but only as an 'experiment'.

That women were now seen as valuable workers was emphasised when, at the start of the month, it was reported that Mr.Miller, the managing director of the Derby lace factory, had, after representations from the Workers' Union, awarded 'substantial increases' to his mainly female staff probably to ensure they stayed in a time of labour shortages. They may have been happy but in the same week some 40 Barnstaple sawyers and woodworkers went on strike after their employer, Mr.Bartlett, refused to go to arbitration over a call for increased wages – although he alleged that the men in the Workers' Union demanded he sack all non-members which he refused to do. Happily after discussions the strike was ended with the men getting a wage rise.

The oddest story this month came from Lynton where a lady was going around the parish soliciting signatures for a 'Peace Petition'. Approaching one farmer he refused to sign and suggested she help with his work – which she did. This reference to pacifism is a rare example at this date though as the war dragged on more voices would be heard.

The First World War in North Devon

July 1916

July 1916 was to go down in history as one of the worst months ever experienced by the British Army. On July 1st General Sir Douglas Haig launched an offensive in France that came to be known as the Battle of the Somme. On that single day there were some 57,470 British casualties of whom 19,240 were killed – a one-day total never exceeded in British history. The battle dragged on until November having degenerated into a series of smaller actions with the final casualty toll of 415,690 for the Allies and 434,500 for the Germans. Needless to say local men were involved and were among the dead.

The first North Devonians knew of the battle was when the War Office announced initial successes though not going as far the editor of the *North Devon Journal* who, in the issue of July 6th wrote that the attack would 'mark the end of the period of purely trench warfare on the Western front.' Sadly the next issue of the newspaper carried multiple reports of wounded local soldiers with the Red Cross Hospital in Barnstaple seeing the arrival of 18 men 'who took part in the recent advance in France'. A week later eight deaths were reported – to be followed a week later by sixteen more names of men either killed in fighting or dead of their wounds – a sharp increase carried on through August. One article in the *Journal* headed 'Five Barumites killed in action' gives some indication of how terrible the news was. The five were Pte.P.Sanders (23), Pte.R.Richards (19), Pte.A.Harding (20), Pte.G.Avery (33) and Pte.F.Holwill (29). Barnstaple wasn't the only place affected, of course, with men from Lynton, Bideford, Chawleigh, Torrington, Marwood, Langtree, Ilfracombe and Appledore amongst other places being listed among the dead.

This slaughter on the Western Front overshadowed other theatres but local men were still dying in Mesopotamia for example, including 19 year old Frank Smallman of Chawleigh. Others were succumbing to disease there such as L/Cpl.Prettejohn of Barnstaple whilst Gunner Frank Sheppard of Lynton died of peritonitis in German East Africa. Lieut.Robert Wiggin from Brendon was killed fighting at 'Oghratina' in Egypt. One death was unusual; Pte.George Cook of Clovelly was wounded on the first day of the Somme battle and couldn't be rescued for many hours. Taken back to England he died in a Manchester Hospital his body being returned to Clovelly and buried in the parish churchyard 'amid many manifestations of grief and sympathy.' Another odd casualty, although not fatal, was that of Langtree's Lieut.G.Hackwill, Royal Flying Corps, wounded in the hip by shell fire whilst flying at a height of 8400 feet in France.

The paucity of eyewitness accounts in local newspapers this month is very noticeable and one wonders if the scale of the carnage was such that censors did their best to keep it hidden? Pte.C.Sollis, however, wrote a jingoistic letter to a correspondent in Ilfracombe saying 'We are giving the Huns something to go on with now, I can tell you….They will wish they had never been born by the time we finish with them.' Training of new recruits continued with ever greater urgency with local men taking part in exercises on Braunton Burrows and Salisbury Plain.

1. Training on Braunton Burrows. The Sergeant in front was William Jewell.

2. Royal Artillery man Reginald Manley from Rackenford is seen here training on Salisbury Plain.

3. Harry Dayman of Hartland of the Duke of Cornwall's Light Infantry with accordion on Salisbury Plain.

For the first fortnight after July 1 local Tribunals carried on as usual thus the first meeting of the Bideford Borough Tribunal dealt with 40 cases - with every one given exemptions ranging from two to six months. The Torrington Rural Tribunal similarly granted exemptions to every applicant but one, most of the men being engaged in agricultural work. At Ilfracombe only one man was told to enlist – though six men granted exemptions were told to join the town's Volunteer Training Corps. The Barnstaple Tribunal refused exemption to more men than the others but did give it to Charles Jewell, son of the Mayor, on the basis that he ran his father's office which organised railway maintenance work. One very unusual case followed this one when Percy Dunning (18) applied. His father appeared saying he had been in the Battle of Handub in 1888 after which he 'vowed before Almighty God that he would never take life again' – views he inculcated into his son. The panel agreed that Percy would only serve in a non-combatant capacity. At the same hearing Bernard Cooke was also assigned to a non-combatant role he being a CO as a member of the 'Exclusive Brethren'. Some COs when told to enlist, even just as a non-combatant, refused. Walter Trebble of North Molton on receiving his call-up papers ignored them, was arrested, fined and handed over to the Army.

Attitudes at Tribunals changed when the numbers of deaths on the Somme became known. There seems to have been two effects in North Devon; firstly men became ever keener to acquire exemption from conscription and secondly the military representatives challenged more exemption decisions granted by local Tribunals. This became obvious when the North Devon Appeals Tribunal met twelve days after the Somme battle started and all applicants, apart from one baker, were instructed to enlist. When the Barnstaple Rural Tribunal sat at the same time Henry Hammett the sub-postmaster/postman of Swimbridge asked for exemption pointing out his four brothers were already serving – only for the panel to say they thought he 'would have wished to join his brothers'. Ordered to enlist one panel member rather heartlessly added that they 'hoped they would live to see him come back safely again.'

The biggest tussles between the local Tribunals and the Appeals panel came with the continuing large number of agricultural workers being given exemptions though they had their defenders. At the South Molton Rural Tribunal one panel member spoke at the beginning of the hearing claiming 'too many men were being taken off the land' going on to say 'he knew a case where hay would be allowed to rot and mangold would be ploughed down, for want of labour.' Even so, agricultural workers continued to be challenged as when John Lee, a rabbit trapper of Alsweare, appeared before the Appeals Tribunal. He claimed to have caught 10,000 rabbits and 1000 rats in one season thus safeguarding the nation's food supply nevertheless he was sent for medical examination to see if he was fit enough to serve. One can understand the military's opposition to these exemptions when at the Bideford Rural Tribunal half way through July of the 56 applicants 47 were given exemptions for varying lengths of time.

This month saw a case directly related to men attempting to avoid conscription when William and Anne Jewell of Barnstaple were each fined 10/- for failing to notify their change of address to the authorities. The case was brought under the rules of the National Registration Act and even though William produced evidence of his medical rejection by the Army he and his wife were still fined. Another man detained for the same reason was Joseph Mehgan who had arrived in Combe Martin in September 1915 and built a hut on Holdstone Common to live in - without notifying anyone. It turned out that he was Irish which seemed to upset the court which sent him to prison for 3 months with hard labour for 'failing to produce his Registration Card.'

July saw the first case heard by the Devon Munitions Tribunal at Exeter. The Barnstaple firm of Shapland and Petter, who were involved in 'munitions work', alleged that their employee James Loosemore had illegally left them having been 'poached' by Morris & Co., timber merchants of Yarnscombe. After careful consideration the Tribunal dismissed the case on a technicality though they warned that any future cases could lead to a fine of £25.

Amidst all the bad news there were a few glimmers of hope. At Bideford the Old Town Boys School had set aside some land which 12 of their pupils cultivated 'splendidly'. The 320 boys in the school were also given an extra week's holiday allowing the older ones to help in getting in the harvest. It was also reported how T.Fairchild the surveyor to Torrington Rural Council was employing four women to break stones for road repairs as well as two school children after the school day had finished. Other working women included four at North Molton employed to deliver the post. When not doing 'men's jobs' women continued to support servicemen with L/Cpl.Horace Raymond writing to the women of the St.Mary Magdalen District Knitting Party in Barnstaple to thank them for his three pairs of socks and 'bottle of milk tablets' they had sent him amongst other things.

Men up to the age of 60 who have had previous military training can now be enlisted in the Royal Defence Corps for home service. For particulars apply to the Local Secretary of the National Reserve, J. H. L. Brewer, Bridge End, Barnstaple.

4. Men aged up to 60 could now serve. NDJ 27.7.1916 5d

Whilst the war was being fought by young soldiers for the most part older men could now do their part as a small note in the North Devon *Journal* made clear. Truly the whole nation was now involved in the war effort.

The First World War in North Devon

August 1916

As the Somme battles continued so the casualty lists became ever larger – with 55 deaths of North Devon men being recorded in the *Journal* this month plus even larger numbers of men who had been wounded. The first death was Richard Eddy of Barnstaple who had been a member of the machine gun section of the Norfolk Regiment he being a nephew of the Chief Constable of Barnstaple. The last was R.Turner who had been a master of Barnstaple Grammar School who had been promoted from the ranks.

Some were very young; Pte.Harry Grant of Clover Rocks, Exmoor was aged just 19 when he died on the first day of the Battle of the Somme and was buried in one of the old trenches on the battlefield. Even younger was Pte.W.Harris from Chittlehampton also killed on July 1st. He had somehow managed to enlist before he was 17 – dying a week after his 18th birthday. The oldest was Pte.Henry Grant of Ilfracombe who was a member of the Royal Defence Corps. He had been invalided out of the Navy in 1884 but joined the Army in 1914 and in 1916 was posted to Ilfracombe where he died from septic poisoning and haemorrhage after having teeth extracted aged 53.

All these deaths tended to merge into one another with only the occasional personal note being struck. Thus when Sergt.Charles Webber of Barnstaple died his friends sent his watch 'smashed by an enemy bullet' home to his widow. When Pte.E.Delbridge of Lynton was killed on the Somme he was the ninth soldier from the village to die – with flags being flown at half-mast to mark his death. Pte.E.Foden from Bideford died aged 22, he having been Head Boy at Bideford Grammar School, who on leaving, travelled to Germany and learnt the language. Pte.Reginald Bettiss of Bideford aged 21 had been shot in the arm and died in York of blood poisoning – with his body returned to Bideford where he was the first war casualty to be buried in the town.

To cope with the huge number of wounded the Red Cross opened their hospital at 'Craigmore' in Ilfracombe. This had 25 beds but increasing demands soon saw the requisitioning of the house next door to provide another 20 beds. It closed at the end of January 1919 having treated 809 wounded soldiers.

1. Craigmore Military Hospital, Ilfracombe.

2. A group touring Bideford raising funds towards a YMCA Hut.

In Bideford the Mayor launched an appeal to collect money to supply a hut to the YMCA who were operating 'rest rooms' behind the lines in France. Such huts gave the troops a welcome break from the hardships of the trenches and the appeal was well supported.

Up until this date medals had been won only occasionally but this month saw a sudden slew being awarded. Military Crosses were won by RSM Fred Miller, whose wife lived in Appledore, Lieut.W.Peters of Chulmleigh, Captain A.Kendrew of Barnstaple and Captain L.Pike also of Barnstaple. When Pte.R.Pound of Bideford was awarded a Distinguished Conduct Medal for defusing a 60 lb trench mortar bomb he was given a civic reception on returning home, he being the third Bidefordian to win this medal. A more exotic award went to Pte.Richard Harris of Barnstaple who was serving on HMS *Jupiter* which rendered valuable but unspecified services to the Russian government in the White Sea – for which he was awarded the Order of St.Stanislas by the Tsar.

The huge number of casualties and the subsequent need for more men saw the local Tribunals becoming ever more hard-nosed in refusing to grant exemptions. Many farmers when applying for their sons claimed they could obtain no workers from anywhere so when Daniel Lawrence of Sheepwash appeared before the Torrington Rural Tribunal and claimed he worked five days a week 'helping farmers' one exasperated panel member said 'How is it farmers never get casual labour? Everyone that comes here cannot get any.' A similar complaint was voiced at the Barnstaple Rural Tribunal when John Manning of Marwood produced a petition signed by local farmers who said he worked for them on different days. One panel member on hearing this exclaimed 'We never hear of these casual labourers when farmers are asking for men.'

At the same hearing the military representative opposed exemption for one man reckoning that 'throughout that district people went into "semi munition works" to avoid military service' whilst in another case he doubted that the man was a 'bona fide tenant'. At an Appeals Tribunal a Lieut.Stirling 'complained that all over Devon older men were allowed to join, and employers then came forward and said their sons were indispensable.' At a later hearing the same Lieutenant, after hearing several cases, observed 'it was a standing joke at Exeter that if the military had all the rabbit trappers and thatchers it would be the finest battalion in the Army!' At a meeting of the Barnstaple Rural Tribunal the military representative after hearing a Combe Martin woodcutter being described as 'indispensable' remarked 'that everyone at Combe Martin appeared to be wood-cutting or market gardening.'

These irritations reached their peak at the South Molton Rural Tribunal when Roland Hulland, the military representative, made a statement that 'At the last seven Tribunals we have had only six men refused' i.e. ordered to enlist, he going on to say he had been called a liar both by applicants and another panel member and so he would resign – which caused embarrassment all round.

This month saw several COs appearing including William Spear from Marwood who was granted an exemption with no explanation recorded. Another CO E.Cann of Barnstaple had his case heard at the Appeals Tribunal when Lieut.Stirling asked if Cann 'would defend his wife from a German?' to which he got the reply 'he would stand between the German and his wife, and receive the bayonet first.' He was ordered to join a Labour Battalion. Fred Mitchell of Langtree appealed on religious grounds and was allowed to continue working on the roads for the Torrington Rural Council. One CO who ignored his call-up papers was arrested. William Milton of Barnstaple claimed he was a Missionary and thus should be exempted but the Tribunal members didn't think this was germane to his case and handed him over to the military.

Interestingly the military authorities were challenged by a Barnstaple Alderman, A.Reavell, who pointed out that he had been relying on men with heart problems rejected by the Army as medically unfit to keep his glove factory running but the men had been sent to Exeter for a second medical. Here 'Exeter, however, seems to have effected some sort of lightning cure, and they have been passed for some sort of service.' Clearly friction between civilians and the military was increasing though the Government had attempted to boost patriotism by releasing two films which were shown in the Barnstaple Picturedrome this month. One was 'Nurse and Martyr' featuring the execution of Nurse Edith Cavell by the Germans (now available on youtube), the other being 'The Dublin Rebellion' about the Easter Rebellion in that city.

Presumably most cinema patrons were women and children – when they weren't working. The *Journal* was carrying more and more reports of women working such as this.

> A good many women in Devon are doing admirable War work. A great many more might join the ranks, but they do not seem to be able to make up their minds in what direction to apply their efforts. Those who are used to country life can render estimable service by doing something to assist in the production of food for the people, and, if an example were necessary, I can give them one from Little Torrington. Here are two young ladies, the Misses E. and B. Bond, of Undercleave Farm, who deserve medals for their War work. They render the greatest assistance to their father, who is 72 years of age, and has over 100 acres under cultivation. They drive the oil engine, thresh and grind the corn, work with the horses on the farm, cut down wood, load the carts with hay, manure the fields, feed the cattle, and drive stock to market. This is a fairly full programme for any women to fulfil, but these young ladies do it in all kinds of weather, and seem to thoroughly enjoy the work. Apparently, they have little to learn in the way of farm duties.—"Exeter Gazette."

3. Women land workers. NDJ 3.8.1916 5d

At Bideford a meeting was held in the Market 'to promote the movement for securing women to work on the land.' To mark women's efforts 'War Workers' Badges' were instituted for those in War Supply Depots and with the Red Cross – in Bideford these were distributed this month by Lady Rosamond Christie of Tapeley Park. Such was the urgency for mobilising female labour that local Suffragettes even decided to support a decision to hold their demand for the vote over until the war ended.

> **WOMEN'S SUFFRAGE.**
>
> DEAR SIR,—Will you kindly give space to the following resolution passed by the Executive Committee of the National Union of Women's Suffrage Societies, after hearing Mr. Asquith's statement on the Registration Bill, and dated 15th August, 1916 :—
>
> "That in view of the national position as set forth by the Prime Minister in his speech of August 14th, 1916, the National Union of Women's Suffrage Societies will abstain from pressing for an amendment to include women in the new Registration Bill, provided that the question of altering the basis of the franchise be not raised by other amendments or alterations to the Bill.
>
> In deciding on this course the National Union is postponing to its sense of the urgent national need of unity, its undiminished resolve to obtain for women the full rights of citizenship, which are more than ever necessary, having regard to the problems of reconstruction bound to arise after the war."
>
> Thanking you in anticipation,
> Yours faithfully,
> HON. SEC. (Barnstaple Branch) N.U.W.S.S.

4. The Suffragettes help the war effort. NDJ 24.8.1916 8b

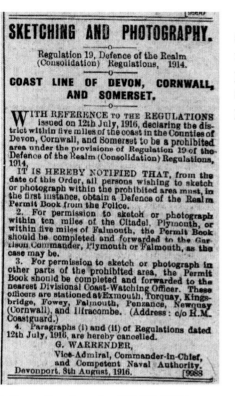

The Government may well have welcomed this hiatus but it was still battling to get people to follow the various rules introduced under the catch-all Defence of the Realm Act. Posters had been put up warning that, given the Zeppelin threat, all lights had to be screened from August 7th and the rules regarding sketching and photographing the coastline were strengthened.

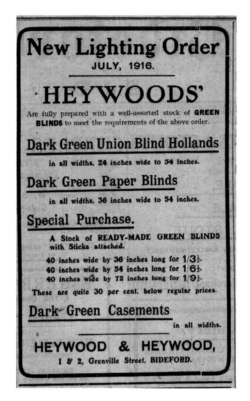

6. The 'black out'.
BG 15.8.1916 2d-e

This new lighting order saw an enterprising Bideford business publish this advertisement.

Another new regulation saw petrol restricted in usage, with the twelve tourist charabancs in Ilfracombe immediately deprived of fuel. E.Tamlyn of Autocars (Ilfracombe) Ltd. claimed that most of their customers were from the 'industrial centres' and trips in their vehicles 'helped them to recuperate more quickly' – and thus the charabanc owners were helping the war effort – but this had no effect. The Bideford Motor Works published an advertisement informing motorists how they might save fuel.

The month finished with an odd advertisement appearing in the local press. Percival Harris a bookseller/stationer of Barnstaple offered 'Regimental In Memoriam Cards' with the crest of the dead man's regiment embossed on the card. A sad keepsake.

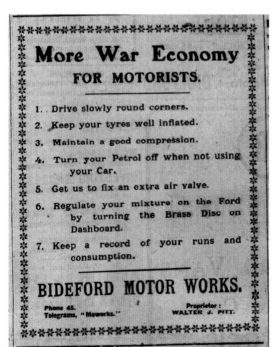

7. Saving fuel. BG 1.8.1916 2d-e

The First World War in North Devon

September 1916

With the ferocious Somme fighting continuing it is no surprise that this month saw the highest number of deaths recorded so far in the war - with some 35 being listed in the *Journal*. Most of these were in France and so numerous were they becoming that the notices in the newspapers were becoming briefer. Not all were killed this month as when Pte.J.Lock was listed it was noted that he had died at Loos a year before - with his body only being found now. Occasionally a few extra details appear. Thus, of Rifleman Cyril Squire, aged 20 from Barnstaple, it was recorded in a condolence letter to his guardian that 'He was shot through the head by a sniper just as we were taking the German second line yesterday.' Needless to say the writer attempted to soften the blow by adding 'his death was instantaneous'.

Rather more unusual was the obituary for Pte.Robert Yeo, also of Barnstaple, who was endeavouring to bring a gun to safety 'when a German aerial dart burst above him, pieces of the dart penetrated his helmet and striking him on the head.' Two deaths were of North Devonians who had emigrated – only to enlist to help the 'Mother country'. Rifleman A.Gibbing came from Ilfracombe but had enlisted in New Zealand, whilst Sergt.Frederick Walter from Parracombe was a member of the Australian Imperial Forces.

These deaths were far outnumbered by reports of wounded soldiers with injuries ranging from flesh wounds to amputations. By this stage of the war it was now acceptable to say a man was 'shell shocked' – with numbers of local men so identified increasing as the fighting continued. An interview with Sergt.James Conibear at his home in Loxhore forcibly demonstrated the deadly nature of trench warfare. Conibear was a professional soldier who had been in the Reserves and thus called up in September 1914. Going to France he was wounded three times – on the last occasion requiring three operations before being sent home to convalesce. He described the front as 'a scene of destruction, desolation and ruin' with his gun battery having once been shelled continuously for 25 hours.

Some particularly sad deaths in this month could only be presumed as no bodies were ever found. The schooner *P.T.Harris* disappeared somewhere off of Land's End though whether this was due to enemy action or extreme weather has never been ascertained. Its five man crew all came from Appledore and consisted of Captain Tom Harris, his two sons aged 16 and 14 along with Walter Leslie

1. The Harris memorial stone in Appledore churchyard.

98

and Ernest Parkhouse. Harris left behind a widow and five other children.

Given this level of casualties the various local Tribunals became even more exacting when challenging men before them. Thus at Lynton George Perkins, the younger son of Mr.Perkins of Ilkerton Farm, was told that 'if the elder brother joined up' he would be exempted. At Ilfracombe James Draper said his wife was about to have a serious operation and they had two children aged 2 and 4 – he was merely given time 'to arrange for the care of his wife and children.' When Mr.Shapland a farmer applied to the Barnstaple Rural Tribunal for his two sons he claimed they worked up to 16 hours a day – only to be told by the panel chairman 'I don't believe any man works 16 hours a day.' At the same Tribunal W.Welch of Orchard Farm, Instow applied on behalf of his horseman; he was refused and told 'that sick men were coming home from the various fronts, and they would be available for farmers.' He could only say 'Sick men are not much good on the farm.' A Molland farmer was told his horseman would have to enlist but he would be sent a 'substitute' sick man – and replied 'I hope you'll get a better substitute for me than was got in another case I know of - that man didn't know wheat from oats.'

Substitution was still a relatively new idea and a public meeting was called in Barnstaple Guildhall this month where Colonel Kirkwood the 'commanding officer of the recruiting area' for the district explained it to a large audience. Simply put it would see 'men who were less capable and less fit for service in the Forces' sent to take the place of fit men in industry. Wounded soldiers were also to be substituted where practical. Kirkwood pointed out how vital this was given that daily casualties for the preceding two months had been running at around 4000 a day. The meeting supported the scheme.

Of course many men enlisted voluntarily and some actually made the best of their time in the Forces. Thus Herbert Harris who served his apprenticeship in Shapland & Petter's factory in Barnstaple joined the Army at the outbreak of war and then in 1916 opted to join the Royal Flying Corps. Here he soon received promotion to Flight Sergeant – and, managing to survive the war, returned home and resumed his pre-war position later becoming a lecturer in Technical Drawing at the North Devon Technical College.

2. Herbert Harris in his Royal Flying Corps uniform.

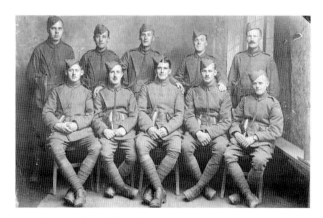

3. Herbert in the middle of the front row – note how they are armed with revolvers.

4. Herbert behind the wing of an aeroplane.

The need for more men was reflected in the action of police when they arrested Henry Foster as an Army deserter in Barnstaple. Henry had changed his address and claimed he had lost his 'papers'. Detained at the same time were two gypsies William and Robert Birch who had evaded the call up. Robert initially said he was 42 – a year over enlistment age – but given his mother was 47 this seemed unlikely. Also arrested was Albert Bennett after police staged a 'round up' at Barnstaple Fair. He too had changed addresses and had even changed his name. All four were fined and handed over to the Army.

This drive to obtain more men saw further friction between the Tribunal members and their military representatives. This came from the insistence by the latter for men initially categorised as being medically unfit to go to Exeter for another medical. When Fred Nicholls appeared before the Bideford panel it was noted he had been sent to Exeter where 'everyone was being passed'. The Ilfracombe Tribunal heard the case of Archibald Rudd who had failed three medicals until sent to Exeter where he was passed they reckoning the 'Medical Board at Exeter very unsatisfactory'. Actually when George Oatway came before the same Ilfracombe panel and said he had now been passed as 'fit' at Exeter even the military representative present thought he 'did not look as though he was capable of carrying a full kit.' Even greater friction was to come when towards the end of September the War Office sent an order to local Tribunals that it was henceforth to be a condition for exemption that the man should join either the Voluntary Training Corps, the Fire Brigade or the Special Constabulary.

Given the level of casualties it was inevitable that people at home would want to honour their death in some way. The Rev.R.Boggis of Barnstaple suggested that a 'War Shrine' be erected in town he envisaging a 'sacred picture' above a list of those serving and those killed the whole illuminated by a 'hanging lamp'. His idea, however, was characterised as being 'papist' by a local religious zealot and didn't get constructed.

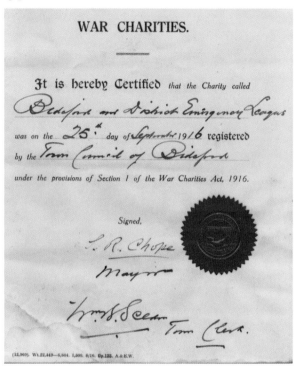

5. The Bideford & District Emergency League is set up.

More positive were the various reports of women taking over men's jobs including one at Fremington driving a coal wagon and two at Winkleigh breaking stones to surface the roads. At Alwington many mothers along with their children helped get the harvest in during the school holidays. Additionally the closed Swimbridge Tannery was being re-opened by the British Electric Tanning Syndicate of Somerset due to the 'enormous demand for leather' by the Forces. Even more cheering was a report on how Pte.Egbert Watts from Ilfracombe had been saved when a bullet hit the New Testament he was carrying in his breast pocket thus saving his life. He had sent it home and it was being displayed in the shop of Mr.Osborn in Portland Street. Also at Bideford the council supported the registration of the Bideford & District Emergency League which would allow it to collect money for the various local wartime charities.

Retailers were not slow to spot selling possibilities as this advertisement from an Exeter tobacconist that appeared in the *Journal*.

Just to show that the war had not stopped politics the *Journal* carried an extraordinary editorial this month which began 'What in

6. Tobacco for the troops. NDJ 21.9.1916 4e

ordinary times would be denounced as Socialism is regarded as quite the natural thing under stress of War conditions' – going on to say that State intervention i.e. Socialism did work in these extraordinary times. The *Journal* had always been a strongly Liberal paper so this statement was unexpected.

The First World War in North Devon

October 1916

The month opened with a long list of men killed in action appearing in local newspapers. They came from all over North Devon including three from Barnstaple, three from Ilfracombe and ten more from other settlements. As the war ground on these sixteen were joined by another twenty nine to give the worst number for any month so far. They included Captain Cecil Martin from Westward Ho!, aged just 22, who was another victim in France of a German 'aerial dart' – after having been wounded and gassed previously. Another 'colonial' soldier died he being Cpl.W.Palmer of the Canadian Engineeers who came originally from Barnstaple. The body of a long 'lost' soldier from Chittlehamholt, Pte.Frederick Blight, was found this month he having been killed in 1915, whilst Lundy saw its first death when Pte.F.Ackland was killed. One of the saddest deaths was that of L/Cpl Thomas Kift from Ilfracombe who was killed in action in France this month aged 19. He had enlisted, illegally, in 1914 when aged just 16 – at a time when Recruiting Sergeants were notoriously lax in enforcing minimum age limits.

This apparently ever-increasing roll of young men killed on the battlefield must have spread grief across the whole of North Devon – but the Tribunals had to continue their work although there was one major change to their rules this month. The War Office sent an instruction that men involved in agriculture or food production be exempted and only called up where substitutes were available or they had special skills needed by the Forces. Such men were easy to identify but the Barnstaple Rural Tribunal stretched it to include William Weighill the 28 year old 'foreman jam boiler' of the Combe Martin Jam Preserve Co.Ltd. though as tinned jam was a staple food in the trenches one can understand his exemption.

In fact the new rule wasn't quite as clear cut as the Tribunal members first thought as at the first Bideford Borough Tribunal this month the military representative, when asked about it, replied that although such men would not be called up the Tribunal should still adjudicate on their appeals just in case their cases were weak and they could be ordered to enlist. The Bideford panel heard 35 cases after this only sending one man to the Army. In one of these cases a man called Darch was noted as having gone to Scotland to work in a munitions factory – leading the military representative to say 'another man slipped through the net.'

Clearly the new instruction was too vague for some Tribunals with the Torrington Rural one deciding to 'adjourn all cases of men engaged in agriculture until the regulations were sufficiently clear for them to work upon.' At the South Molton Rural Tribunal sitting the same week as these other two some 100 cases were heard with 'agricultural exemptions' being granted in virtually every one. The *Journal* was intrigued by this and provided a breakdown of the occupations listed which included 45 horsemen, 13 farmers, 2 thatchers, 3 shepherds, one rabbit trapper and a miller.

The North Devon Appeals Tribunal was less accommodating ordering six men to enlist within a few weeks. One case concerned Albert Mitchell a 20 year old single man from Barnstaple of whom it was explained that the Ministry of Munitions had 'placed him in a controlled munition works'. William Watts, a horseman of

Umberleigh, was exempted until 'the military can get an efficient substitute'. When Henry Shore, a Bampton saddler, appeared he 'expressed the hope that he would not go before Bampton Fair' to which the chairman replied 'Has the war got to wait for Bampton Fair? It will be good news for the Kaiser if everything is to be stopped like that – join up.' With so many men away it wasn't surprising to read cases like that of two Torrington glove cutters. Here their employer W.Vaughan & Sons claimed that if they were taken 'it would be exceedingly difficult – indeed impossible – to provide work for the workers in the town and district around.' Each was exempted for 4 months 'with power to appeal again.'

That the Tribunals had been thorough in getting men to enlist can be seen from the last meeting of the Bideford Borough Tribunal this month when 34 cases were heard. Ten were ordered to retake the medical and 21 others were exempted being in the 'C' class – the lowest category of fitness. The three others were all exempted for a few months. Given the War Office stipulation that exempted men should join one of three local bodies it is interesting that the Northam Urban Tribunal heard from the local Volunteer Training Corps commander that 'there had been an improvement in the attendance of conditionally exempted men since the warning issued by the tribunal.'

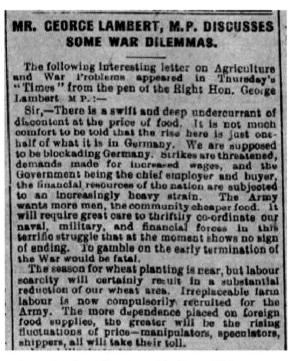

MR. GEORGE LAMBERT, M.P. DISCUSSES SOME WAR DILEMMAS.

The following interesting letter on Agriculture and War Problems appeared in Thursday's "Times" from the pen of the Right Hon. George Lambert M P.:—

Sir,—There is a swift and deep undercurrent of discontent at the price of food. It is not much comfort to be told that the rise here is just one-half of what it is in Germany. We are supposed to be blockading Germany. Strikes are threatened, demands made for increased wages, and the Government being the chief employer and buyer, the financial resources of the nation are subjected to an increasingly heavy strain. The Army wants more men, the community cheaper food. It will require great care to thriftily co-ordinate our naval, military, and financial forces in this terrific struggle that at the moment shows no sign of ending. To gamble on the early termination of the War would be fatal.

The season for wheat planting is near, but labour scarcity will certainly result in a substantial reduction of our wheat area. Irreplaceable farm labour is now compulsorily recruited for the Army. The more dependence placed on foreign food supplies, the greater will be the rising fluctuations of price—manipulators, speculators, shippers, all will take their toll.

1. George Lambert MP writes to The Times. NDJ 5.10.1916 2e

The most unusual case before any Tribunal this month was when 29 year old, George Branch, a Barnstaple electrician appeared. He had been classified as 'C3', the lowest possible, but on being examined at Exeter 'he applied to be placed in a sufficiently high grade to enable him to do something in his own trade for his country' but the military turned him down. His patriotism can be compared to George Pow, also of Barnstaple, who was arrested as a deserter from the Devon Regiment this month.

That agricultural exemptions were needed became clear when the local MP George Lambert wrote to *The Times* about the farming situation in North Devon. The points he made in this letter were to resurface in many other letters he wrote.

This October saw milk rise to 5d a quart with the poor said to be subsisting on cream which was more affordable than meat. At Lynton councillors heard that around 1300 acres in the parish was not being cultivated. They suggested planting trees so the soil doesn't sound that good but even that idea was deemed impossible given the scarcity of labour.

One way of tackling wartime price increases was for workers to strike and when 60 employees of W.Vaughan & Sons' glove factory at Torrington walked out demanding an increase of 1d a dozen for completed gloves they were soon joined by another 100 workers from other Torrington glove factories. Their employers soon capitulated and they returned to work. In Barnstaple the cabinet workers asked for a rise of 1d an hour but the employers prevented a strike by quickly agreeing to an increase of ½d an hour.

Women Workers' Series.—No. 1.

"*I used to laugh at him a little.*"

MY husband has taken cocoa for years, and I used to laugh at him a little because he set such store by it. He's a big strong man, and I did not think he needed cocoa. It never struck me that his good health might have something to do with the cocoa. But when I went into the factory I began myself to feel the strain. "Take a cup," he said to me one day when I was making his cocoa, "it will do you a power of good." I did—and I felt a warm glow all over me. It put new life and strength into me. I wasn't nearly so tired when I got to bed that night; and next day I started with another cup of cocoa; and the work seemed far lighter than before. I don't laugh at my husband any more—we have our cocoa regularly together.

a cup of Rowntree's *Elect Cocoa* makes a biscuit into a meal

This Illustration shows one of the Women workers at Port Sunlight in her becoming and workman-like costume.

2 & 3. Women take on men's jobs. NDJ 19.10.1916 2b-d + 19.10.1916 6d-g

Women continued to enter the job market it being noted in one Tribunal case about a Barnstaple baker that he asked to be exempted until he could finish training the six women he had taken on. Two advertisements appearing in the same edition of the *Journal* reflected these new workers.

Women were actively being encouraged to take jobs and even pre-war Suffragettes were urging them to do this – as when Mrs.Millicent Fawcett of the National Union of Women's Suffrage Societies addressed a public meeting in the Forester's Hall in Barnstaple. Her subject was 'The position of women after the War' and she was introduced by the Mayoress Mrs.F.Jewell who set the tone by saying of her sex 'In connection with the

War they had done a brave and noble work, and they were going to have their places when the present struggle was over.' Mrs.Fawcett spoke of how women had taken on many industrial jobs and 'they had not only done it well, but in a great many cases better than the men'. She noted that the Government had 'induced the Trade Unionists to suspend their rules under which an embargo was placed on the employment of women in trades. At present this applied simply for the period of the War.' Unfortunately they were to find that the men wanted the embargo to return after 1918.

An event which probably attracted far more people than Mrs.Fawcett's talk was the screening of what became

FORESTERS' HALL, BARNSTAPLE.

— A —

PUBLIC MEETING

Will be held in the above Hall,

On SATURDAY NEXT, OCTOBER 7th,

AT 7.30 P.M.

MRS. FAWCETT

(Widow of the late Henry Fawcett, Post-master - General in 1880) will Speak on

"**The Position of Women after the War.**"

The MAYORESS (Mrs. F. A. Jewell) will preside.

ADMISSION — — — FREE.

Collection will be taken for Mrs. Fawcett's Hospital Unit in Russia. [428

4. Millicent Fawcett.

5. A Suffragette meeting. NDJ 5.10.1916 4e

a famous film at the Torrington Cinema. 'The Battle of the Somme' was a powerful piece of propaganda being viewed by some 20 million people in its first six weeks of exhibition with many people going to see if they could spot their loved ones in the sometimes harrowing footage.

Both women and men were still being brought before the courts for flouting the lighting regulations. When Arthur Baker of Combe Martin was summonsed he offered the rather odd excuse that 'he did not know the regulations referred to back windows' – and saw his case dismissed. More unlucky was Rhoda Ayling a chambermaid at the Ilfracombe Hotel who was fined £1 for showing a 'brilliant light' that could be clearly seen from the sea.

6. The film of the Battle of Somme.
NDJ 19.10.1916 4e

The First World War in North Devon

November 1916

As the Autumn gave way to Winter the news was as chilling as the weather with some 32 local men appearing in the list of deaths. Again there were several very young men including Pte.Horace Wood, aged just 20, he having been a Bideford postman before enlisting. Another 20 year old was Pte.J.Ayre of Halsbury Mill, Parkham who 'succumbed to wounds received in action.' The youngest was Pte.Archie Incledon of Braunton who was a member of the Ambulance Section killed aged 19 whilst tending the wounded. Pte.Walter Norman, aged 23, from Ilfracombe, 'was killed on his first time in the trenches.'

Lists of wounded servicemen were even longer and though most notifications were brief occasionally other details are provided. Thus in the *Journal* for November 2 we read how Pte.W.Goss of Bradiford was in hospital 'suffering from severe chill'. Rifleman P.Thetford from Barnstaple had 'a gunshot wound in the groin', whilst Lt.F.Jewell, third son of the Mayor of Barnstaple, was home 'suffering from severe shell shock'. Poor Trumpeter Percy Ffoulkes, also from Barnstaple, had been in the Gallipoli campaign after which he 'underwent fourteen operations for frostbite.'

News items like these doubtless increased the desire to avoid conscription but the Tribunals were still processing men as fast as they could – and seemed to be casting their net ever wider. Thus when Samuel Found, a 21 year old machine minder at Barnstaple's lace factory, came before the Tribunal he related how he was the only support for his blind mother, that his brother had already been wounded in the war and he added that 'he was only 4 ft 11 inches out of his boots' – notwithstanding which he was ordered to enlist. Frank Edwards a Parracombe farmer was ordered to provide a copy of the lease for his farm and the cheque he claimed to have given his brother for the tenancy as the panel members of the Barnstaple Rural Tribunal had suspicions as to the legitimacy of his tenancy. P.Cowie was a 'traveller and designer' for Shapland & Petter who had been granted 6 months exemption to allow the firm to get orders from the USA. When the firm asked for a further 6 months the military representative said he would like to take the issue to the 'Central Tribunal' as a test case for, as he saw it, a man was avoiding enlistment by going to a foreign country.

Occasionally the Tribunal could be slightly more lenient as in the case of Alfred Cann, a lace twister of Barnstaple. After he pointed out that his five brothers were already serving as were his sister's three sons and one brother's two sons – not to mention his brother-in-law who had already been wounded three times. Given 'the good record of the family' the panel exempted him until January - when he would have his place at the factory taken by a substitute. The South Molton Rural Tribunal hit an unexpected problem this month when, following a snowstorm, it proved difficult for some of the 72 men to be examined to actually attend.

Whilst interviewing many previously medically exempted men the military representatives on the various Tribunals were demanding a new medical examination – which, as noted, seems to have seen an almost inevitable up-grading of the man's classification. Indeed so notorious did this become that H.Woodcock the military man on the Barnstaple Rural Tribunal actually went to Exeter to see the examination process for himself – which he was thoroughly satisfied with. This came out during the hearing of William Gould's appeal; he recounted how he had suffered from 'gastric trouble' for 16 years – to which Woodcock replied 'one of the finest things he could do, would be to go into the Army. Regular food and regular exercise would do him a power of good.'

These Tribunals were being held by at least one of our allies as shown when this month Dr.Vermylen, a Belgian doctor who had been working for 18 months as House Surgeon at the North Devon Infirmary in Barnstaple, was summoned before a Belgian Tribunal – where he was granted exemption to stay in his post.

Presumably as a form of encouragement and in order to maintain local morale more brave North Devonians were awarded medals. Thus Lt.L.Rathbone of South Molton received a Military Cross to go with the DSO he had already won. Another MC went to Acting Captain S.Norrish of Instow. When Pte.Arthur Tout of Ashreigney won the DCM his fellow parishioners clubbed together to purchase a silver tea service for him.

Such awards may have helped but civilians were faced with the day-today struggle to cope with increasing food costs. George Lambert, the South Molton MP, again wrote to *The Times* pointing out the problems being experienced by farmers who were trying to cope with far fewer workmen. He suggested that 'fair maximum prices for farm produce might be fixed' adding that the country was at risk from German submarines sinking ships bringing food to Britain. He didn't want to quote figures obviously but 'That they are formidable is beyond doubt.' In fact shipping losses had been appalling. In 1914 some 312,000 tons of Allied (and Neutral) shipping had been sunk by U-boats. This rose to 1,308,000 tons in 1915 and 2,327,000 tons in 1916 hence Lambert's concerns.

His views were echoed at a meeting called by the local Trades and Labour Council in Barnstaple with several speakers alleging profiteering on the part of 'some people' at the expense of 'the working class'. The sixteen Trade Unions then operating in Barnstaple which represented some 1000 workers, were each asked their views – with a decision that 'a resolution of protest against the present inflated prices be sent to the Government.' A week later the Government in a 'momentous statement' announced the appointment of a Food Controller to tackle fixed prices, address food waste, regulate the distribution of some foods and draw up a census of food stocks. Additionally 'War Bread' was to be introduced in January 1917 which would see less 'white flour' used to make loaves.

As prices rose so more trades saw demands for wage increases. This month bakers in Barnstaple again demanded a rise – their representatives pointing out that their weekly wage was 27/- whereas bakers in most parts of the country were being paid £2. Builders in Barnstaple asked for and received an extra 1d an hour and when the 'operative painters and decorators' requested a similar rise on top of their existing rate of 6½d they were offered and accepted an extra ½d.

Increasing prices saw ever greater pressure on women to take a paying job. Already, of course, many women were working in agriculture and this month saw a meeting in Barnstaple designed to boost their numbers with Lady Fortescue distributing 'armlets' to 100 women who had already completed more than 248 hours' work on the land. One of the speakers at this meeting, F.Horne from the Board of Agriculture, spoke of women as an 'untapped source' of labour noting that 'so far from women finding farm work difficult, they were learning it abnormally quickly.' As if to prove his point the *Journal* carried a report of how Mrs.J.Curtis and Mrs.S.Harris working in Fremington had 'pulled six acres of mangolds and dug 236 bags of potatoes'.

Interestingly though women were helping farmers the Bideford War Agriculture Committee suggested that German prisoners of war be used for agricultural labour – an idea not followed up for some months. At the end of the month it was noted that several women had been taken on by the Barnstaple Cabinet Works – a hitherto all-male establishment. Another outlet for female labour was announced this month – a new Red Cross hospital at Torrington based in 'Mr.Vaughan's house Enderby' though this didn't actually open until April 1917.

Amidst all these worries locals could still go to local cinemas – so long as they didn't mind seeing war films.

The Theatre Royal in Barnstaple was still operating showing films and they clearly realised that official war films weren't for everyone when they proclaimed 'You have had an opportunity of witnessing the gruesome spectacle and its effects of this horrible War but in these dull and dreary days of depression you require something bright and cheery to take you out of yourself.' This came with an advertisement for 'Look out for Cabiria' – 'a screaming Comedy' and 'Children of Cappan Grant' – a wonderful photo play'. Another welcome diversion from the War was the arrival of post from men serving abroad – especially the extremely decorative 'silk' postcards which became a large 'cottage' industry on the Western Front with many thousands being sent home. They varied from the personal to the patriotic as these example show.

1. *The Theatre Royal, Barnstaple shows war films.*
NDJ 9.11.1916 5g

This happy note wasn't common and a report on a 'Lady's death from misadventure at Barnstaple' would have left many downcast. Given the carnage on the battlefield it might be thought surprising that this case was covered at all – but the lady in question was Miss Emily Hawken the sister-in-law of Sir Arthur Conan Doyle. What made it even more newsworthy was that she was addicted to the drug chlorodyne 'which was similar in its effects to laudanum' (opium) and had swallowed a whole bottle-full of the drug on the day she died at Grenville House in Barnstaple's Boutport Street.

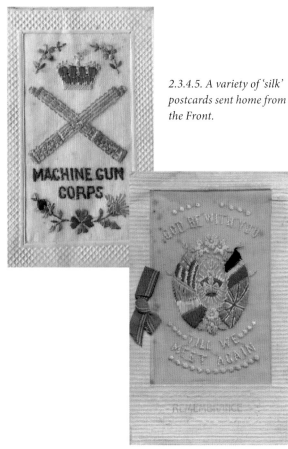

2.3.4.5. A variety of 'silk' postcards sent home from the Front.

The First World War in North Devon

December 1916

As the third Christmas of the War came around so the number of deaths reported fell slightly as if to mark the 'Season of Peace'. Some twenty men were reported killed with the usual much higher number of wounded. The very first to be recorded were two brothers from Barnstaple. L/Cpl.Albert Stephenson and Pte.William Stephenson died within a fortnight of each other – with the report in the *Journal* gloomily noting of the parents 'the general hope will be expressed that their only remaining son in the Army will be spared to them.' Another double bereavement in the same family happened when Pte.Jack Lovering and Pte.C.Lovering were both killed within weeks of each other. Both had emigrated to Canada just before the war but both had enlisted into the Canadian forces, with the pair coming to England together and travelling on to France together.

Just above the report of the Loverings' deaths is another report headed 'Well-known North Devonian killed in action'. This concerned L/Sergt. Hector Munro, aged an astonishing 45, who had enlisted at the start of the war after presumably lowering his age. After being raised in Barnstaple he became a writer under the pen-name 'Saki' and authored many articles and stories with his barbed satires still being read today. Famously his last, possibly apocryphal, words before being shot by a sniper were to a soldier in a shell crater 'Put that bloody cigarette out.'

1. H.H.Munro better known under his pen name 'Saki'.

As always many of the deaths were poignant. Thus Mr & Mrs.Gibbs of Ilfracombe first heard that their son Pte.W.Gibbs had been wounded, this was then changed to 'Missing' with finally the chaplain of the 1st Guards Brigade writing to them to say 'there can be no doubt he was killed.' Another referred to Pte.Bertie Ball who came from Frithelstock leaving there to join the Police Force and being stationed in Bideford. He volunteered for the Army in 1915 and was posted to France where he was killed, it being noted 'He was expecting leave shortly to return home to be married.' At least seven deaths this month were from disease rather than fighting. Thus Pte. Leonard Baker (of the local Rawle, Gammon & Baker family firm) died in Egypt of 'dropsy and heart trouble'. Pte.W.Boundy from West Putford died from dysentery at Basra whilst Pte.Robert Tolley of Bishops Tawton died

2. Cpl.Charles Slee from Filleigh.

in India from 'fever'. Of course many men seemed to acclimatise very quickly – one of them being Charles Slee seen here riding his camel in Egypt.

Against these sad deaths was the happier news of men being awarded medals. So, for example, five Military Medals for personal acts of bravery were awarded to local servicemen. Sapper Gush and Sergt.B.Jeffery of Ilfracombe, Cpl.S.Heath of Bideford, Pte.F.Hocking of Northam and Sergt.F.Clements of Torrington were all proud recipients of this mark of honour. Even if men returned home without a medal they often brought souvenirs. Thus Driver J.Snow came home on leave to South Molton bringing with him a Prussian Guards officer's helmet with a bullet hole 'showing how its owner met his fate' – plus the officer's revolver. He also had a German Private's belt with the motto 'Gott mit uns' (God with us) on the brass buckle. One wonders where these are today?

Apropos of equipment at the beginning of this month the Government passed The Volunteer Bill which saw men in the Volunteer Training Corps who agreed to 'undertake certain duties in connection with national defence' and be 'subject to military law' receive a bounty of £2 to cover costs of their uniforms whilst being given rifles 'as they became available'. This new force was to number 150,000 and provide 'a home defence force in the event of invasion.'

The North Devon Tribunals weren't quite so busy this month though, as ever, some of their decisions seem odd. Thus when Tom Davey, a 35 year old Lynton plumber, appealed the military representative said that as a mechanic he should go to a munitions factory. The very next case saw T.Sydenham's appeal adjourned after he claimed to be the sole support of his aged mother. He had one brother in the Army whilst 'another had died in munition making' which must have cheered Davey up. At the Barnstaple Borough Tribunal Charles Williams, a carpenter aged 32 with seven children, was given a week 'to voluntarily enrol as a munitions worker.' Williams replied 'he did not want to go in munitions if he could help it' – but he was then ordered to go.

Queries about the fitness of men resurfaced; at the Barnstaple Rural Tribunal Arthur Robins a 19 year old shepherd of High Bray was described as 'very delicate' he having been rejected by the Army notwithstanding which he had now been reclassified as fit for service – which one panel member reckoned 'an extraordinary thing.' At the same hearing James Harris, a 22 year old baker from West Down, applied for exemption but was told 'being a young, single man' he 'ought never to have come before the tribunal at all' but should have enlisted voluntarily. He was ordered to join up. Frank Edwards, a Parracombe farmer, whose case has already been mentioned, saw the military representative present 'a report from the police, expressing the opinion that Frank Edwards did not cultivate the farm as he should.' He was refused exemption. These harsh decisions can be seen as necessary when the chairman of the Barnstaple Rural Tribunal said 'men were very badly needed for the Army. It was all nonsense to say the Germans were beaten, and now the enemy had entered Roumania [sic] the position was worse than before.'

If the fighting was going less well then here in North Devon more discussions were being held about growing more food. Lynton council heard several councillors suggest areas which might be used to produce crops. One was near the 'isolation hospital' whilst another was the 'Pleasure Ground in the valley' – but the shortage of labour and seed potatoes militated against these ideas. At their meeting this month the Barnstaple Farmers' Union debated the employment of German PoWs on the land. William Dunn from Ashford 'urged that the matter should be looked upon from a national standpoint, and their opinions should be devoid of prejudice and sentiment' adding that employing PoWs would help Britain win the war. The chairman R.Sanders of Bishops Tawton then suggested 100 PoWs could be

3. Victoria Park, Bideford

used to clear Codden Hill but members thought the Germans would be more constructively employed on local farms experiencing labour shortages. The meeting then passed a motion strongly supporting the idea of utilising PoW labour. When Bideford town council met this month they didn't go so far as this but some councillors did suggest turning over the town's Victoria Park to growing potatoes, though this didn't gain total support.

They also discussed approaching the rector and the town's Bridge Trust charity to see if any land was available for allotments which could help tackle the perceived future food shortages.

Food prices were continuing to rise and so there were more demands for pay increases with a threatened strike of masons in Bideford defused by an offer of a 'war bonus' of an extra 1d an hour. In Barnstaple the bakers' strike dragged on with the men giving a week's notice to their employers which ran out on December 16th. The Mayor stepped in to act as an arbitrator and the employees finally agreed to an offer of a rise of 4/- a week for both male and female labour with a reduction in their working week to 48 hours.

This extra money would have helped get them more food though they could have spent some on going to the pictures. The Palace in Barnstaple offered 'a thrilling 3 act detective drama' and 'three screaming comedies' suggesting 'Come and have a laugh, and forget the War for a time.' At the same time, however, the Barnstaple Watch Committee recommended that all the public houses in town close at 10 p.m. to restrict drunkenness and keep workers fresh. At Bideford the Electric Palace Cinema was showing two war films.

Christmas itself saw local shops advertising just as heavily as in peacetime

ELECTRIC PALACE, BIDEFORD.

The Latest War Film—

The King's Visit to his Troops at the Front,

Will be shown on

Thursday, Friday & Saturday,
December 7th, 8th & 9th.

AND

The original and authentic Film of

The Battle of the Somme

ON

Thursday, Friday & Saturday,
December 14th, 15th & 16th,

Commencing at 8 o'clock.

No advance in prices, but Season Tickets will not be available for these dates. No half-price.

Usual Prices for Children Saturdays only at the Matinees. Doors open at 2, commence at 2-30.

even if their stocks were not so plentiful. Servicemen sent greetings cards home – including this one from Barnstaple man Herbert Harris who was serving with the Royal Flying Corps.

In addition children were still funding the presents sent to servicemen by the Overseas League. This 'thank you' card was presented to Jack Easterbook of Bideford.

The month ended with the unveiling of another individual war memorial when a new stained glass window to

4. The Bideford Electric Palace programme. BG 5.12.1916 2c

the memory of Captain H.R.H.O'Brian of the Royal Field Artillery was placed in the Roman Catholic church in Bideford. He had been killed in action at Ypres on 1 June 1916 aged 25.

5. A Royal Flying Corps Christmas card sent home to Barnstaple.

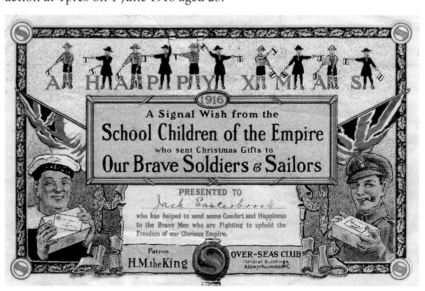

6. An 'Overseas League' thank you card for Christmas 1916.

The First World War in North Devon

January 1917

The month began with the *North Devon Journal* publishing a 'Roll of Honour' listing all the North Devonians (the definition was elastic) who had been killed in 1916. Stretching over seven columns it brings home the sheer wastage of lives – mainly those of young men. Sadly this month saw an extra 21 names added to this list though nine of these deaths were due to illness. Thus both Pte.J.Lashbrook of Clovelly and Pte.W.Barnell died of dysentery in Egypt. The Barnstaple brothers, Pte.William Dennis and L/Cpl.P.Dennis, who had been taken prisoner when the Kut garrison surrendered, both died from sickness in prison camps. The youngest was Pioneer S.Buckingham of Bittadon who was 19 his passing being marked with a fulsome obituary unusual at this stage of the war which reckoned he had been 'a young man who was assured of a brilliant future.'

The oldest was Lieut.Q/Master Tuffrey who had been a Regular serving as Regimental Sergt.Major to the Royal North Devon Hussars. He retired in early 1914 but rejoined on the outbreak of war aged around 52! He left on active service with the regiment but illness forced him home again and he entered into a munitions factory in Cumberland where he died aged 54.

The 'Roll of Honour' shows why more men were needed – a need fulfilled by the Tribunals where the military representatives were pushing for every men they could garner. Thus when 18 year old William Waldron, the 'wash-house engineer' at the Ilfracombe Laundry appeared before the town's Tribunal he was given a temporary exemption until March 1st his employers noting that 'all the other men in the employ of the firm had been called up.' When William Petherbridge, a Bickington blacksmith, applied for exemption it was pointed out that local farmers 'had been asked to plough up thousands of acres more, and more ploughs would be required and more horses wanted to be shod.' The panel chose to ignore this and he was ordered to enlist by March 1st.

Forty year old William Sampson, a road builder employed by the South Molton Rural District council, appeared at the North Devon Appeals Tribunal saying he wished to go into munitions work but the military representative pointed out that 'this man would be extremely useful in making roads abroad' – and his appeal was rejected. One man, Charles Eddy, who had been exempted before, asked the Torrington Borough Tribunal for a renewal – but was questioned as to why he had not attended drills of the Volunteer Training Corps as he had agreed? He said he had been ill but this didn't appear to carry much weight with the panel as he was only given 3 month's exemption.

One case at the Barnstaple Rural Tribunal was unusual. Samuel Parker, a 19 year old horseman on a High Bickington farm, applied for exemption as he was a member of the Plymouth Brethren. The panel members accepted his conscientious objection to military service but ordered him to another district to do farm work 'to be paid at the rate of army pay'. At this Tribunal meeting the military unsuccessfully challenged six exemptions granted to agricultural workers whilst nine other men were to enlist when the Army had found substitutes for them.

Up until now substitutes were difficult to find many wounded soldiers being incapable of doing the work but this month the War Office announced that 'C3' civilians (the lowest medical grade) were to be used on the land as substitutes.

A further change to the rules followed a week later when it was decided that all youths would be immediately called up on their 18th birthday – though none would be posted overseas until they attained the age of 19. Their eighteenth year would be spent in training and on home defence.

As in earlier months awards of medals were reported with three local officers being so honoured. Captain Hugh Ebrington from Filleigh and Captain G.Doe from Torrington both won a Military Cross whilst Major H.Molesworth, whose father was a General from Bideford, was awarded a Distinguished Service Order. Most medals were awarded to Army men but Leading Seaman George Manley of Braunton won the Distinguished Conduct Medal along with 'a special money prize' for his service.

Hand in hand with the demand for more men went demands for more food to be grown - with the Government establishing a Food Production Department this month whose orders were implemented by County War Agricultural Committees and local councils. Barnstaple led the movement at the start of the year by advertising for land to grow potatoes on – and requesting the Ashleigh Road School to grow more food 'in their gardens'. Sadly not much land was offered and that which came forward was deemed to be too far from the town to allow allotment holders easy access.

The clerk to Lynton council explained to his councillors that they could 'simply walk in and take' unoccupied land whilst occupied land could be 'acquired by agreement' and common land could be taken 'subject to the consent of the Board of Guardians'. When the South Molton Rural Council discussed this topic the possibility of employing German PoWs on farms came up but as was pointed out by a Mr.Harding 'Many people in the district had lost sons in the War. They could hardly be expected to "swallow" the coming of Germans to do the work these sons had formally done.' At Bideford three areas owned by Mr.Stucley were to be made available as allotments – with 70 people putting their names forward to take them on. Unfortunately the most popular site, in Abbotsham Road, had to be taken out of consideration owing to a disagreement about its letting price.

The Torrington Farmer's Union heard calls for more land to be cultivated though one member's call for 'an Act whereby no syndicate or middleman should be allowed to tamper with the nation's food' wasn't supported. At Parkham a parish meeting saw a committee formed by the Rev.S.Hensley to grow more potatoes and keep more pigs. When the Barnstaple War Agricultural Committee met they heard that the Government were sending 4-5 new-fangled 'motor ploughs' to North Devon to help farmers. Additionally the Devon War Agricultural Committee had agreed that the first two 75-strong batches of German prisoners were to be supplied for farm work in the county.

Also this month the price of wheat, oats and potatoes was fixed by the Government to stop 'profiteering'

1. The least fit men are 'called up'. NDJ 18.1.1917 5d

2. Grow more potatoes. NDJ 4.1.1917 1f

by some farmers. This was all very well but local MP George Lambert wrote another of his sharp letters to *The Times* pointing out the need for agricultural labour was paramount and its shortage would derail any moves to obtain larger crops.

If Barnstaple led the way in growing more food the council's move to close public houses at 10 p.m. was copied by South Molton and Bideford this month. This was probably unpopular with the working class for whom public houses provided a community centre. One wonders if this was the spur to the decision by the Barnstaple Trades and Labour Council to announce they were to stand six candidates in the next election to the town council? The Workers' Union held a meeting at the Barnstaple

In a letter to the "Times" Mr. George Lambert M.P., writes :—"Quill-waving in Whitehall won't produce a singlegrain of corn or a single potato. Prompt practical action is essential. Land can only be cultivated by labour. Unless drastic steps are taken tens of thousands of acres of first-class arable land will not be tilled for want of labour. Ploughing up parks, old pasture, and the like will be well enough when the arable land is thoroughly well cultivated. For the first season an old pasture, unless skilfully handled, will produce more wireworm than wheat. Skilled agricultural labour is the vital need."

3. Another of George Lambert's letters to The Times. NDJ 11.1.1917 8b

Oddfellows Hall to hear A.Trickey of the Railwaymen's Union, discuss 'When peace comes and how it will affect the workers.' It was interesting that some were already looking to the future although the speaker reckoned there would be huge male unemployment after the war – with no mention of what might happen to wartime women workers.

Another speaker turned up in North Devon this month when the American D.Thomas Curtin gave his lecture entitled '300 days in Germany' in Barnstaple's Albert Hall. He described the 'long, long lines' of people waiting for food due to the blockade of Germany by the Royal Navy and further major problems in the country. After praising the stoicism and community spirit of the British he ended by saying 'Argument was of no use when dealing with the German people, they must be smashed.' Not all citizens were as public minded as he made out. Maud Chapple, the wife of a serving Barnstaple soldier, was gaoled for one month after defrauding the local War Pensions Committee of £7.4.0. She was receiving 19/6 a week 'separation allowance' whilst her husband was at the Front which the court thought 'ample to keep a woman with no encumbrances'.

The month ended with a 'magnificent memorial tablet' to the memory of Captain R.P.Dunn-Pattison being placed in Braunton church he having fallen 'gallantly leading an attack on the Turkish lines in Mesopotamia' on 8 March 1916. In addition a 'War Shrine' was erected in the parish of Fremington church this being the first in North Devon. Executed in walnut and beaten brass (taken from an old battleship) it contained the names of 14 dead parishioners and around 100 names of men still serving in the Forces. Many more community memorials were to follow.

The First World War in North Devon

February 1917

The freezing weather affecting the European battlefields seems to have caused the fighting to decline but even so another 14 local servicemen are reported as dying this month with two passing due to illness. The Salonica theatre of war is often overlooked but Pte.T.Bamford, a 19 year old Ilfracombe soldier, died from his wounds there this month. One especially sad death was that of Pte.C.Gant, also from Ilfracombe, who had apparently been 'delicate' even before enlisting and had suffered ill-health for all his Army career and died in Colchester Military Hospital.

Most North Devon men were in the Army but not all; Leading Stoker Tardival of Clovelly was serving on HM Auxiliary Cruiser *Laurentic* – this being a transatlantic liner converted to an armed merchant ship.

The vessel hit a mine and sunk with most of the crew escaping in lifeboats – though 354 died of hypothermia following the sinking, including Tardival. A more cheery if surprising story was the detailed coverage of the escape from Crefeld, a German PoW camp, of Captain H.Lloyd of Bideford this noting 'he ran and walked all night' he having been a cross-country runner whilst at Cambridge University. He managed to reach Holland where he had to cut his frozen trousers off with a knife!

1. The Laurentic.

The number of servicemen killed might have been lower this month but the Tribunals were as active as ever in examining men trying to avoid the fighting. The various local Tribunals in North Devon adjudicated on 205 cases this month whilst the North Devon Appeals Tribunal heard 40. Fewer and fewer arguments for exemption were being accepted – as shown in the case of Ernest Allen a wood turner at the Barnstaple Cabinet Company. His employer A.N.Oliver said Allen was an expert working full-time on work for the Ministry of Munitions. Notwithstanding this the panel members ordered him to enlist. At the Torrington Rural Tribunal his father applied on behalf of V.Parkhouse he stating that three other sons had enlisted, one had been killed and the other two 'invalided out'. The Tribunal adjourned the case to allow him to produce a medical certificate for one of these invalid sons which seems fairly heartless.

When the South Molton Rural Tribunal met they heard a War Office telegram read out which instructed all military representatives to immediately appeal against any exemptions granted by local Tribunals to any man of Class A or passed for garrison duty abroad. Local panel members, however, still ignored these military challenges – and sometimes with good reason. At a Barnstaple Rural Tribunal when the case of John

Westlake, a Combe Martin blacksmith, was being heard the Army man present queried how vital John was to local farmers as he had heard there was another smith called Lerwill in the village who could do the work. It was then pointed out, to laughter, that Lerwill was 84 years old – John was granted exemption.

Two North Devon Appeal Tribunals were held this month mainly hearing challenges from the military although when Frank Gunn, a horseman of Bishopsnympton, appeared and the panel heard he 'had accidentally blown off his "trigger" finger' they sent him for a medical report after which he was to be cross-examined. The previous month had seen the High Bickington CO Sam Parker given exemption – whereupon his employer Mrs.Bedford applied to retain him even though he had been ordered to leave and work elsewhere. The military representative said 'The idea was to make these conscientious objectors feel that they must be put to some inconvenience and make some sacrifice for the sake of their country.' The case was sent to the Central Tribunal.

Poor G.Tucker, a farmer of Challacombe was told that one of his two sons should enlist but 'he said he preferred to make no choice between the two, and left it to the tribunal to decide' – a terrible predicament for a parent. When William Baron, employed by his father W.L.Baron manufacturer of 'Barnstaple Ware' pottery, appeared the military demanded he enlist even though his father said his products would 'cut the German and Austrian trade'. The panel expressed sympathy but ordered him to join up.

While these cases were being heard the looming food crisis was being addressed with some urgency. At Lynton a 'co-operative potato growing scheme' was instituted by three local councillors – Messrs. Vogel, Pulkinghorne and Hodges. They had set aside two acres of land by the golf course where a local farmer would plough and plant potatoes – with members of the scheme weeding and lifting the crop – and paying 6d a week for 32 weeks before they got the crops. A similar municipal scheme was suggested for Barnstaple whilst at Ilfracombe a field at Bicclescombe had been taken over by the council and let as allotments. Local War Agricultural Committees were given powers under the Defence of the Realm Act to both encourage/order the ploughing of pasture land in order to grow crops – possibly presaging serious changes in North Devon. At Arlington the major landowner Miss Chichester ploughed up pasture land to grow corn even before the order came into force.

The first motor-plough arrived this month and created great interest.

A NOVEL feature in the development of the agricultural industry in the district was the arrival at the station during the week-end of a motor-plough. The plough, which was ordered through Messrs. W. J. Isaac and Sons, by Mr. G. M. Style, of Pickwell, has four shares, and is capable, under the direction of only one man, of ploughing ten acres a day. The machine, which has attracted a large number of interested agriculturists and others, is detached from a motor which in the harvest season can be attached to two self-binders. At an early date a demonstration will be given at Pickwell.

2. The arrival of the first tractor. NDJ 15.2.1917 2e

That this mechanisation was needed was highlighted at a meeting of the Bideford District Agricultural Committee where it was explained that in the Bideford and Torrington districts 'labour returns show a shortage of 37½ per cent below the standard' – mainly due to the War Office taking men away. Bideford town council took a pragmatic approach when they opened a Soup Kitchen and served out over 800 quarts of soup on the first day. In Barnstaple a group of ladies had published the 'Barnstaple Book of Cookery' which included 'a fine collection of tested recipes' all provided by 'Ladies' – and raised money for the 'Mayor's Samaritan Fund'.

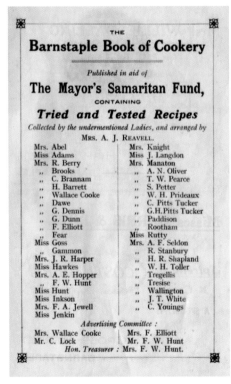

3. The title page of 'The Barnstaple Cookery Book'.

BOROUGH OF BIDEFORD.

FOOD SUPPLY.

Dear Sir (or Madam),

IMPORTANT.

I think it is my duty to remind you that His Majesty's Government, through the Food Controller, has issued an appeal to the Nation to reduce its consumption of Food, and that **EVERYONE** is expected **AT ONCE** to conform to the conditions laid down in the Order.

The Order provides that the Heads of Families should endeavour to limit themselves to the weekly purchase for each person comprising the household of the following quantities per head per week :—

1. **BREAD, 4 lbs. (or its equivalent in FLOUR, 3 lbs.)**
2. **MEAT, 2½ lbs.**
3. **SUGAR, ¾ lb.**

A **special** appeal is made to the **Women** of the land, and notice has been given that if the voluntary system is not a success compulsion will be established.

Yours obediently,

S. R. CHOPE, Mayor.

Bideford, 8th February, 1917.

Coles & Lee, Printers, "Gazette" Office, Bideford.

4. A Bideford flyer urging people to reduce their food intake.

In Bideford the Mayor issued this poster exhorting his fellow citizens to limit their food intake voluntarily.

This local money raising effort was matched by the Government who had introduced a 'Victory War Loan' to raise funds to fight the war. Meetings were held across North Devon to explain why it was so important for people to subscribe to this 'Loan'. Within a fortnight residents of Barnstaple and the surrounding area had raised an estimated £500,000. At Ilfracombe the total was around £106,000 whilst Bideford raised £184,000 and confidently expected that to rise to £250,000 before the end of February. Even small places responded well with Combe Martin managing £2000 whilst Woolacombe raised £158 just from its school pupils. Local War Savings Associations set up in factories helped boost the totals with the Pilton glove factory doing especially well.

HAVE YOU INVESTED
IN THE
WAR LOAN?

You Have Only Three Days More.

The Last Day is Friday, the 16th, and Germany is watching us.

If you have not already invested every shilling you can scrape together—do so now.

IF you have £5 or any amount up to £50 to lend go the nearest Money Order Post Office and they will invest it for you in War Loan. You will get a receipt for your money and afterwards they will send you your stock.	**HAS IT** OCCURRED TO YOU that you can help to end the War by borrowing on your Life Policies OR by obtaining a Loan from your Bank OR	IF you have £50 or over to lend to your Country go to your Bank Manager. He will help you to increase your lending power. The Bank Managers have intimated their desire to do everything in their power to make the Victory Loan an overwhelming success.

BY CONVERTING YOUR TREASURY BILLS INTO WAR LOAN.

The Bank will accept the War Loan it buys for you as security for what it lends to you.

WAR SAVINGS COMMITTEE—
J. H. OSBORN, Hon. Secretary, Town Hall, Bideford; or
E. J. LABBETT, Hon. Secretary, 6, Castle Street, Northam.

5. An advertisement for the War Loan. BG 13.2.1917 2c-e

Much of this money was contributed by ordinary people – including cabinet makers at Shapland & Petter in Barnstaple who were now wanting a raise of 1d per hour – only four months after their previous increase in wages of ½d an hour. The Barnstaple Trades and Labour Council met this month to hear rousing speeches attacking the 'capitalist class' and others stressing the need for the working class to 'recognise the potential power they had in co-operation'. Such fiery statements would never have been published by North Devon's newspapers before the war.

If food was short then another product was also in such great demand that special measures were having to be taken to secure it. Timber for use in the war effort was being cut everywhere as a special illustrated story in the *Bideford Gazette* showed. The text accompanying these three photographs talks of the process of 'wood distillation' producing acetone for use in munitions – with a passing reference to 'factories for wood distillation having been 'erected in Devonshire' i.e. at Bideford.

Temporary Saw Mill — The first thing to be done is to cover the engine.

Cutting the first log.

Tuning up a circular saw. The men are inside the skeleton shed.

6a,b & c. Illustrations of timber workers. BG 13.2.1917 4a-d 1-3

The First World War in North Devon

March 1917

Although there was the usual dismal list of casualties and the never-ending parade of men appealing to local Tribunals against conscription the news this month was dominated by the shortage of food and other goods – a shortage reflected by the *North Devon Journal*. The newspaper printed an apology that 'due to War conditions' the paper was having to be reduced in size. In the same edition appeared a report on the speech of Prime Minister Lloyd George which succinctly summarised the problems facing the nation – including the stark warning that there could be 'Less beer'.

If these were the new national rules what was happening in North Devon? A set of figures published this month showed how local farmers had responded to the call for more food.

Hopes to increase these figures even more were boosted by the first use of a 'motor plough' at Pickwell in Braunton this month.

Unfortunately there was a major shortage of drivers leading Lord

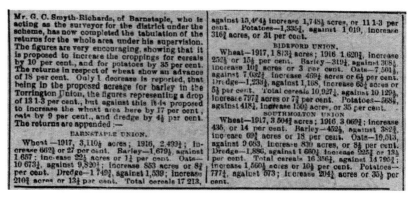

1. Local farmers respond to the call for more food. NDJ 8.3.1917 6b-d

2. The first use of tractors attracts a crowd.

3. An advertisement about farm tractors.
BG 20.3.1917 2d-e

Fortescue to issue an appeal to 'any persons, male or female, with experience of driving motors or tractors' to offer their services using these machines. A fascinating advertisement appeared in the *Bideford Gazette* this month discussing 'Farm Tractors' but note its reference to the Russian Revolution and Henry Ford.

Barnstaple town council contracted with Thomas Hogg to rent his field adjoining Raleigh Park for use as allotments. Later in the same month it was reported that some 12 acres had been acquired, including the playing fields of the Boys' Grammar School – with three-quarters of the land being given over to potatoes. The council in Bideford was to rent a field at the bottom of Northdown Road for the same purpose, this following receipt of a petition from townspeople requesting allotments. At Braunton villagers 'seem to be grimly intent on accelerating the supply of food especially potatoes' through intensive cultivation whilst 'even the brakes on the hills have been turned up ready to receive the crops.' The parish council at Bishops Tawton were making moves to take the glebe land over to cultivate whilst at Fremington 26 allotments were to be established at Bickington.

Local MP George Lambert returned to his complaint that too many farm workers had been enlisted which only exacerbated food shortages. He had been told that 2400 ploughmen and horsemen had been released from the Army to help farmers – but they could be recalled at 24 hour's notice – a situation Lambert characterized as 'crass stupidity'. In the event just 33 such men were sent to North Devon, it being announced at the same time that no German PoWs would be coming to the area.

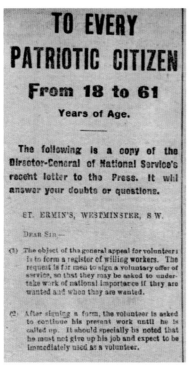

4. A call for volunteer workers.
NDJ 8.3.1917 3a-b

This shortage of labour extended to many other areas and not just farming hence the launch of 'National Service' this month the first advertisement calling for volunteers appearing in the *Journal* of March 8.

Amongst the first to enrol were the Rev.W.Jordan, Lynton's Congregational Minister, who offered to help with the parish's Cliff Railway, and F.Erridge who took on a Lynton postal round. The Barnstaple Rural District council in discussing this new scheme noted that in many areas denuded of men of military age only 'old crocks' were left to volunteer although it was stated that all Government officials between the ages of 18 and 61 would have to enrol, and many clergymen had already done so.

Public meetings in local towns heard from A.Trewethy the National Service 'Sub-Commissioner for North Devon' explain the scheme. Apparently the National Registration returns from July 1915 were to be used to identify possible 'volunteers'. At Ilfracombe after hearing details of what was involved one of the speakers, a Mrs.Hudson Lyall, talked about austerity as a way of coping with shortages suggesting that women cut back on new clothing and 'not mind being old frumps but look as nice as possible in their old clothes' adding that the National Service scheme needed as many women as men to offer their services.

Very quickly it seems to have become clear that volunteers were not coming forward in the numbers required and by the end of the month payment was being offered with the new rules being spelt out in an advertisement signed by Neville Chamberlain.

That all these moves to address shortages weren't an over-reaction was seen when police in Barnstaple were called to the Market following accusations of over-charging for potatoes but no evidence was found though the supply was soon exhausted. One enterprising Barnstaple shopkeeper had secured a ton of potatoes from Braunton and as soon as the news spread his

5. National Service. NDJ 29.3.1917 8

FOOD ECONOMIES.

Sir,—In these days of food shortage a few hints as to the prevention of waste may not be out of place.

The common habit of peeling raw potatoes and throwing away the peelings is extravagant and wasteful since the most nourishing part of the potato is to be found immediately beneath and adherent to the skin. Potatoes should be boiled or baked in their jackets, and those who have good teeth will find that by eating the skins they will find that appetising resistance which renders meat attractive, and they will not only obtain a much greater proportion of nutriment, but they will find it possible to dispense with meat with less feeling of deprivation.

Those who find that they cannot masticate and digest potato skins should partly boil potatoes and then peal them, when the thin exterior coating will peal off, leaving the inner coatings of the peel with all the nutriment preserved, the cooking can then be completed.

The almost universal habit of throwing away pea pods is equally wasteful; they can be employed to make an appetising soup with a delicate flavour, quite equal to that of the pea itself, and if grated and passed through a sieve a thick and nourishing soup can be prepared with or without the addition of a little stock.

Bread, which is the staff of life and the chief food of millions of our population, should be prepared from flour containing a larger proportion of the branny elements than is even provided for in the Government regulation bread, and the "germ," properly treated, should be included. There are various breads upon the market which

any baker can supply made from such flour which are even richer in the proteids, phosphates and enzymes obtained from the inner surface of the bran than is " G.R." bread.

The habit of putting a spoonful of salt on the side of the plate is extremely wasteful, and the same applies to mustard; the requisite quantity of either of these condiments should be sifted upon the plate so that nothing is lost.

When tea or coffee are made in a pot there is often a greater proportion wasted than consumed. If these beverages are strained off from the leaves or grounds respectively, they can be heated up and used again. No thrifty French peasant throws away coffee liquid, she rather heats it up and pours it through a small quantity of fresh coffee, and in many farmhouses in Normandy and Brittany even the coffee grounds are preserved and used a second time.

Soap is not a food but it is a valuable commodity, and if small pieces are collected and mixed with a small quantity of hot water the mixture being heated till solution is obtained, a new cake of soap can be made from the leavings which are commonly thrown away.

In these days we can afford to waste nothing, and wastage due to thoughtlessness is as serious as if it resulted from deliberate extravagance. Perhaps these hints may stimulate your readers to think of others.

Yours obediently,
C. R. RUTLAND.

London, W., March 7th, 1917.

6a & b. Hints on making food go further.
NDJ 15.3.1917 3e

shop was 'literally besieged, the crush being so great that customers had to leave by a side door.' Another Barnstaple shopkeeper rationed potatoes 'according to the size of the families requiring them' which implies a good knowledge of his customers. At South Molton Market similar scenes were witnessed with stalls being 'besieged by thirty or forty customers clamouring to be served at the same time' whilst Bideford Market experienced 'scrambles' for potatoes. This shortage led to accusations of profiteering with Bideford councillor Mr.Fulford announcing that 'he knew potatoes were being held back for higher prices' and certainly there were constant complaints as to the increased cost of foodstuffs. One way of countering this was to use food more economically as suggested by a correspondent to the *Journal* this month.

Barnstaple town council went further when they opened the Municipal Canteen and School of Cookery in the High Street to supply 'munition and other workers' with cheap meals and to provide cookery lessons about 'economical dishes'. A meal cost 4d with soup at 2d the food being produced by 'a ladies committee'.

As noted whilst all this activity was occurring in North Devon local men were still dying on the battlefield – with 21 deaths being reported this month in the *Journal* including several very young ones. Thus Pte.S.Sheppard of Bideford was killed in action aged 20 as was Pte.Alfred Salter of Ilfracombe. When Bertram Watts, an apprentice on the ss *Rosalie* died after his ship was torpedoed he was just 18. Even younger was John Ash of Appledore who died at Shotley Naval Barracks of 'brain fever' aged 16.

Amidst all these concerns over food and the continuing litany of deaths the work of the Tribunals continued. It is very evident from the reports on the many appeals they were dealing with that the military were challenging virtually every man – and where there was a hint of deliberate evasion were especially strenuous in their efforts. Thus when William Kift, a Braunton tailor, applied it came out that he had applied for munitions work locally which would have allowed him to carry on his business in the evenings. The military representative characterised this as 'a very serious case' where Kift was trying to 'scoot off'. He was ordered to enlist by April 1st. The Barnstaple Tribunal heard an appeal from the town's Borough Accountant Frank Grocott who claimed to be in a 'reserved occupation' – and had been granted an exemption on this basis earlier in the war the council saying he was 'indispensable'. He had now secured a similar post at Buxton and the military panel member pointed out this rather undercut his claim to be 'indispensable' – and when the rest of the panel renewed his exemption the military said they would take it further. They did and his appeal was dismissed though he was given permission to take his case to the 'Central Tribunal' – where he was allowed exemption.

Poor C.Blackmore appeared before the Ilfracombe Tribunal to explain how he had gone for his Army medical only to be told to see an eye specialist. This he did and he was given a certificate pointing out his inability to serve – which he sent to the Army doctors who ignored it and told him he had to enlist. This annoyed the local panel who sent him back to the Army medical board for another examination. The Bideford Tribunal heard how an unnamed man had been kept waiting in the nude for 45 minutes at the medical centre and as a consequence 'had been seriously ill ever since.' This was denied by the President of the Exeter Medical Board but the Tribunal chair pointed out 'there had been other complaints, not only from the Bideford Tribunal, but from many others.' When the Ilfracombe Tribunal heard the case of William Guard, a tailor, he was told 'He should join the Royal Flying Corps as a sail maker' – presumably this meant he would be making the fabric wings of these early aircraft.

In many cases heard by the rural Tribunals panel members often disallowed military challenges citing personal knowledge of the worth of the farms the men worked on. At one Barnstaple Rural Tribunal this month, for example, of eight cases challenged by the military representative only two men were told to enlist. But in one of these cases the man had disappeared - although the Army officer present said 'We will find the man.' At the Bideford Rural Tribunal of 42 cases 14 were exemptions being claimed for agricultural workers – with nearly all being allowed.

Perhaps the most unusual case was that of Ivan Ridge, a 24 year old 'comedian' and travelling actor classed as 'C3'. At his appearance in Bideford he noted that 'according to Mr.Neville Chamberlain he was in an essential occupation' – and he had five brothers in the Forces. He was ordered to 'find work of national importance'. Why a comedian should be viewed as essential might seem odd but at the time more serious issues were exercising most people.

This month three Barnstaple shopkeepers were taken to court for exposing lights in their premises at night – with the Borough's Chief Constable saying 'it is very distasteful to me to take proceedings.' Each was fined 2/6. At Bideford 'official notification' was given that the Bideford, Westward Ho! and Appledore Railway was to be closed whilst at Barnstaple twenty women passed a medical allowing them to work in munition factories. Also in Barnstaple painters went on strike for an extra ½d an hour whilst cabinet makers received 1d an hour extra they had demanded. Local newspapers also noted, not entirely approvingly, that many local farm labourers were joining a Union.

In September 1916 tanks made their first appearance and this month the Palace Cinema in Bideford showed 'at great expense' the official Government film – 'The Battle of the Ancre and the Advance of the Tanks'.

In Barnstaple when Mr & Mrs.Venn visited the town's Picturedrome and were watching 'Pathe's Animated Gazette' they were delighted to see their son L/Cpl.W.Venn 'prominently represented in a group of Tommies just leaving the trenches at the Front.' A few weeks later the Barnstaple Theatre Royal was showing a variety of films including one entitled 'Our Russian Friends' which was unfortunate as in the adjoining column was the news that there had been a revolution in Russia and the Tsar had abdicated – with unknown results for the Allied war effort.

One seemingly innocuous letter was published this month - an appeal for more beds for the 'Commons Auxiliary Hospital' in Northam. It did, however, have the chilling line that more beds were needed as the 'Authorities' i.e. the War Office were 'anticipating a very heavy casualty list'.

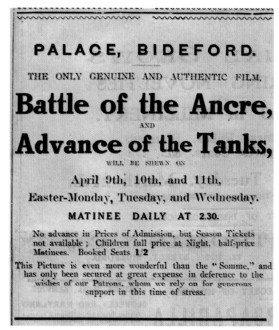

7. Films in Bideford. BG 27.3.1917 2d-e

The First World War in North Devon

April 1917

With the news of the Russian revolution still fresh another astonishing but better piece of news came when, on April 6, President Wilson announced that the USA was at war with Germany. Given the relatively tiny size of the US Army at this date – 127,500 – and the need to train up a new force, clearly the American entry into the war would have little effect in terms of fighting for some time. It must, however, have been extremely heartening to the Allies to have the economic might of the US join them. Wilson announced immediate plans to increase his Army by half a million men – who were badly needed as the carnage on the battlefields continued with another 25 deaths of local servicemen being recorded this month. Of these, three died in Turkish prison camps, an ominous and on-going fate of many such prisoners. One of these unfortunate deaths saw a longer report than usual in the newspaper.

The homes of these casualties were usually scattered across the area, as it were, so it must have been extremely upsetting when three Lynton soldiers were reported killed in the third week of April. Pte.F.Murley, Pte.A.Gardener and Pte.S.Ridd brought the total of Lynton and Lynmouth men killed in the war to fourteen. A Barnstaple casualty was Pte.Herbert Eller who died aged 26 – whose eye-witness accounts of the war were often published in the *Journal*, one of which has been quoted in this book.

This month saw the dedication of the first 'War Shrine' in Barnstaple it being a glass cabinet lit by an oil lamp and set up in the doorway of No.19 Vicarage Street. Unveiled by the Rev.R.Boggis no letters of objection were published this time. The 'Shrine' contained a list of the 233 men serving in the Army and Navy from Vicarage

REPORTED DEATH OF BIDEFORD SOLDIER.

A passage in a letter from a prisoner of the Turks at Afion Kara Hissar, about 200 miles east of Smyrna, leaves little doubt that Corpl. Laurie B. Finnegan, of the Devon Regiment, who was captured after the battle in the attempted relief of Kut on March 8th, 1916, has died in captivity. Pte. W. Aze, of Barnstaple, also of the Devons, has been able on several occasions to send brief postcards to his relatives from Afion Kara Hissar, and his parents in communicating with him have asked for information of other Devons missing. Hitherto, Pte. Aze had apparently been prevented from answering the questions, but at length he was permitted to write a letter, a passage of which, after referring to a number of casualties, reads:— "Finnegan, of Bideford, and Hill, of Woollacombe, got captured when I did, but only Farnham is left now." It appears that Pte. Aze, with the others, went out on the night after the battle to see if they could succour or rescue any of our wounded. They were overtaken by darkness, and seeing a light some of them made for it, thinking it was in our lines. Instead of that it led them towards the enemy's camp, and they were captured. It will be recalled that Corpl. Finnegan was reported by the War Office as missing, and that some months afterwards a card was received from him through the Red Crescent Agency stating that he was a prisoner. The fact that several cards have been received from other prisoners and only one from Corpl. Finnegan rather points to the conclusion that he died some time ago. He was the only son of Mrs. O. Allin, of Myrtle Grove, Bideford, was a popular member of Bideford Boy Scouts and subsequently of the Bideford Volunteers, with whom he was called up at the commencement of the War, going to India for over a year and then proceeding to Mesopotamia. He had just served his apprenticeship at the printing and monotype operating at the "Bideford Gazette" Office.

1. The death of Cpl.L.Finnegan.
NDJ 12.4.1917 3d

The rank and file and names of the men included in the lists on the War Shrine are as follows :—

CORSER STREET.—Private Thomas Henry Burnell, Pioneer William Featherstone, Private William Kidwell, Private Arthur Turner.

HIGHER MAUDLIN STREET — Lance-Corporal William John Bamson, Private William Barnes, Private Horace Berry, Gunner Alfred Cann, Private Thomas Cann, Private George Chugg, Private Bertie Davis, Private Frederick Delbridge, Private William John Delbridge, Corporal John Dookott, Private Frederick W. F. Fry, Sergeant George Kingdon, Sergeant John Kingdon, Private William Loosemore, Private Albert Edward Parkin, Private Abraham George Smale, Private Frank Stribling, Private Fred Taylor, Sergeant James Shaddick.

LOWER MAUDLIN STREET. — Private George Barrow, Driver Samuel Berry, Private John Edward Bryant, Sapper Henry Cann, Driver George Casinelli, Sapper Edward Clapp, Private Frederick Dadds, Seaman Wilfred Dadds, Leading Seaman Richard Ell Fisher, Lance-Corporal Charles Folland, Private Henry Ford, Private Joseph Ford, Corporal Charles Henry Found, Private Frederick Fry, Private William Fry, Private Arthur Charles Harris, Private Arthur Henry Knight, Farrier Harold Lateman, Private Frederick James Laud, Private Robert Burvill Mackie, Private Arthur Marles, Private Sidney Marles, Corporal Alfred Pickard, Private Arthur Popham, Private Herbert Rottenbury, Sergeant Bill Rottenbury, Private Frederick Taylor, Private Albert Ward, Private Frank Westacott, Private Walter Wollen.

2. Some of the names on the 'Shrine'.
NDJ 26.4.1917 7d

3. A Bideford 'Shrine'.

Street and adjoining streets, part of the list is shown here.

A similar one from Bideford is shown here.

Once conscription had been introduced reports of families having multiple men in the Forces largely disappeared so it is surprising to read this month in the obituary of Mrs.Mary Stevens of Fremington, who died aged 92, how she 'had the proud satisfaction of witnessing at the outbreak of the War the enlistment of 15 of her grandsons' – which could well be some sort of record.

At this stage in the war conscription was universal – with the Tribunals continuing to hear claims to be exempted. Such claims now followed a well-worn routine with men claiming to be vital to their employers or businesses - with the military challenging their veracity. Thus when Richard Williams, a farmer of East Ashford, appealed on behalf of his son Robert at the Barnstaple Rural Tribunal it was alleged the son was 'rabbiting a good deal of his time and is the talk of the parish', and when Richard denied this the military representative asked 'Would you like me to call the police to support this evidence?' Robert was ordered to enlist by June 1st – although in a letter in the *Journal* a fortnight later he was defended by the Rev.Charles Williams, rector of Ashford. In the next case a man claimed to be a rabbit trapper only for the Army panel member to exclaim 'everyone who came there said they were rabbit trappers.'

At the first South Molton Rural Tribunal of the month it was announced that the need for men was 'so urgent that exemption is not justified on any ground, whether of employment or hardship unless there are specially strong reasons which make the case clearly exceptional' – with men classified as low as 'C2' now being liable to conscription. This might have been the new ruling but panels nevertheless continued to exempt many agricultural workers. Given the perception that farmers were trying to keep their own family members at home (as with Robert Williams above) one case was interesting. Walter Barry of Knowstone, who worked on his uncle's farm, had been told to enlist - with his employer and uncle James Barry hiring a substitute. The military representative claimed that a substitute had been found but refused to take the post as James

SIX REASONS

Why we should adopt National Rations

1. **BECAUSE** there is a shortage of food all over the world.

2. **BECAUSE** most of our food comes to us in ships which are being sunk daily by German Submarines.

3. **BECAUSE** if we eat more than our share we are eating somebody else's share.

4. **BECAUSE** if we eat all we can obtain now we shall go hungry later.

5. **BECAUSE** we must not waste an atom of the food which is so scarce, and Rations help to check waste.

6. **BECAUSE** if we are fighting for honour and freedom surely we can be put on OUR honour and trusted to use OUR freedom rightly.

Scale per Week for each Person :—

BREAD	-	-	-	**4 lbs.**
	(or its equivalent in Flour 3lbs)			
Meat	-	-	-	2½ lbs.
Sugar	-	-	-	¾ lb.

Substitutes for Wheat Flour obtainable locally are Rice, Rye, Maize and Barley Flour, Oatmeal and Maize Meal.

Circulars, giving practical recipes for the use of Maize Meal and Flour for making Bread, Porridge, Cakes, Puddings and Biscuits may be obtained, price One Penny each, from Messrs. Coles & Lee, " Gazette " Office ; Mr. G. Fluck, and Messrs. Harper and Son, High Street ; Messrs. Pearse & Son, Allhalland Street ;

Or from **Mr. J. H. OSBORN,** Hon. Sec. War Savings Committee, Town Hall, Bideford ;

Mr. E. J. LABBETT, War Savings Committee, Castle Street, Northam.

expected him to work a 14 hour day for £1 a week – thus allowing James to say he had to keep Walter working for him. A novel claim was put forward by 40 year old William Heard the sexton and gravedigger at Appledore church. The panel heard that the vicar and one of the two churchwardens had enlisted and 'as no one had a plan of the Churchyard, the sexton was the only one who knew where there were available spaces for fresh graves.' He was given three weeks to show the remaining churchwarden where graves could be dug before he had to enlist.

When the Barnstaple Tribunal met this month all the cases heard were ones where the military were challenging exemptions given by the panel members These included 19 men from Shapland & Petter who had been exempted as 16 were 'on Government work' and the other 3 'on export work' – in the event 9 were ordered to enlist. The clerk to the Tribunal did say that 'This was, he believed, the last combing out that the military could possibly have at the works, the remaining men being either over military age or rejected.'

Casualties and Tribunals were being reported on in some detail but even more space in the newspapers was now being given over to the continuing problem of food shortages. The first notice concerned a Barnstaple court case where eight men were charged with selling/ buying seed potatoes above the fixed minimum price. After a long hearing the magistrates dismissed them saying they 'had already been penalised by the prices they had paid' which seems an odd decision. A second case saw Thomas Richards of Bishops Tawton fined 10/- for the same offence as was Martha Rowcliff of West Down. A fortnight later Francis Davey junior of West Anstey was fined the very heavy sum of £11.10.6 for exactly the same crime.

If this seemed harsh worse was to come when the Food Hoarding Order came into force this month. This allowed 'an authorised person' to enter any premises to ensure owners weren't hoarding supplies. At the same time new regulations were brought in under the Defence of the Realm Act to control the consumption of food in hotels, restaurants and clubs which included 'a weekly meatless day' and 'five potatoless days'. An editorial in the *Journal* reckoned the waste of bread 'is a crime' and if everyone ate one pound of bread less every week 'the submarine peril would be vastly mitigated.' A local initiative in Bideford saw 'Six Reasons' spelling out why people should try to adopt the suggested 'National Rations' food intake.

On the domestic front suggestions as to economies in cooking began to appear.

FOOD ECONOMY.

TESTED RECIPES FOR THE WEEK.

POTATO SUBSTITUTE.—Boil 1 quart of water, and add a little salt. When it boils, put in by degrees 8½ozs. of maize meal. Cook it, stirring often, until it does not stick to the sides of the saucepan. When cooked, put it in a pie dish until it is quite cold, then cut it in thick slices and fry in boiling fat.

JOHNNY CAKE (Canadian).—2 cups of white flour to 1 cup of maize meal ; 2 ozs. of fat, salt and sugar to taste ; 1 teaspoonful of baking powder, 1 egg. Mix flour well together with the salt, sugar, and baking power, add the egg well beaten (yolk and white separately), mix with milk, bake in a fairly hot oven.

Maize meal is better sifted before using.

To soften these blows more and more allotments were being made available by local councils – with Bideford reporting they now had 200. At Lynton as an encouragement an unnamed gentleman offered three prizes for the best allotment produce. On a more commercial basis 'a large crowd witnessed the motor-plough at work on the Pickwell estate' in Braunton. It was completing seven acres a day and during the night was 'working by the aid of electric light'. In March 1917 the Women's Land Army was established in order to organise female labour on farms – with an advertisement appearing this month in the local newspapers appealing for women to come forward. By the end of the war some 23,000 women had joined the WLA – which was to be revived in the Second World War.

Given all this it is astonishing to read a letter from J.B.Chamings arguing that North Devonians should not be working the land on Sundays as 'Sabbath breaking' would apparently lead God to 'cause the crops to fail'. Presumably he hadn't noticed that the war didn't seem to stop on Sundays?

This month the Barnstaple Theatre Royal 'At a big expense' was screening 'The Battle of the Ancre' film. If one didn't fancy seeing war films then you could go to see 'Broncho Bill's Great Wild West Exhibition and Mammoth Circus' which visited South Molton, Barnstaple, Bideford and Torrington. Presumably many young people were attracted to this show but when three boys aged from 13 to 15 were brought to court in Barnstaple for 'Disorderly conduct' the borough's Chief Constable said 'This sort of hooliganism was going on all over town' and he blamed a lack of parental control – though as so many fathers were away at the war this wasn't surprising.

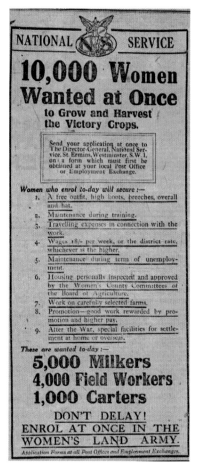

6. A call to join the Women's Land Army. BG 10.4.1917 4b-c

The First World War in North Devon

May 1917

This month saw the highest number of deaths being recorded so far during the war with some 75 men killed in action or dying of their wounds. The reason for this seems to be that the Devonshire Regiment was heavily engaged in the Battle of Arras and at Vimy Ridge where the Allies advanced some distance only to come up against prepared German defences in depth – with the inevitable slaughter.

Many of the dead were young, thus Pte.V.Taylor of Bideford was 22, his fellow Bidefordians Pte.L.Colwill and Pte.L.Hocking were both 20 whilst Pte.W.Sage and Signaller R.Sanders both of Barnstaple were 20 and 21 respectively. At the other end of the age spectrum was Pte.Henry Thomas of Barnstaple who died of pneumonia aged 45. Most of the men listed were Privates or at most Sergeants but this month saw a report that Lt.Col.McConaghey of 'Rock House, near Bideford' had been killed at the Front. Two other senior officers, also from Bideford, died in action this month. Lt.Col.Meredith Magniac and his brother Lt.Col.Erskine Magniac were killed within 3 days of each other, Meredith in France and Erskine in Mesopotamia.

The dangers of the Front were again brought home to North Devonians when the death of Pte.W.Hobbs from Lynton was reported. Aged 32 he was a member of the Machine Gun Corps and was killed after being in France for just 3 weeks. When Pte.H.Grant of Ilfracombe was wounded and had both his legs amputated he wrote to his mother 'You cannot realise at home what it is like going over the parapet....I had no sense of danger until I was right over the German trenches and found the snipers at work. Then it was nothing but digging. We were up to our waists in water and mud.'

Such descriptive letters had become unusual by this stage of the war but such correspondence and the dreaded War Office telegram were the only means of communication between servicemen and their families. Obtaining news of prisoners was even harder as shown when Flight Sergt.John Hollis from Ilfracombe was brought down over the Front.

ILFRACOMBE AIRMAN MISSING.

Mrs. Hollis, of 27, Chambercombe-road, Ilfracombe, has received information that her youngest son, Flight-Sergeant John Kenneth Hollis, Royal Flying Corps, had been brought down behind the enemy lines in a combat with German machines. The fate of the intrepid young airman is unknown at present, except to the Germans, and the utmost sympathy is felt with Mrs. Hollis and family in their anxiety.

The information was conveyed to Mrs. Hollis by the following letter from Major C. T. Maclean, R.F.C. :—

April 23rd, 1917.

" Dear Mrs. Hollis,—The War Office will have informed you that your son, Flight-Sergeant J. K. Hollis was posted as missing yesterday, when he did not return from a flight over the German lines. I have been unable to obtain much information except that your son's machine was shot down in a combat with German machines. He was clearly seen to land under control behind the German lines. I am of opinion that your son is a prisoner of war, and if wounded probably not seriously, and I hope you will soon hear from him from Germany. Should I obtain any more information I will at once write to you.—Yours sincerely, C. T. Maclean, Major."

Flight-Sergeant Hollis, who is only 22 years of age, joined the Royal Flying Corps in November, 1914, as second-mechanic. He was rapidly promoted to first-mechanic, to Corporal and then to Observer. Whilst an observer he did much valuable and clever work, on one occasion being highly complimented by his commanding officer. At the end of last year he was sent home for three months' training, and obtained his " wings " on February 27th last, and qualified as an instructor. He returned to the front about a month ago, and practically ever since has been making daily flights over the enemy lines.

Two other sons of Mrs. Hollis hold commissions in the Royal Flying Corps, having returned home from the Solomon Islands early in the war for the purpose of joining up.

1. The downing of a pilot. NDJ 10.5.1917 3b

2.3.4.5.6. A wonderful series of photographs showing wounded soldiers relaxing in Ilfracombe.

A more optimistic note was struck by a report from the 'Commons' Auxiliary Hospital at Northam where, of the 600 patients treated there, only one had died. At Ilfracombe wounded soldiers being treated at the 'Craigmore' hospital were taken on motor trips around the area in both private cars and charabancs. At the same time patients and staff featured in a series of photographs.

With this number of casualties, however, it is clear that the Tribunals were being pressed to send as many men to the Forces as they could - but there weren't that many left who could be spared from vital work. That this was true was noted in Lynton where the town had 'been so cleared out of eligible men for the Services that there has been no Tribunal for six weeks. The majority of the men enlisted voluntarily.'

Other men were not so willing with one widely reported court case concerning Richard Cann, a 'grocer's porter' from Barnstaple, who was charged with being unlawfully absent from the Army. At the hearing a Cpl. Trevenen from the town's recruiting office produced 'the daily record calling up book' showing that Cann had been contacted on March 15 and told to report for duty on March 29. The records of the Barnstaple Tribunal for 22 June 1916 were then referred to where it was noted that Cann claimed to be a CO and 'Pastor of the International Bible Student's Association' (the Jehovah's Witnesses) and thus was ordered to do non-combatant duties in the Army. He declined these and applied for full exemption through his claim to be a church Minister, which was refused, the next step being his non-appearance at the enlistment centre. After a very long discussion over whether Cann could be considered a genuine clergyman the magistrates decided he wasn't and he was handed over to the military. Taken to an Army camp in South Devon he was ordered to don a military uniform, unsurprisingly he refused - and was court martialled for disobeying an order.

Another man charged as being an absentee from the Army was Abraham Benson who had been arrested at Shirwell. In court he produced an Irish birth certificate which he believed absolved him from serving in the British Forces. Unfortunately by living in England he had made himself liable which he was probably aware of as he had actually altered the date on his birth certificate to make it appear he was too old to be called up. The magistrates handed him over to the military. Also this month the Barnstaple Rural Tribunal heard the case of 18 year old James Butt who claimed to be a CO on religious grounds. After a long presentation of his beliefs he admitted he was a member of the No Conscription Fellowship and the similar Fellowship of Reconciliation – though as the Army man present pointed out he had only joined them in 1916. He added that as Butt was under 21 'he did not think he was responsible for his statements.' Ordered to undertake non-combatant duties Butt refused and said he would take his case to the Appeals Tribunal. His brother George then appeared, he being another CO. He admitted to passing on anti-war leaflets and, surprisingly, the panel allowed him exemption – with the Army representative saying he would challenge both cases at the Appeals Tribunal.

Apart from the CO cases the local Tribunals continued with their usual work although applicants were being routinely challenged. Thus when 39 year old Frederick Drodge of Barnstaple, who had 9 children under the age of 15, appeared this carried no weight with the Tribunal members and he was ordered to enlist – unlike 41 year old Henry Taylor also of Barnstaple who had 9 children and was granted exemption. This lack of consistency became ever more obvious when agricultural workers were questioned - with older men being sent to the Army before younger men who were often much fitter than these older men. One class of worker, however, was now regularly being given exemption – bakers – who were supplying large numbers of customers, their occupation being regarded as vital even if not so recognised in law.

Another reason for exemption was now being regularly ignored as when Miss Chichester of Arlington (herself a member of the Appeals Tribunal) argued that her employee 18 year old Frederick Kiff should be exempted as his five brothers had all enlisted. Panel member the Rev.J.Dene made what he presumably thought was a humorous comment but which now appears callous when he said 'It's a pity to spoil the batch; send him along.' Many cases were argued by farmers and market gardeners attempting to keep at least one son at home but often the panel would order the son to enlist once a substitute had been found, although as will be seen, this was in reality giving an open-ended exemption as skilled substitutes were very scarce.

There were the usual odd cases as when A.Clive, who ran the Victoria Hotel in Ilfracombe, came before the Appeals Tribunal. He had been granted exemption by the Ilfracombe Tribunal but the Army challenged this – and lost, whereupon Lieut.Stirling said 'It's the same old thing, Ilfracombe looking after its visitors; it puts visitors before the Army in the field.' When W.Jenkinson, the manager of the Strand shirt and collar factory in Bideford, argued for his foreman W.Stacey he pointed out that 75% of their output was for export thus bringing in vital foreign exchange. Lieut.Stirling then came out with a slightly surreal comment, 'This is one of the penalties we have to pay for civilization. A starched collar does add a finish to one's appearance, especially when it has a glossy white face.' Stacey was granted exemption until July 1st.

Running in parallel to concerns over the strength of the Forces was the worry over food supplies. Food economy tips were now a staple of local newspapers and even King George V became involved with his call to reduce bread consumption.

Several weeks later this Royal Proclamation was publicly read out by the Barnstaple town clerk before large crowds at four sites in town, this being backed up by a speech from the Mayor F.Jewell in which he emphasised 'the submarine menace' pointing out that in April some 174 Allied vessels had been sunk. Similar events were held in Bideford and Torrington. At the same time the *Bideford Gazette* published two advertisements, one stressing the submarine menace and linking it directly to the need to cut food intake, with the second pointing out the personal responsibility of every citizen to act.

7. King George V becomes involved in saving food. NDJ 10.5.1917 3b

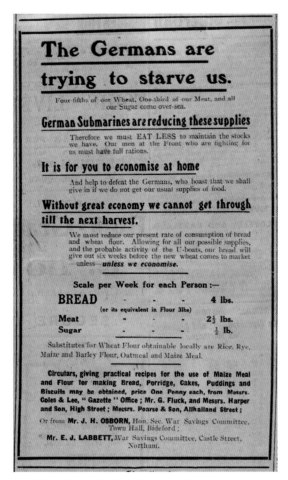

8 & 9. Two advertisements about food shortages. BG 1.5.1917 2d-e + 8.5.1917 1c-f

Many other suggestions were being made to tackle food shortages including a letter in the *Journal* from an invalided soldier commenting that 'frugal inhabitants' of Northern France all grew haricot beans which were easy to produce and use. Barnstaple town council heard from the Devon Food Production Committee that sparrows were responsible for 'large depredations' on food crops – and decided to declare a 'War on Sparrows'. At Bideford the council received a 36 name petition requesting the disused railway garden at East-the-Water be compulsorily purchased for use as allotments, this being immediately agreed to. At Ilfracombe the town's War Savings' Association staged a competition for 'economy in foodstuffs' along with a cookery demonstration. In a speech in Barnstaple by Earl Fortescue the new powers granted to local War Agricultural Committees to compel farmers to plough up pasture land and grow crops were outlined, these being termed 'epoch marking' by the editor of the *Journal*.

Other goods were becoming scarce hence the launching this month of a municipal waste paper collection in Barnstaple by the Mayor, something taken up in most other North Devon towns. Scarcities of labour were now being extensively met by women, with the Barnstaple Theatre Royal screening the Government 'National Service Film – Women on the Land' to encourage more volunteers. Even the local Salvation Army, when experiencing a shortage of men, formed a female band who made their first appearance in Barnstaple this month.

A report in the *Journal* reckoned that the hundreds of women volunteering to work on Devon farms 'have been carefully selected for the work, both as regards character and physical health.' This reference to 'character' might seem odd in wartime but similar thoughts were echoed at a meeting of the North Devon Association for Rescue and Preventive Work. Apparently the members 'were always asking ourselves what effect the war would have on our morals' – although they comforted themselves with the belief that Britain was more 'moral' than our enemies and 'Happily, North Devon was differently situated from other places where trouble had arisen from men in the Services. In North Devon they had something very different – the tone of the public mind.' Lady Florence Cecil in addressing the meeting didn't quite accept this and blamed the local lack of morality on cinemas where girls 'often picked up acquaintance with a total stranger – and very often with regretted results.' One wonders what cinema goers and owners made of this?

The First World War in North Devon

June 1917

After the carnage recorded in May the number of fatalities reported amongst local servicemen fell to around 35 this month although some of these were 'historical' including that of Pte.William Gooding from Chittlehampton whose death in a Turkish PoW camp was only now known about – 13 months after his passing. The obituary for Lieut.W.Miller, son of the director of the Derby lace factory in Barnstaple, notes he was killed at the end of April – aged just 20. Other youthful deaths included Pte.H.Woollacott of Barnstaple aged 21, Pte.A.Sanders of Ilfracombe aged 21 and Pte.S.Thomas of Combe Martin aged just 19. Much older was Pte.H.Wybron of Ilfracombe who died of his wounds aged 43 he being a member of the Canadian forces who had returned to Britain to fight. Three more men were recorded as dying in Turkish prison camps with a few more men dying of disease usually in Mesopotamia or India.

Generally these deaths were noted in the newspapers in very brief notices but occasionally longer obituaries were given often focusing on the men's younger years as their lives were so dominated by service in the Forces. Two of these longer notices give the flavour.

As well as the lists of the killed there were many reports of men 'missing in action' or 'presumed killed'. Many of these were never found and are only recorded on post-war memorials as soldiers with no known grave. Many relatives must have hoped that their 'missing' man would be found – and occasionally such hopes were realised. This month, for example, Pte.James Parker from High Bickington was reported as killed but then his parents received a letter from him saying he was a PoW in Germany and, even though his leg had been amputated, at least he was still alive.

Some 18 months after they had started the various local Tribunals were still sitting, though most cases were of men already exempted presenting arguments to have their exemptions extended. At the first meeting of the Barnstaple Tribunal this month, however, there was a very public argument between the panel and the long-time military representative H.Woodcock. It hinged around instructions allegedly received by the latter to immediately challenge any men exempted by the Tribunal which seemed to be pre-judging cases no matter what the evidence. The panel listened to Woodcock's explanation but were so dissatisfied that 'as a protest against the action of the military they had decided to adjourn the sitting sine die [indefinitely].'

ILFRACOMBE SOLDIERS KILLED IN ACTION.

We regret to record the death in action of Gunner Stanley Millman, R.G.A., second son of Mr. and Mrs. W. Millman, 152, High-street, which took place in France on June 18th last. He was a young man of good promise, and was for some time a scholar in the Wesleyan Sunday School (having been educated at SS. Philip and James' School) afterwards becoming a member of the choir. For seven years he was with Mr. H. Palmer, of Lynton, managing a hair-dressing business, and became engaged to Miss Stella Palmer. He was medically rejected three times, but voluntarily joined up in October, 1915, crossing to France in June, 1916. The sad news reached the parents on Monday last in a letter from a comrade, who said that death was instantaneous, from the explosion of a shell. This letter was followed by one from his Chaplain, who wrote a sympathetic letter, giving an account of the funeral. Great sympathy is felt for the parents and relatives of this bright and brave lad.

We also record with much regret and the death of Rifleman Lindon Goldsworthy (London Rifle Brigade), eldest son of Mrs. Goldsworthy, 8, Adelaide-terrace, and the late Mr. H. Goldsworthy. For some time he was on the staff of the "Ilfracombe Chronicle," and for eleven years was on the Parliamentary reporting staff of the "Pall Mall Gazette." He was killed by a bomb on June 19th, and the news came from the widow in London; official news was not to hand at the time of writing. He began his training in August, 1916, and went to the Front on Christmas Day last. He leaves a widow and two children. The deceased was a young man of much literary ability, and besides having the faculty of clever draughtsmanship, he was of a most genial temperament, and very much liked by all who knew him.

1. Two Ilfracombe soldiers. NDJ 28.6.1917 5e

It was clear that nerves and tempers were becoming frayed from the never-ending demands for more men to enlist as shown by a case at the Barnstaple Rural Tribunal. When 18 year old horseman Samuel Down who worked on his father's farm at Atherington appeared the panel heard that his 27 year old brother who might have helped on the farm had gone into munition work. Samuel's father, who had accompanied his son, was then asked if he had other sons and said yes – one aged 14 the other 9 – whereupon the military representative said 'You are like some other farmers, keeping your son at school when he might be helping you on the farm. He thought it a clear case of defying the military.' The Tribunal decided Samuel had to enlist once the Army had found a substitute for him. Even substitution, however, was now being challenged with the Bideford Rural Tribunal hearing that there were 80 cases outstanding where farmers were waiting for substitutes to be provided. Clearly the issue was becoming a problem – not helped by the South Molton Rural Tribunal deciding this month that 12 agricultural workers required substitutes to take their place before being called up. The number of substitutes available wasn't the only problem with them apparently. When T.Pearse appealed on behalf of his baker and motor delivery driver William Sexton he noted that an earlier substitute from Plymouth crashed the vehicle on his first day!

At a Barnstaple Rural Tribunal hearing Percy Moon, a 37 year old house decorator of Braunton, was told his job was a luxury in wartime though one of the panel remarked that Moon could undertake painting duty in the Army – to which he got the reply 'surely if painting was a luxury in civil life it was equally so in the Army.' He was ordered to enlist but not until August 'having regard to an impending domestic event' – presumably his wife giving birth.

An indication of how desperate the need for men was became clear when George Bratcher, a Barnstaple tailor, appeared before the reconvened Borough Tribunal. He pointed out he had an artificial leg and had also lost one finger though when Woodcock argued he could become a tailor in the Army one of the panel members lost patience saying what was the point of hearing cases like this? – only for Woodcock to claim that 'many men escaped service through fraud.' Bratcher was exempted. A hint at what type of 'fraud' was being referred to came out at a meeting of the Barnstaple Rural Tribunal. Here William Annis, a Bickington schoolmaster, asked for exemption on medical grounds. He had gone to Exeter for his examination and 'After he had hopped round the room, however, the military doctor asked "what pills have you been taking to make your heart beat like this?" ' His appeal was dismissed though the Tribunal ordered another medical examination before he would be called up.

The on-going dissatisfaction with medical boards was referred to in Parliament this month by Barnstaple MP Sir Godfrey Baring. He had had 'some very remarkable experiences of the work of medical boards, and his confidence in them had been rudely shaken' – especially when Army doctors were calling some men 'shirkers' and accusing them of 'shamming'. He reckoned such military doctors were biased – and he wanted civilian doctors to carry out examinations noting 'associations were being formed to protect the interests of men who had to go before these boards.'

One unexpected case was heard at Barnstaple when Arthur Perryman, the 23 year old clerk to the Tribunal appeared. He said 'he was quite ready to go if the Tribunal thought fit' but the Town Clerk A.Seldon argued they needed him as not only was he clerk to the Barnstaple Tribunal but also served as clerk to Lynton council and their Tribunal. Lieut.Geen for the military reckoned a woman could do the work, indeed 'it was astonishing what work women were doing at present. There were special colleges in which they were being trained for this very kind of work.' Perryman was exempted for a month.

Many men having their previous exemptions overturned took their case to appeal and the North Devon Appeals Tribunal sat three times

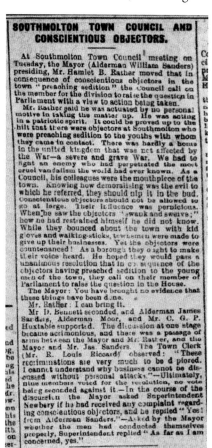

SOUTHMOLTON TOWN COUNCIL AND CONSCIENTIOUS OBJECTORS.

At Southmolton Town Council meeting on Tuesday, the Mayor (Alderman William Sanders) presiding, Mr. Hamlet B. Rather moved that in consequence of conscientious objectors in the town "preaching sedition" the Council call on the member for the division to raise the question in Parliament with a view to action being taken.

Mr. Rather said he was actuated by no personal motive in taking the matter up. He was acting in a patriotic spirit. It could be proved up to the hilt that there were objectors at Southmolton who were preaching sedition to the youths with whom they came in contact. There was hardly a home in the united kingdom that was not affected by the War—a severe and grave War. We had to fight an enemy who had perpetrated the most cruel vandalism the world had ever known. As a Council, his colleagues were the mouthpiece of the town. Knowing how demoralising was the evil to which he referred, they should nip it in the bud. Conscientious objectors should not be allowed to go at large. Their influence was pernicious. When he saw the objectors "swank and swerve," how he had restrained himself he did not know. While they bounced about the town with kid gloves and walking-sticks, townsmen were made to give up their businesses. Yet the objectors were countenanced! As a borough they ought to make their voice heard. He hoped they would pass a unanimous resolution that in consequence of the objectors having preached sedition to the young men of the town, they call on their member of Parliament to raise the question in the House.

The Mayor: You have brought no evidence that these things have been done.

Mr. Rather: I can bring it.

Mr D. Bennett seconded, and Alderman James Sanders, Alderman Moor, and Mr. C. G. P. Huxtable supported. The discussion at one stage became acrimonious, and there was a passage of arms between the Mayor and Mr. Rather, and the Mayor and Mr. Jas. Sanders. The Town Clerk (Mr. R. Louis Riccard) observed: "These recriminations are very much to be deplored. I cannot understand why business cannot be discussed without personal attack."—Ultimately, nine members voted for the resolution, no vote being recorded against it.—In the course of the discussion the Mayor asked Superintendent Newbery if he had received any complaint regarding conscientious objectors, and he replied "Yes" from Alderman Sanders."—Asked by the Mayor whether the men had conducted themselves properly, Superintendent replied "As far as I am concerned, yes."

2. South Molton council and Conscientious Objectors. NDJ 14.6.1917 8d

this month though the demand for men was now so imperative that earlier grounds carried no weight. Thus Walter Roberts, a 40 year old Bideford butcher with 7 children and 'a delicate wife' was ordered to enlist if his medical examination found him fit to serve. Somewhat unexpectedly this saw him being reduced from a 'B1' category to 'C1' and being exempted for three months. When James Butt, aged 19, appeared again at the Appeals Tribunal he claimed to be a CO on religious grounds adding the rather incendiary and ill-judged statement that 'Germany was not the sole cause of the War.' Dismissed as 'immature' and having 'cold feet' he was ordered to enlist immediately - a decision greeted with applause. Taken to Exeter he refused to put on an Army uniform, was then tried by Court Martial and sentenced to 112 days in prison. At South Molton town council the subject of COs came up this month with an extraordinary claim by councillor Hamlet Rather which is presented on the preceding page. Note that the police didn't support his claim.

Preaching 'sedition' was almost as bad as profiteering apparently according to 'WB' who wrote to the *Journal* this month to denounce traders at Barnstaple Market who charged him 'sixpence for an immature cabbage and ninepence for a cauliflower, with a melancholy flower.' The following week another correspondent pointed out that cabbages had actually been dearer in 1916 – and at Lynton they were selling for only 3d each.

Food, however much it cost, was now a major item of interest. At Fremington a public meeting was called in advance of an official census of possible corn growing land, the idea being that if local farmers planned next year's planting now it would give them a head start and yield good results. C.R.Chanter, who acted for Miss Yeo, Miss Quartly and Mrs.Langdon who between them owned four fifths of the parish, had agreed to the idea the only problem being a shortage of labour. Chanter had been told that the Government would be providing motor ploughs and the necessary workers. At Hartland farmers undertook to put an extra 1000 acres under corn with smaller parishes agreeing to increase the percentage of land growing the crop e.g. Woolsery 55%, Abbotsham 68%, Monkleigh 34% and Parkham 35%. A similar meeting at Torrington saw increases promised from many more parishes.

The shortage of labour was attempted to be addressed locally when John White, Secretary of the Barnstaple Food Control Committee, wrote to the *Journal* suggesting a list be drawn up of local people who would be willing to work one day a week on farms. Farmers would apply for such workers – and pay them 4½d an hour. The idea was taken up and a list began to be prepared.

NORTH DEVON FARMERS AND THE FOOD PROBLEM.

Earl Fortescue Thanks the Farmers at Torrington.

3. North Devon farmers respond to food shortages. NDJ 21.6.1917 6e

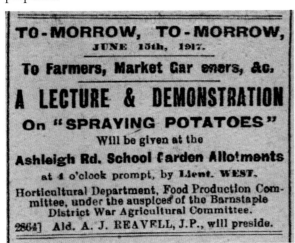

4. Tackling potato disease. NDJ 14.6.1917 4d

A meeting in Barnstaple was put on for allotment holders who heard D.Moule of the Royal Horticultural Society lecture on 'The Management of Vegetable Gardens'. Here councillor G.Andrew announced the town council would be buying equipment for spraying potatoes to prevent disease – the spraying to be free of charge. An advertisement in the local newspapers announced a lecture on and demonstration of 'Spraying Potatoes' at the Ashleigh Road School Garden Allotments.

Another series of meetings across the area this month saw Miss Lahee from the Board of Agriculture demonstrating 'Fruit Bottling' and how to make sugarless jam. Also this month saw the inauguration of the collection of waste food to feed pigs and poultry.

All this emphasis on food is understandable but other goods were also becoming scarce. In May an order had been put in place by the Government limiting the use of petrol to ambulances/doctors or journeys taking munitions workers to their factories. At South Molton when this was announced in the Police Court those present heard that the Government had made the order less draconian by allowing private cars to be used in country towns where there were no taxis for a limited number of exceptions – for which fuel was provided. The Mayor of South Molton suggested that a 'rank' be set up for private vehicle owners wishing to provide these services to the town.

One major innovation this month was as a direct result of the number of women taking part in the war effort - when Parliament voted by 385 to 55 to introduce an Act to extend the vote to women over the age of 30 – the law actually coming into force in November 1918. It may have taken a World War to win this concession but at least the door was now open to full enfranchisement. There was also some mixed news for local men when following their demand for an increase in wages Barnstaple cabinet makers saw a raise. Unfortunately it was then announced by their representatives 'There is absolute dissatisfaction with the award' as the two main factories in town had different rates of pay. Only a week or so after this the workers employed by Barnstaple town council asked for an increase in wages.

If adults had mixed news then so did children. Thomas Dyke Acland wrote to the *Journal* asking them to help the nation by collecting foxgloves and dandelion roots for use in medicine. At the same time there was a sad report about the death of a child she being Seraphine Wijenberg, a Belgian refugee, who fell over Capstone Hill at Ilfracombe whilst collecting flowers. Her mother was dead and her father missing so there was no-one to mourn her. On the other hand communal grief was being addressed at Lynton where it was decided to erect 'a plain but appropriate memorial' at the summit of Lynmouth Hill. This was planned to be a stone 5 foot by 3 bearing the names of local servicemen killed in the war. At Braunton a rather less ambitious scheme saw J.Yeo Tucker collecting photographs of the roughly 300 local men serving in the Forces prior to them being displayed in the village.

5. A Bruce Bairnsfeather cartoon recycled. NDJ 7.6.1917 8a-b

Given all this war-related news it is sometimes difficult to realise that everyday life was continuing albeit in a very restricted form. This included local businesses advertising their wares in the local papers and this month saw a very rare illustrated example. The Brinsmead piano firm had been founded by a man from Weare Giffard around 1835 – whilst Bruce Bairnsfeather, whose original cartoon had been used here, went to the United Services College at Westward Ho! – so there were two local connections for this advertisement.

The First World War in North Devon

July 1917

While the 'In Memoriam' column in newspapers grew longer as families commemorated the deaths of their sons and fathers in action over the preceding three years so the contemporary casualty lists continued to grow. This July saw thirty more deaths recorded including four cases where this was the second, and in one case third, son to have been killed – a pattern that became commoner as the fighting continued. As ever many of the dead were relatively young including two 19 year olds. One, Pte. Albert Waldron from Tawstock, was killed by a shell he having been 'very popular throughout the district' whilst Pte.

1. Pte.C.Powe's grave in Appledore churchyard.

William Cutcliffe from Ilfracombe, a member of the Royal Naval Division, was 'killed after one day's experience in the trenches.' One 20 year old died here in North Devon and was buried in Appledore churchyard.

When 36 year old Leading Seaman Isaac Knill from Ilfracombe died after his minesweeper was sunk by a mine the *Journal* printed his photograph – a very rare accolade.

Two other sailors who died when HMS *Vanguard* accidentally blew up at Scapa Flow did not have their photographs published. Seaman W.Gammon, aged 19, and Chief Petty Officer W.Seal, both from Barnstaple, were among the 843 crew members, out of 845, who lost their lives. One piece of good news concerned John Hollis from Ilfracombe whose plane had been downed behind enemy lines with his relatives not knowing if he was dead or alive. News reached them this month that he was in a German PoW camp.

By now the Tribunals were figuratively 'scraping the barrel' as when Alfred Wood, a 40 year old baker of Ilfracombe appeared before that town's tribunal. As

2. Leading Seaman Knill.
NDJ 5.7.1917 5d

noted previously bakers were often given exemptions as their job was of great community benefit – and in any case Alfred was only 4 foot 9 inches in height. He was exempted. The Army often now suggested substitutes or 'casual labour' in place of fit men but when they did in the case of an Ilfracombe gardener Donald Kipling his employer Thomas Garnish said 'That is no good. They are more of a hindrance than a help when you have got them. It is a waste of time running about after them.' Kipling was given an exemption for 6 weeks to allow Garnish to find another man. This didn't stop H.Woodcock, the military representative at the Barnstaple Rural Tribunal, reckoning 'The recruiting net is full of big holes through which men are escaping' – though many had good cases.

When the Barnstaple Tribunal had Charles Ferrier, a general dealer, appear before them he alleged his medical examination at Exeter was 'entirely farcical and misleading' as although he told them he had 'rheumatism in his eyes' none of the doctors checked his eyesight. He was ordered to go back to Exeter for a 'special medical re-examination'. The same thing was ordered in the case of Edgar Piper who had been in hospital for two months 'suffering from an ulcerated stomach'. Even more extreme was the case of Alfred Calo, a Barnstaple insurance agent, who was arrested as a deserter. He had been ordered to go to Exeter for examination but as he had doctor's certificates saying he had a fractured and dislocated shoulder he didn't think he had to go. Brought before a magistrate's court he pointed out that his shoulder had been dislocated around fifty times and every time 'he had to go under chloroform' and indeed had to sleep in bandages. Handed over to the military he was taken to Exeter and there 'rejected as being absolutely unfit for military service.'

To add to the military's frustrations Tribunals often now exempted even fit men if they were deemed indispensable as when the Bideford Rural Tribunal met to adjudicate 31 cases most of whom were 'young farm hands of high medical category but often the only capable labour on the farm.' The panel chairman went so far as to say 'it was quite ridiculous to require farmers to be continually coming to the Tribunals to apply for men who it was well-known were quite indispensable.' It appears that all the men were granted exemptions.

This attitude clearly annoyed the military panel members. At the North Devon Appeals Tribunal when J.Metherell, a farmer on the panel, pointed out that 'the Government was asking for three millions of acres more land to be tilled in food, and this could not be done without the labour' a member of the public present applauded him. This led Lieut.Stirling to say 'That's a very popular decision in North Devon – it's far away from the firing line. I think when a man who should be doing his duty and is at home, the person who claps is not a patriotic citizen.' One case where the Tribunal and the military were in agreement was that of Hastings Butt, a 19 year old CO from Braunton who appears to have been a relative of James Butt an earlier CO. He claimed to be a member of the Pacifist Church in London whose minister was chaplain to the CO prisoners in Wormwood Scrubs. Queried what he would do if a German was assaulting his sister he 'did not give a direct answer.' He was ordered to enlist as a 'combatant'.

Some who had enlisted were awarded gallantry medals this month. Six men won Military Medals and Capt.H.Keene of Bideford was awarded a Military Cross for services in East Africa. Gunner F.Screech from Appledore won a Distinguished Service Medal for gallantry when his transport ship was attacked by a submarine in the White Sea. One of two gunners on-board his mate was killed but he continued firing the ship's gun alone from 10 a.m. to 5 p.m. although twice wounded.

As the growing season was well under way there was an appreciable lessening of Government demands to grow more. Rather this month saw the Barnstaple War Agricultural Committee discussing the figures for the newly cropped areas plus the estimated figures for 1918, many of which were extremely impressive – with even more yet to be reported.

INCREASED CORN ACREAGE, THE RETURNS:
MR. PROTHERO'S VIEWS.

Returns were presented showing the increased area to be devoted to corn in the year 1918. The figures were:—Arlington, 1916, 270 acres, 1917, 360 acres, 1918, 390 acres, increase 44½ per cent; Ashford, 8, 17, 19, 137½ per cent; Berrynarbor, 540, 647, 830, 53½ per cent; Bratton Fleming, 355, 477, 596, 38½ per cent.; Braunton, 1,282, 1,422, 1,572, 23 per cent.; Brendon, 152, 191, 233, 53 per cent.; Challacombe, 212, 229, 307, 44½ per cent; Eastdown, 305, 345, 444, 45½ per cent.; Georgeham, 657, 733, 860, 30½ per cent.; Heanton Punchardon, 558, 626, 693, 24 per cent.; High Bray, 196, 228, 314, 60 per cent.; Horwood, 163, 193, 254, 56 per cent.; Kentisbury, 213, 307, 429, 101 per cent.; Landkey, 417, 463, 568, 36 per cent.; Marwood, 581, 663, 782, 34 per cent.; Martinhoe, 165, 184, 242, 46 per cent.; Morte Hoe, 349, 393, 524, 50½ per cent.; Newton Tracey, 126½, 171, 213, 69 per cent.; Pilton East, 13, 20, 50, 276 per cent.; Shirwell, 505, 557, 693, 37 per cent.; Stoke Rivers, 269, 333, 387, 43 per cent.; Tawstock, 1,192, 1,320, 1,619, 35½ per cent.; Trentishoe, 106, 136, 155, 46 per cent.; West Down, 451, 481, 543, 20 per cent.; Pilton West, 16, 25, 48, 200 per cent.; Westleigh, 276, 476, 581, 54½ per cent.

3. Increases in corn acreages. NDJ 5.7.1917 2a

Similar large increases were recorded by the South Molton War Agricultural Committee where the average parish increase in corn land was 52½%. A rare photograph shows some of this corn stacked in South Molton market hall.

This month also saw the first requests to the volunteer labour scheme established by the Barnstaple Food Control Committee - which saw a rapid response by 'patriotic citizens' going into the countryside to help farmers get in the hay harvest. Unfortunately not enough people had signed up to the scheme and as a result it was said that the fruit in 'large mazzard orchards' was rotting

4. Corn stacked up in South Molton Pannier Market.

on the trees. Even worse was the news that 'The dread potato disease had made its appearance in certain parts of North Devon.' The Government's Food Production Department immediately offered to send 20 soldiers with spraying equipment to tackle the outbreak – and to provide equipment to those wishing to treat the disease themselves.

Other moves to extend food supplies came when the Mayors of both Bideford and Barnstaple wrote to the Taw and Torridge Conservators asking that the season for catching coarse fish in the rivers be extended and also that nets with smaller meshes be allowed to increase catches. After a long and tendentious discussion the idea was turned down on a technicality – doubtless leading to an increase in poaching. More easily achievable was bottling fruit, as a letter and an advertisement this month explained.

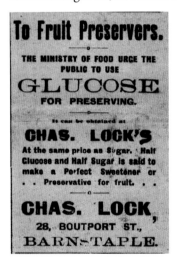

5. Tackling food shortages. NDJ 5.7.1917 1f

6. NDJ 12.7.1917 2e

The ever increasing costs of food went hand in hand with an expansion in membership of the local Workers' Union to over 500, whilst even the Barnstaple police force ask for a salary rise.

More community projects were developing with the Ilfracombe War Saving Committee boasting 1000 members whilst in Bideford the council decided to set up a Maternity and Child Welfare Centre for the benefit of the borough's mothers and children – a fairly revolutionary idea for the area at this date. Also in Bideford the Church of England put forward a proposal to erect a memorial to local men who had been killed in the war though, strangely, this was not to be a 'town' memorial – and one wonders why the church authorities were thinking of a memorial long before the war was to end.

Perhaps the saddest story this month was when Sarah Richards a barmaid at the Bath Hotel in Lynmouth was taken to court for serving wounded soldiers who were out on a day trip with alcohol. Under the Defence of the Realm Act this was illegal and was made worse as two of the men were 'found drunk' and four more were 'under the influence of liquor'. Both she and the landlady of the Hotel, Jessie Parsons, were fined £1 each which seems unduly harsh.

The First World War in North Devon

August 1917

As the third anniversary of the War passed, this month saw another 52 local men dying in the various theatres of war. As ever there were some teenagers recorded – such as Lieut.Maurice Bate, son of the vicar of Chittlehampton, who died aged just 19, who seems surprisingly young to be an officer. Also just 19 was Pte. Reginald Price who before enlisting had worked at the Rapparee Bathing Beach in Ilfracombe. He was so young that his father, a Staff-Sergt., was also serving in France. There were others just a year older including Pte.George Mock of Braunton, Pte.Walter Blight of Chittlehampton who died from dysentery at Basra – the third of his parents' four sons to be killed in the war. His wasn't the only death at Basra this month as eight other fatalities are noted. The oldest to die this month, at 48, was Herbert Perrin. He volunteered for the National Reserve and then joined the Royal Defence Corps whilst still working as a decorator.

One man who was killed this month was Harry Dayman from Hartland who had enlisted into the Duke of Cornwall's Light Infantry. He was killed on the 16th of this month aged 29 though his body was never found. His mother received various items to mark his passing including his identity disc and the so-called 'death penny'.

1. Harry Dayman on right, P.Heard on left.

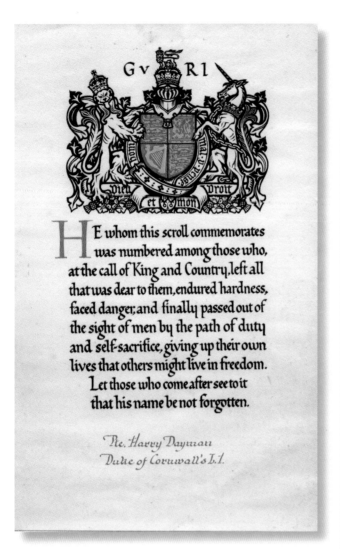

GᵥRI

HE whom this scroll commemorates was numbered among those who, at the call of King and Country, left all that was dear to them, endured hardness, faced danger, and finally passed out of the sight of men by the path of duty and self-sacrifice, giving up their own lives that others might live in freedom. Let those who come after see to it that his name be not forgotten.

Pte. Harry Dayman
Duke of Cornwall's L.I.

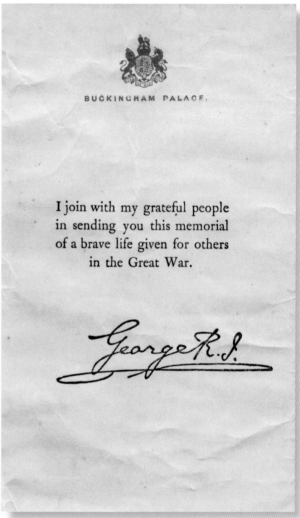

BUCKINGHAM PALACE.

I join with my grateful people in sending you this memorial of a brave life given for others in the Great War.

George R.I.

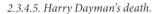
2.3.4.5. Harry Dayman's death.

When the vicar of Newport in Barnstaple published the parish 'Roll of Honour' in his church magazine this month it revealed that there were 300 of his parishioners in the Forces whilst some 23 had been killed and 31 wounded. The Barnstaple Grammar School also compiled its 'Roll' and this was printed in the *Journal* and it is interesting to note the very varied regiments and corps these 'Old Boys' had joined.

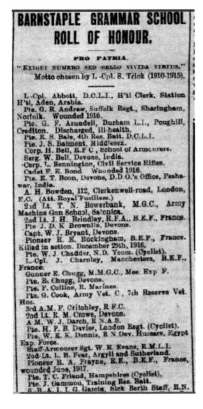

6a,b,c. Barnstaple Grammar School 'Roll of Honour'. NDJ 2.8.1917 7b-c

As the odds of dying on the battlefield rose this must have spurred many men to apply for exemption from service – and the Tribunals were now becoming rather desperate as when Frederick Sluman, a Combe Martin carrier, appeared. He was blind in one eye but this didn't stop the military representative demanding he should enlist so he could be used as a substitute in timber hauling. He was exempted. Another man exempted on grounds of poor eyesight was Charles Ferrier who we have met before. At his appearance before the Barnstaple Borough Tribunal in July he had been ordered to have another medical which found him unfit for the Army. Ferrier now demanded an apology from Woodcock the Army man who had accused him of 'wearing dark glasses to deceive the Tribunal' at his previous hearing – Woodcock declined.

Not every health claim succeeded. When Herbert Partridge of Witheridge appeared before the North Devon Appeals Tribunal he produced a doctor's certificate 'stating that he was suffering from heart trouble' but Army doctors classified him as 'C1' and his appeal was dismissed. These glaring differences between civilian and military medical men were the subject of many complaints as related earlier so it was no surprise when this month the Government acted on a Select Committee report on Medical Boards. This saw the responsibility for medical examinations 'removed from the War Office and placed under civilian control, in order to restore public confidence.' It should be pointed out that the Tribunals weren't only just hearing the cases of clearly unfit men – there just weren't enough suitable men left in the general populace. Thus it was reported 'There is a considerable falling off in the work before the South Molton Rural Tribunal. Formerly the monthly agenda usually contained about 60 cases. There are now less than twenty.'

Doubtless the military panel members would much rather that men appearing before them were more like the members of the Glover family of Bideford whose story was published this month.

The reference to Signaller Glover's DSM and gold watch was echoed when J.Y.Tucker of Braunton presented privately minted 'gold medals' to Sergt.Maj.Pile and Pte.Ackland of the village to honour their services. Other medals awarded this month included a Military Cross to 2nd Lieut.R.Smyth of Barnstaple and Military Medals to Sergt.H.Crocombe of Lynton and Gnr.E.Townsend of Combe Martin whilst Lt.Col.W.Favell of Barnstaple won a DSO and the Serbian 'Order of White Eagle'.

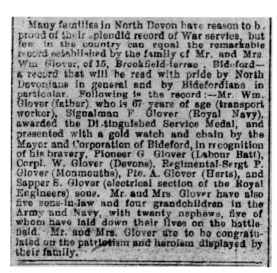

Many families in North Devon have reason to be proud of their splendid record of War service, but few in the country can equal the remarkable record established by the family of Mr. and Mrs. Wm Glover, of 15, Brookfield-terrace, Bideford—a record that will be read with pride by North Devonians in general and by Bidefordians in particular. Following is the record :—Mr. Wm. Glover (father), who is 67 years of age (transport worker), Signalman F Glover (Royal Navy), awarded the Distinguished Service Medal, and presented with a gold watch and chain by the Mayor and Corporation of Bideford, in recognition of his bravery, Pioneer G Glover (Labour Batt), Corpl. W. Glover (Devons), Regimental-Sergt P. Glover (Monmouths), Pte. A. Glover (Herts), and Sapper S. Glover (electrical section of the Royal Engineers) sons. Mr. and Mrs. Glover have also five sons-in-law and four grandchildren in the Army and Navy, with twenty nephews, five of whom have laid down their lives on the battlefield. Mr. and Mrs. Glover are to be congratulated on the patriotism and heroism displayed by their family.

7. The proud record of the Glover family.
NDJ 30.8.1917 5d

THE CROPS IN NORTH DEVON.

First reports relating to the crops in North Devon this season are on the whole highly gratifying. Of the cereals, oats and barley are the leading crops, wheat being very light in many cases and variable on the whole. Hay was comparatively light, but there is now an abundance of grass. All farm stock is doing well, and cattle has for some time fetched exceptionally high prices. In view, however, of the Government proposals restricting the price of beef, somewhat of a reaction has set in, quotations showing a downward tendency. Bush fruit has been abundant, and apples and plums are plentiful in some parts of the district, but light in others. Onions are showing more rust or mildew than usual this year, and potato disease is widespread. In spite of the urgent requests of the Board of Agriculture, many have neglected both spraying and the pulling up of the haulms, in order to save the crop. In different parishes, many growers are strongly prejudiced against spraying, and advance the opinion that even if diseased haulms are not removed the tubers are not affected! Experiments and demonstrations have, however, proved conclusively that spraying in early stages of growth or the pulling up of the haulms later as an alternative is absolutely essential; and particularly as sprayed crops have entirely withstood disease, the question is raised as to whether another year the Government should not issue an order providing for the compulsory spraying of all potatoes.

8. A crop report. NDJ 16.8.1917 2b

These military matters ran in tandem with the on-going food problems. The potato blight that had hit North Devon 'to an alarming extent' saw widespread spraying by soldiers with both letters of advice appearing in the local newspapers and lectures with demonstrations as to how to tackle it. At Bideford eighty allotment holders had their potato crops sprayed by the council. Though potato growers were experiencing serious problems other crops were doing well as shown by this report.

The on-going shortages of labour were being met now by schoolboys who, too young for the Forces, were being utilised to help gather in the harvest – at 4d per hour. Some 22 from Blundell's in Tiverton were billeted at Barnstaple Grammar School from where they cycled to local farms on a daily basis. They were joined by 31 boys and 3 teachers from Swansea Secondary School, their food being prepared by five military cooks under a Quartermaster-Sergeant. A further 30 boys from King Edward School at Bath camped in a meadow at the end of New Street, Torrington whilst 25 boys from Tavistock Grammar School and 14 from Newton Abbot Secondary School camped at South Molton where, headed by a fife band, they attended church parade. At Bideford boys who were tending their school allotments were doing so well that the town's Bridge Trust presented them all with new spades.

9. Mr.Hooper of Old Town School, Bideford with his 'Garden Boys'.

10. *Newly arrived tractors by Ford House, Bideford.*

All these extra hands were welcome but at Westleigh the largest landowner, A.L.Christie of Tapeley Park, purchased a motor plough. First used at Bradiven Farm it attracted a large crowd of local farmers who saw it working at a speed of 2½ miles per hour it being capable of ploughing up to 10 acres a day.

11 & 12. *The tractors are deployed.*

LOCAL FOOD COMMITTEES.

Their Constitution and Duties.

The Ministry of food has issued the following:—Lord Rhondda, through the courtesy of the Local Government Board for England and Wales and of the Scottish Office for Scotland, has approached local authorities throughout Great Britain with a request for their co-operation in the work of Food Control, and forwarded to them certain detailed information as to the method of control to be adopted. The authorities approached for England and Wales are—in London, the Common Council of the City and the Metropolitan Borough Councils; outside London, the Municipal Borough Council and the Urban and Rural District Councils. These authorities are asked to appoint Food Committees which will administer a new scheme of sugar distribution, continue the campaign for food economy, and, when their organisation is complete, deal with other foodstuffs, including bread and meat. They will also be asked, at an early date, to assume special responsibilities in regard to food prices. For all imported foodstuffs the Food Controller will fix a general scale of prices, based at each stage on the reasonable profits of traders. The Committees will be entrusted with the enforcement of this scale, and will be asked to advise on any modifications of it that may be shown to be necessary in their districts.

The Food Control Committees thus to be constituted will consist of not more than twelve members each, some of whom may be co-opted, and each Committee must include at least one woman and one representative of labour. Their necessary expenses will be a charge on the Exchequer; for, while free to delegate work as they think fit to sub-committees, they will need a special staff and will be put to other cost. It will be their first duty to safeguard the interests of consumers.

Immediately the Local Committees are constituted they will proceed to register grocers and other retailers of sugar, and after October 1st no retailer who remains unregistered will be allowed to deal in sugar.

13. *Food Committees are set up.*
NDJ 16.8.1917 5d

These innovations were helping but the distribution of food was now becoming a problem with the first prosecutions of 'residents for obtaining quantities of preserving sugar to which they were not entitled' taking place at South Molton. Seven residents were fined £11 between them for this offence. The answer to shortages would have been wholesale rationing but the Government recoiled from such a draconian move opting to set up local Food Control Committees which only covered sugar supplies in the first instance.

When the South Molton Rural District Council established their committee one member couldn't resist asking 'Is it worth all this trouble – just for sugar?' This was greeted with laughter but it was then explained the move was necessary so that supplies would be 'shared equally by rich and poor'. Similar sentiments were voiced at other councils but all set their committees up. In fact this month actually saw the introduction of 'rationing' for coal although this relied on the honesty of consumers and merchants - with rations being based on the number of rooms in a house and ability to pay. People with less than four rooms got 2 cwts per week whilst those with more than fifteen rooms received 2½ tons.

Sugar and coal may have been rationed but lack of money was forcing cutbacks on many people. This month saw employees of Barnstaple Cabinet Works seeking a raise of 2d per hour for both males and females to bring them in line with other cabinet makers in the town. Not getting a satisfactory answer the workforce went on strike but following a meeting with the Works manager decided to go back to work until arbitration took place. The ever growing Workers' Union held a fete at Torrington to raise funds and attract members and followed it with a dance at the Albert Hall in Barnstaple in aid of the Fund for Wounded Soldiers which was under the patronage of the Mayor. At the same time the Mayoress was the patron of 'Women's Day' at Barnstaple held to collect funds to equip canteens and clubs for women 'doing Munitions and other War Work in England and France.' Women, of course, were doing more than just work in munitions factories; at Braunton two women were delivering meat on bicycles whilst another was driving a 'self binder' in the harvest fields – and yet another was actually mowing corn with a scythe.

This loosening of the old gender boundaries was reflected in a very unexpected way when it was announced that the play 'Damaged Goods' would be staged in various places in North Devon.

This story dealt with the 'hidden plague' of syphilis, the incidence of which was increasing amongst servicemen who were then passing it on to wives and sweethearts. It is hard to imagine the play being staged in pre-war North Devon and it was only allowed now due to the impacts venereal disease was having on both troops and the civilian population. In 1917 it is estimated that 32 out of every 1000 British soldiers were found to be infected and it is thought that at any one time 40-50,000 servicemen were out of action due to VD.

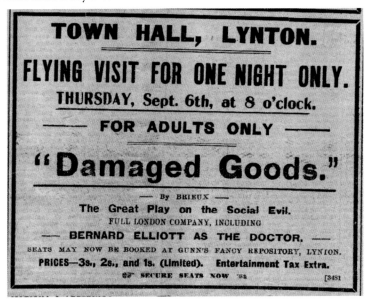

14. A morality play. NDJ 30.8.1917 4c-d

If this was unexpected then an upsurge in Spiritualism belief was more understandable. With massive numbers of deaths amongst servicemen it was only natural their families would turn to a system offering 're-union after death'. A series of lectures were staged by a Miss Clara Codd and Edmund Russell bearing titles such as 'The Secret of Death' and 'The Significance of the World War'. These probably helped grief-stricken relatives come to terms with their losses however spurious their claims might be seen by some. Mainstream churches were, of course, also offering comfort but they were in the difficult position of preaching peaceful Christianity of the sort espoused by COs whilst at the same time supporting the war effort. Typical was an all-denominational service held at Bideford to mark the third anniversary of the 'righteous war', as the clergy termed it, with the rector of St.Mary's church preaching on the Biblical verse 'If God shall be for us who can be against us.'

Amidst all these social issues was one very physical one when a crowd several hundred strong gathered to see the three engines of the Bideford, Westward Ho! & Appledore Railway be taken across Bideford Bridge on specially laid track prior to being taken away to help the war effort. No-one knows for certain what happened to them and the line and equipment was sold off in 1918 and 1921.

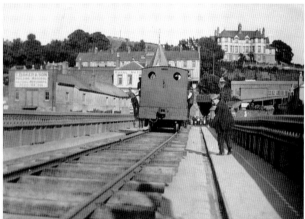

15.16.17. The engines of the Bideford, Westward Ho! & Appledore Railway are taken to help the war effort.

One thing that hinted at a return to the normalcy of peace time was the announcement that Barnstaple Liberals had chosen Lieut.J.Tudor Rees as their Prospective Parliamentary candidate for whenever the election was held. He was a Welsh solicitor and the *Journal*, a Liberal supporting paper, printed a portrait of him clad in khaki. If politics were returning could peace be far behind?

The First World War in North Devon

September 1917

By September 1917 over 500,000 tons of Allied shipping had been sunk much of it whilst bringing food to Britain and the Government was becoming ever more aware of the looming food crisis. The convoy system for shipping had been introduced in May 1917 which reduced losses and the harvest was looking good but clearly these crops would only last so long. Sugar was rationed with 'Sugar cards' being issued by local Post and Food Offices which were to be used at peoples' usual suppliers as shown in these advertisements.

1. Sugar rationing in Barnstaple. NDJ 6.9.1917 1c-d

2. Sugar rationing in Bideford. BG 18.9.1917 1c-d

To emphasise the gravity of the situation several people at Bideford were fined from one to three guineas for contravening the orders concerning sugar.

Following the rationing of sugar the Government announced the prohibition of imports of bacon, ham and lard by private persons or companies. Henceforward purchases were to be done by the Ministry of Food and then 'distributed on fixed terms' thus enabling the public to buy them at 'prices excluding any unreasonable profit'. This move to apparently attack profiteers in fact also gave the Government control over a large segment of the market. The 'fixed terms' that came with this were extended to other foodstuffs which saw the price of Cheddar cheese, for example, fixed at £6.12.0 per cwt with cheesemongers told to keep records of all their sales. Butter and bread also had their prices fixed as shown in these advertisements – and within a week potatoes became a fixed price item as well.

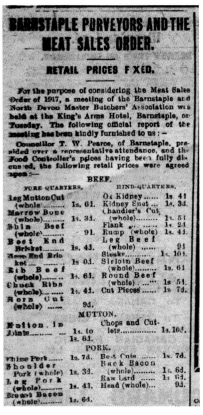

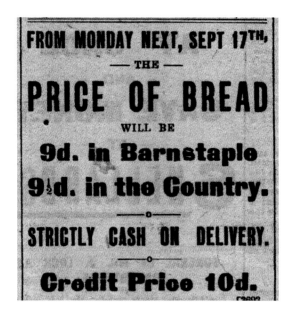

3. Meat rationing NDJ 6.9.1917 8a
4. Bread rationing NDJ 13.9.1917 5d

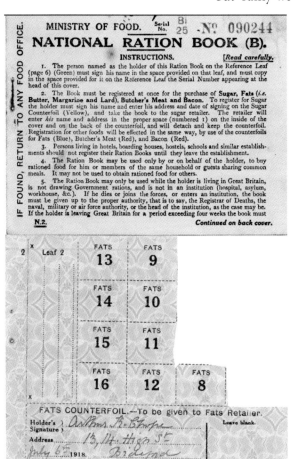

5. A ration book

At the end of the month the various schoolboys who had been drafted in to help with the harvest returned home. Their work had been valuable but 'rainy weather' restricted how much they were able to do, but local farmers said they would be very welcome to return in 1918.

The concentration on food supplies rather overshadowed other news though as always the work of the Tribunals heavily featured in local newspapers. It was now common that panel members were granting exemptions to agricultural workers – and just as regularly the military were challenging them. Given the shortage of fit men it is interesting that at the Barnstaple Rural Tribunal the Army man Woodcock said that 'his instructions were to press for 'C3' men for the Flying Corps' which seems an odd requirement given such men were the least fit. At the Bideford Tribunal of the 27 cases heard 18 were thus challenged but in 24 cases exemption was given though some of these were taken to the Appeals Tribunal by the military where they were overturned.

When brothers Charles and John Brannam of the Barnstaple Pottery, both 'C3' men, appeared to have their earlier exemptions extended they pointed out that 74% of their orders were from the Government's Food Production Department with the other 26% being for export. Of their pre-War workforce 51 had enlisted leaving 17 men, 4 boys and 13 women. Even given this Woodcock said 'that 'C3' men had not previously been required so badly as they were now' – the panel, however, sided with the brothers and extended their exemption.

When in June the Barnstaple Tribunal adjourned as an act of defiance against the military's over-enthusiastic challenges this was surprising but this September saw a meeting in Bideford Town Hall of men protesting over the recent actions of the local Tribunal. One of the reasons for exemption was where a tradesman running a business on his own would face financial ruin if called up. This exception did not apply to many but attendees at this meeting passed a resolution to write to the North Devon Appeals Tribunal demanding 'that all single men and those sheltering in Munition Works should be called up before those with greater responsibilities.' The vote was 22 – 10 in favour though some who opposed the motion 'expressed themselves strongly'. The meeting was slightly farcical as when attendees turned up at the Town Hall they found a meeting of the Workers' Union was already going on – and they refused to leave forcing the tradesmen to go to a much smaller venue.

While this protest was going on the desperate need for men saw several ex-servicemen who had been discharged as medically unfit being hauled up before Tribunals to have their cases re-examined. Thus the Lynton panel members questioned W.Rowed who had served some 8 months in the trenches and was now classed as 'C3'; he was only exempted as he had become chauffeur to Dr.H.Edwards enabling the doctor to visit his widely scattered patients.

Deserters were now becoming more numerous. This month saw Gilbert Braund, a labourer from Woolsery, taken to court in Bideford as a deserter. He had been in the Army, been discharged and then ordered to rejoin which he chose not to do hence his arrest. He was handed over to the military authorities. When stopped by L/Cpl.Hodgkins of the Military Foot Police on the Strand in Barnstaple Pioneer Thomas Williams admitted he was absent without official leave from the Royal Engineers and was remanded in custody to await an escort. At Barnstaple Fair a 'round up' was carried out and three deserters arrested. Two came from Bristol and one from Newton Abbot. All three were handed over to the military.

The need for these men can be seen when one considers that this month another 34 local men were recorded as being killed in action or dying of their wounds including some whose deaths occurred as long ago as June 1916 their bodies having only just been located. Amidst all the deaths by shell, sniper or disease was one very unusual one. Forty year old Air Mechanic Charles Murphy from Bideford was in the 5th Balloon Corps of the Royal Flying Corps and when, during a storm, an observation balloon broke loose he grabbed its rope tether to try and prevent it blowing away. Unfortunately he was carried aloft and 'being unable to retain his hold fell to the ground and was instantaneously killed.'

MILITARY CROSS FOR BARUMITE.

Lance-Corpl. Harry Richard Collins (of Barnstaple), serving with the Devons in France, has been awarded the Military Cross for conspicuous gallantry, the accompanying parchment certificate being as follows :—
' For devotion to duty in the trenches near Ypres on 21st June, 1917. Under very heavy shell fire, with the help of two other stretcher bearers, he evacuated six casualties to the field ambulance. Later, hearing that an officer was unaccounted for, he returned and searched the locality in daylight. He has previously done fine work."
Lance-Corpl. Collins, who has been promoted to full Corporal, is a brother of Mrs. A. Fureeman, of Well-street, Barnstaple. Corpl. Collins's many friends at Barnstaple will warmly congratulate him on the honour which has been bestowed upon him.

6. Harry Collins wins the Military Cross. NDJ 6.9.1917 5e

7. Mrs.Harding with clock, sugar basin and photograph of her husband.

One wonders if he had lived he would have been given a medal for his brave but foolhardy act? Various local men were awarded decorations this month including Percy Adkins of the Royal Naval Air Service who won a Distinguished Conduct Medal. One whose actions were published in the *Journal* was L/Cpl.Harry Collins of Barnstaple who won the Military Cross.

Sadly within a week Harry was dead, killed by a shell. Two slightly unexpected decorations went to L/

Cpl.W.Davis and L/Cpl.E.Colwill both of whom had been in the Bideford Territorials before the war and as such ended up fighting in Mesopotamia. Here they both won the 'Russian Order of the 2nd Class of St.George' – which, given that Russia was in a state of revolution and chaos strikes one as odd. When Bidefordian Sergt.W.Harding of the Royal Engineers won a Military Medal a subscription was opened in the town which collected enough money to allow the Mayor to present him with an 8-day marble clock – with a plated sugar basin for his wife.

One novel military unit was formed this month, not for duty abroad but for deployment at home. The Devon Motor Volunteer Corps was set up based around people who owned motor vehicles. Of the 300 members there were 50 in North Devon with their headquarters in Barnstaple. The aim for the local group was to raise two sections each being able to provide five 3 ton lorries, four 30 cwt lorries, six 45 cwt vans 'and a corresponding number of cars and cycles.' It is unlikely many of the Corps drivers were women but they were busy elsewhere with a Miss Robins being appointed as Relieving and Vaccination Officer for the Combe Martin-Lynton district whose duties included tackling poverty in the area – a very responsible post. In addition children were sent out to collect horse chestnuts which could be 'utilised for War purposes' – with Barnstaple council employees securing 'a big supply from the fine avenue of chestnut trees in Victoria Park.'

The month also saw another 'War Shrine' being set up, this one being in Northam church, whilst at Chittlehampton a 'beautiful brass tablet' was placed in the Wesleyan chapel by his parents in memory of Lieut.Percy Cole of the Royal Field Artillery who was killed in France in September 1916 being buried close to where he fell. One wonders if he would have survived if he had been wearing 'The Chemico Body Shield' which was now being heavily advertised, but how effective it might have been is hard to say.

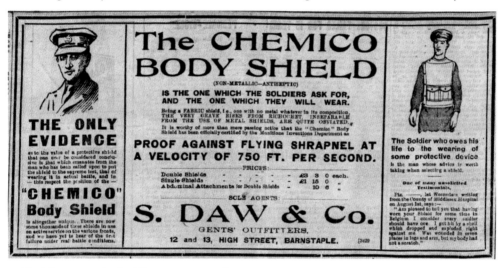

8. The 'Chemico Body Shield'. NDJ 13.9.1917 8b-e

The First World War in North Devon

October 1917

This month saw another 30+ casualties (some were only now being recorded after dying earlier in the conflict) with the first to be noted being that of Lieut.A.T.Shapland of North Molton. He had spent two years in the trenches and just weeks before he was killed wrote to his aunt saying 'he felt sure he should be killed or badly wounded, but thought he could not wish for a finer death than to be killed in the service of his country' – he was 23 being the fourth serviceman from North Molton to die. One less than 'fine' death was that of Cyclist Leonard Long of Barnstaple who 'was killed by a bomb dropped from a German aeroplane whilst he was taking messages to the Front.'

Several other deaths stand out. When L/Cpl.Leslie Court of Barnstaple died of meningitis in Mesopotamia he was just 19 he having enlisted at the outbreak of war aged only 16. The oddly titled Lieut.Sir Burton Williams of Barnstaple had become a Baronet on the death of his brother in 1913 he then being a rubber planter in Ceylon. On the outbreak of war he returned to Britain and enlisted it being noted in his obituary that his mother had made the family house at Pilland available to New Zealand war nurses 'in need of rest'.

This month's casualties were not being replaced by men sent from the Tribunals – indeed the six local boards sitting this month only heard 63 cases – the lowest number for many months, with most being granted exemption. At the two sittings of the North Devon Appeals Tribunal some 35 appeals were considered with the military winning 12 of these, again one of the lowest figures recorded with 21 being exempted as doing 'indispensable' jobs or in agriculture.

This combination of low enlistment numbers and high number of deaths was very concerning to those directing the country's military effort. Possibly in order to boost morale one record was achieved this month when twenty local men were awarded medals. Seventeen of these were men in the ranks who won the Military Medal, including Signalman A.Gunn of Ilfracombe 'for bringing in a wounded comrade under shell fire and gas'. Cpl.S.Goodenough of Bideford was awarded the Italian Bronze Medal 'for military valour' in Mesopotamia. Rather grander was the bar awarded to the Distinguished Service Order that Major L.Reynolds of Bideford had already won – whilst Stephen Slade of Appledore was awarded a Distinguished Service Medal 'for bravery' whilst serving on an unnamed Royal Navy ship.

Turning to the food situation the 'promising' harvest turned out to be disappointing owing to 'deplorable' weather at harvest time which had left large expanses of corn uncut and if it had been stacked it was feared it would go mouldy. Hopes for a better crop in 1918 depended on increasing the acreage under the plough and it was reported how the Torrington district had 'the best return of any district in Devon'. The area had been given a target quota of 17,500 acres but had seen 18,860 acres pledged. At the same meeting of the Torrington War Agricultural Committee where this was reported it was also noted that 'motor ploughing up to the present had not been very successful' presumably owing to the muddy state of the fields due to the weather. Members of the Barnstaple War Agricultural Committee voiced similar experiences though they blamed the high price of hiring motor ploughs – at £1 an acre – 'a preposterous charge' according to one farmer.

The rationing of coal according to the size of one's house was clearly unfair and Bideford town council decided to address it by fixing a maximum price for coal – with no limits being placed on amounts people could purchase. This lead was immediately followed by Barnstaple and Torrington town councils.

1. A tractor working at Moortown, Torrington.

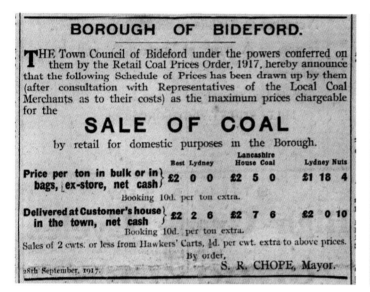

2. Bideford fixes the price of coal. BG 2.10.1917 2c-d

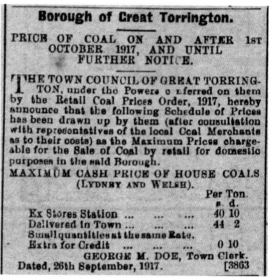

3. Torrington follows suit. NDJ 4.10.1917 4e

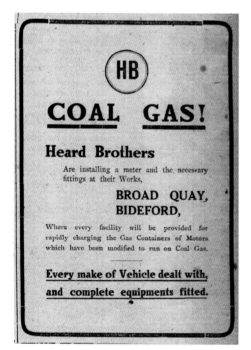

4. Gas fuelled cars make their appearance. BG 28.10.1917 1f-g

Another item that was now in short supply was petrol which lead to this unusual advertisement for gas-fuelled cars – and idea that was to resurface in the Second World War.

Sugar rationing was now a reality and the police began cracking down in earnest on people trying to circumvent the rules – with 17 women and 1 man summonsed to Barnstaple magistrate's court in one go this month. Bizarrely the solicitor defending several of the women blamed their 'errors' in applying for excess sugar on 'female psychology' it being well-known that 'when women get a form of application with the magnetic word 'sugar' on it, they, being already obsessed and influenced by misleading statements in the Press did not take the trouble to examine documents and find out what restrictions were imposed.' This didn't impress the magistrates and they fined all 18 in sums ranging from 10/- to 30/-. These cases were followed by that of Frederick Ridge a Barnstaple grocer who was accused of failing to keep proper records of those customers he sold sugar to – he was fined 10/-.

Another case concerning rationing came before the Braunton Division magistrates when John Barnes of Mortehoe was charged with the misuse of petrol in taking a passenger from Mortehoe to

Caffyns Halt. In court, however, he produced a Board of Trade permit and the charge was dismissed. Oddly as this case was being heard it was suggested that North Devon was likely to be a site for oil exploration as 'oil escapes' had been noted in the past – notably on the site of the Derby lace factory in Barnstaple when in 1874 a foundation trench for an extension of the factory exposed a layer of soil heavily impregnated with crude oil.

The impact of food shortages was highlighted in a shocking report this month by the Managers of the Bideford Council Schools who found that 33% of infants in their schools were underweight rising to 75% of girls at Geneva School. Dr.Adkins who was at the meeting suggested supplying a mid-day meal to 20 'of the worst cases'. Mr.Stucley, a governor, thought that 'in some cases the men being away the mothers did not prepare such substantial cooked meals.' The governors did add that the cost of the meals, if supplied, should be recovered from the parents 'otherwise they would only be encouraged not to provide meals themselves.'

Given comments like this when taken in conjunction with the rise in food prices it is no surprise to read that building workers in Barnstaple decided to press for a rise in the wages of 3d per hour. They also moved a resolution 'deploring the condition of a large number of the working classes in Barnstaple' brought about 'almost wholly by the extraordinary rise in the cost of living, calling upon the men and women workers to organise with a view to improving their present position, and urging employers to give the best possible consideration to demands that might be put before them.' At Torrington an open-air meeting in the Square was held by the Workers' Union, being followed up several weeks later by 'a splendid entertainment' staged by Union members and soldiers in the Drill Hall. A further meeting was held in Frithelstock where the Union was said to already have twenty members whilst in Barnstaple printers held a meeting to organise a branch of the Typographical Association.

Given these continuing high rate of deaths of servicemen, shortages of food along with labour unrest it perhaps is not surprising that this month saw the Government launch a 'National War Aims Campaign' to bolster the nation's resolve to see the war through to the finish. Barnstaple saw the first two 'Mass meetings' on 26th October with more meetings in North Devon scheduled.

5. *The National War Aims meetings. NDJ 25.10.1917 4c*

6. *The looming 'Sex War'. NDJ 18.10.1917 8b*

A rather different kind of war was envisaged by one correspondent to the *Journal* – a 'Sex War'.

7. Female window cleaners. NDJ 25.10.1917 6e-f

Somewhat oddly the next week the newspaper carried an advertisement for Rowntree's Cocoa entitled 'Women Workers' Series No.1' showing a female window cleaner which probably infuriated 'Ex-Service'.

Not all female workers were lionised. In Bideford Lily Elliman was taken to court 'not being a woman certified under the Midwives' Act, 1902 she did unlawfully and for gain habitually attend women in childbirth.' Four mothers appeared in her defence and when Dr.E.Toye, a Bideford physician, said there were no certified midwives in town the prosecuting solicitor said 'As a matter of fact there are three' to which Toye replied 'There are none that will take on these kind of poor cases.' The magistrates dismissed the charge – a decision received with applause. This evidence of community solidarity was also seen when an advertisement appeared inviting men to form a local branch of the 'Comrades of the Great War and Old Comrades'. At Lynton the vicar produced a 'Roll of Honour' for the parish containing the names of 95 local men in the Forces, 8 of whom had been killed – one of many such memorials being compiled across North Devon. Further evidence of community feeling came from Northam where the rector the Rev.Payne-Cook organised a collection to purchase presents for local men abroad.

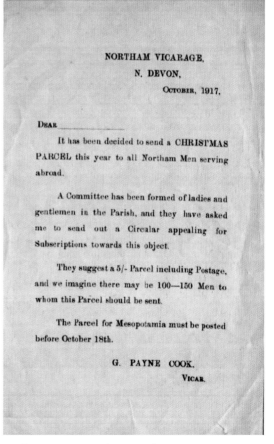

8. The Rev.Payne-Cook appeals for donations.

The First World War in North Devon

November 1917

As the Christmas season approached many North Devon families must have been devastated by the news that a member had been killed. This month saw the highest number of local servicemen's deaths recorded with some 80 being listed. Every death would have been a tragedy but whole communities would probably have known the young men and shared the grief. Thus Barnstaple saw 13 recorded deaths, Bideford and Ilfracombe 10 apiece, Holsworthy 5 with even a small place like North Molton seeing 5 deaths. Some of these were 'historical' as with Pte.E.Arthur of Bideford and Pte. Albert Gould of Barnstaple both of whom were killed in Mesopotamia in March 1916 but whose death was only now being confirmed. Another soldier who died in the same place in the same month was Pte.Ernest Alford of Barnstaple. The notice of his death records that he enlisted aged just 16 with his younger brother having joined aged just 15. The *Journal* terms these two 'plucky lads' but makes no comment about how they managed to enlist when so under age. Another young recruit was Pte. Powlesland from Chulmleigh who enlisted in 1915 aged 17 – and was killed in September 1917 he being the second son of his parents to die in action.

Most of these deaths were reported in just a few lines in the local newspapers but occasionally short obituaries appeared many quoting letters received by the men's families which seem to follow a common template as for example these;

With 'wastage' rates like these in the Forces the Tribunals were urged to find any men they could but the first sitting of the Barnstaple Tribunal saw just one man ordered to enlist with another three having their applications for exemption turned down by the Barnstaple Rural Tribunal. When John Bussell, the Relieving Officer, Registrar of Births, Marriages and Deaths and Vaccination

NORTHAM OFFICER KILLED IN ACTION.

Lieut. Harold Allin, of Northam, son of Mr. and Mrs. N. Allin, of Leonard's House, Northam, and a cousin of the Mayor and Mayoress of Barnstaple (Councillor F. A. and Mrs. Jewell) was killed in action in France on the 23rd ult., while leading his men. He was shot through the head by a sniper and killed instantly. The Colonel, Captain and two officers have written to the deceased's parents letters of sympathy, in which they speak of him as being a brave and fearless soldier, much beloved, and his death is deeply regretted. "He was one of the very best" they add. The deceased was only about 22 years of age.

ILFRACOMBE SOLDIERS KILLED IN ACTION.

Lance-Corporal A. E. Few.

Lance-Corpl. Albert Edwin Few, Royal West Surreys, eldest son of Mr. and Mrs Few, 35 Greenclose-road, Ilfracombe, has, it is unofficially reported, been killed in action. Last week Mrs. Few received from the front a pocket book belonging to the deceased, accompanied by the following letter :—"October 18th. Madam,—It is with my deepest regret that I have to write these few words saying that Lance-Corpl. A. E. Few fell in action, and I took the liberty of returning to you the various articles found on him. I am not one of his regiment, but feel it my duty to do for others as I should wish to be done, by and as a British soldier should do. . . . . You have my deepest sympathy in your great loss —Yours, &c., Gunner J. L. Wilson." Lance-Corpl. Few, who was a promising young man, was 25 years of age. He went right through the battle of the Somme last year, and has taken part in subsequent fierce fighting. A brother is at present serving in France.

1 & 2. Reports of deaths NDJ 8.11.1917 3a-b

154

Officer for Ilfracombe appeared he was reminded that a woman had taken over as Relieving Officer for the Combe Martin/Lynton area and what was stopping a woman doing his job? He pointed out he also had to deal personally with 'lunatic cases' he having had 25 of these in the last twelve months. He reckoned such 'lunatics' couldn't be handled by a woman – and then, almost as an afterthought, added he was the Commanding Officer of the 50-strong Ilfracombe Volunteer Training Corps. He was exempted. The Bideford Tribunal produced one man whilst no recruits at all were produced by the South Molton Rural Tribunal and only one more from the second sitting of the Barnstaple Tribunal. The North Devon Appeals Tribunal met three times this month and ordered seventeen men to enlist - their questioning of the men appearing before them becoming noticeably harsher.

No COs had appeared at any North Devon Tribunals for some months now so one wonders why the Government suddenly announced that COs were to have their right to vote in elections removed. The vote in the House of Commons to do this was 209 to 171 – so not really a massive endorsement of what might be seen as a purely vindictive scheme.

Further news about the food situation came this month. At Bideford local butchers complained that farmers and their wives were selling large quantities of pork in the Pannier Market above the fixed price. The council agree to enforce the rules referring to a bye-law limiting stallholders to only being allowed to sell 20 lbs of meat on any one market day. At Barnstaple the Food Control Committee decided to fix the price of butter and announced it via the Town Crier 'at an early hour' on a Friday market day. Unfortunately the price was lower than usual so traders didn't bother bringing it to market. The National Food Control Office then banned the sale of cream which was widely consumed across North Devon.

This was preceded by Sir Arthur Yapp the 'Director of Food Economy' announcing 'the new scale of voluntary rations' which suggested that men employed in heavy industrial or agricultural work could eat 8 lbs of bread a week with sedentary workers having 4½ lbs. Meat consumption was suggested at 2 lbs a week for both men and women along with 10 ounces of butter and fats plus 8 ounces of sugar. This was only a voluntary target the Government still being wary of introducing compulsory rationing for a much wider range of foodstuffs.

Farmers were again encouraged to grow as much corn as they could in 1918 with Lord Fortescue delivering speeches in several places to that effect, though it was noted that not a single parish in the South Molton district had met its quota of new crop land. Overall the district was 6000 acres below requirements though some farmers pointed out that farms on high, exposed areas would not be very useful as arable land. Not just food was being affected, serious coal shortages were beginning to be experienced and the Barnstaple Rural District council decided to set up a 'Coal Control Committee' to take over fuel distribution. Even the *Journal* had to announce this month that they would only be printing enough copies to supply subscribers owing to shortages of newsprint.

If farmers were being encouraged to produce more and people to consume less then everyone was asked to join War Savings Associations and

CREAM PROHIBITION.

The Food Controller has issued an Order prohibiting the sale or use of cream between Dec. 8, 1917, and April 30, 1918, except for the purpose of making butter or for consumption by invalids, young children, or other persons upon a doctor's order.

The Order has been issued in order to conserve as much full milk as possible, and because the use of cream, except for the purposes above mentioned, has been chiefly a luxury.

The principal clauses of the Order read as follows:—

1. No person shall after Dec. 8, 1917, use any cream except for the purpose of making butter or for such other purposes as the Food Controller may from time to time authorise; and no person shall after Dec. 8, 1917, sell, supply, or acquire or offer to sell or supply or attempt to acquire any cream except for such purposes.

2. Clause 1 of this Order shall not affect:—(a) Before January 15, 1918 the use, sale, supply, or acquisition of preserved or sterilized cream made before November 20, 1917; (b) the consumption of fresh cream by children under the age of five years, patients in hospitals and other similar institutions, and invalids or other persons needing cream in the interests of their health, or the sale, supply, or acquisition of cream for the purpose of such consumption, or with a view to its sale or supply for such consumption.

Where cream is required for the purposes referred to in Clause 2, the person selling or supplying it must have from the customer a statement in writing, giving details of the name and address of the child or the invalid for whose consumption it is needed and of the doctor who authorizes the supply. These written statements are to be kept by the seller and produced if required by the Food Controller or Food Committee.

3. The new rules on cream. NDJ 29.11.1917 7d

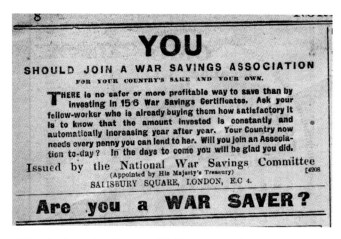

YOU

SHOULD JOIN A WAR SAVINGS ASSOCIATION
FOR YOUR COUNTRY'S SAKE AND YOUR OWN.

THERE is no safer or more profitable way to save than by investing in 15/6 War Savings Certificates. Ask your fellow-worker who is already buying them how satisfactory it is to know that the amount invested is constantly and automatically increasing year after year. Your Country now needs every penny you can lend to her. Will you join an Association to-day? In the days to come you will be glad you did.

Issued by the National War Savings Committee
(Appointed by His Majesty's Treasury) [4908]
SALISBURY SQUARE, LONDON, E.C 4.

Are you a WAR SAVER?

4. War Savings advertisement. NDJ 8.11.1917 8a-b

'participate in this patriotic movement' whose aim was to provide money in the form of redeemable loans to the Government to fight the war. Some were already in being with 220 members having enrolled in the Combe Martin Council Schools Association and 134 in the Fremington Schools one. The Lynton Association had 210 members and they had purchased £1592 of 'certificates' in just 14 months. Following the war plaques were awarded to towns who had done especially well in their 'Savings' drives. This photograph shows the Bideford example.

5. The 'Savings' plaque presented to Bideford.

Savings were one thing but wages were another and this month saw continuing unrest amongst groups of workers. Bakers in Barnstaple met with their employers and won an increase of 3/- per week taking their income to a minimum of 34/- per week. Barnstaple furniture makers who had applied for a rise were offered an extra 2d per hour by one factory but less by the Barnstaple Cabinet Company. Their employees decided to ask for 'a similar advance' and this was agreed a week later. At Ilfracombe mechanics and labourers also demanded a rise and when employers suggested an extra 2d per hour for all this was accepted. Barnstaple printers applied for a wage of £2 for a 50 hour week but compromised on a minimum wage of 35/- plus a 'War bonus of 2s 6d'. Builders in Barnstaple were also offered an acceptable rise with the *Journal* noting 'This makes the second advance granted within twelve months.'

Under the auspices of the Local Trades and Labour Council a meeting was held in Barnstaple to hear Professor A.Morgan from University College in Exeter talk on 'Why the Workers must demand Facilities for a University Education'. The Mayor presided over an audience of teachers and ordinary citizens who heard the Professor, 'who was in khaki', stress the importance of education if the working class was to improve its lot he paying tribute to H.G.Abel who had, singlehandedly, run the Workers' Educational Association in Barnstaple. Merely discussing a post-War future must have boosted the hearers' morale and feelings of hope.

All through his talk the Professor referred to 'men' – apparently not having noticed the now widespread takeover of men's jobs by women. This month, for example, saw Miss Calmady Hamlyn speaking at Combe Martin to female land workers on the importance of cultivating every piece of land possible – and then presenting several women with 'two stripes to be attached to their armlets, representing two years' work on the land.' In Barnstaple a Miss Quare was appointed the Health Visitor for the Borough whilst at Westward Ho! a Miss F.Newcombe was leaving to go to France as a telegraphist 'under the auspices of the Women's Army Auxiliary Corps' a body formed in February 1917. Another uniformed woman was featured in a Rowntree's Cocoa advertisement this month – the postal worker.

6. Female postal worker. NDJ 1.11.1917 6a-b

A nod to 'normality' came when the Ilfracombe Hotel Company held its AGM and even though there had been a 'diminution in tourist numbers' the hotel still recorded a sizable profit. Additionally 'The Barnstaple Sensation' filled many column inches of the *Journal*. John Harvey, a post office sorting clerk, was arrested for stealing £1 from a registered letter – the last of a whole series of thefts over the preceding 18 months. He was caught when passing the money to Richard Sercombe a town councillor and licensee of the Three Tuns in Barnstaple High Street. Both were found guilty with Harvey being gaoled for 4 months and Sercombe sentenced to prison 'with hard labour' for a month.

As if to remind people of the continuing war a meeting of the Lynton War Memorial Committee decided to erect a tablet recording the names of the township's sixteen 'heroes who have given their lives for God, King and Country'. At the same time a Calvary Cross war memorial was erected and dedicated in Bideford parish churchyard.

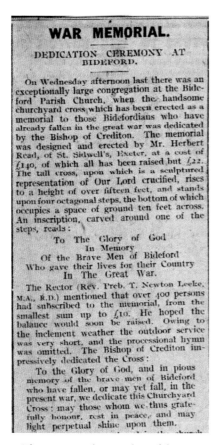

7. The report on the unveiling of the Bideford Calvary cross. BG 6.11.1917 3d

8. The cross today

Designed and made by Herbert Reed of Exeter and paid for by public subscription there seems to have been no real reason why it was erected at this point in the war – which still had another year to run though subscribers would not have known that.

The First World War in North Devon

December 1917

Christmas month was not happy this year with 47 deaths of servicemen being reported. One of these was that rarity – an 'Old Contemptible' named after the Kaiser's sneering remark about the 'contemptible' British Expeditionary Force who nevertheless fought his army to a standstill in 1914. Sgt. T.Clark of the Royal Engineers came from Bideford and had served with distinction in the Boer War and rejoined the colours when war broke out landing in France on August 29 1914. There were few men from the BEF left by this stage in the war.

As noted before some families were now losing their second or third son. Amongst these this month were Mr & Mrs.Albert Stephenson of Barnstaple who had lost two sons in November 1916 and now lost their third son, Pte.David Stephenson, in France. At Ilfracombe a full military funeral was held for W.F.Gage of the Canadian Forces who was buried in the churchyard. He had been badly wounded in France and brought back to England where he died. His mother decided he should be with his two brothers – Edward who had been an engineer on a

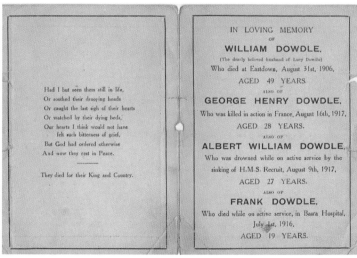

1. The memorial card for the Dowdle family.

In page 3 we record the death from pneumonia of Mr. Wm. Miller, of Stoodleigh, West Buckland, eldest son of Mr. Thomas Miller, of the same parish, and with profound regret we have to state that this respected resident at Buckland received news on Tuesday (when the funeral took place) of a further bereavement, his second son, Sergt. Fred T. Miller, having been killed in action. Prior to the War Sergt. Miller was for eight years in the employ of Messrs. Tromp and Son, seed merchants, &c, of High-street. Barnstaple, by whom he was held in the highest esteem, the news of his death being read by the firm with the deepest sorrow. He joined the Royal North Devon Hussars, and went through the Gallipoli campaign. For some time he had been serving with the Egyptian Expeditionary Force, and he was killed in the course of the operations in Palestine. He was going to Egypt this month for a course of instruction, having volunteered for the Flying Corps. Mr. Miller's youngest son was killed in the Vimy Ridge action last April, so that within a few months he has lost his three sons. The family have the heartfelt sympathy of the community throughout a wide area in their terrible affliction.

ship sunk by the Germans whose body had washed up on the Tunnels Beach in Ilfracombe and was interred in the churchyard – where the name of another brother killed at the Battle of the Falklands was added to the gravestone. One family recorded its dead on a simple memorial card – note how two of the men died just a week apart.

Just as sad was the account of the death of Sgt. Fred Miller of West Buckland.

2. The Miller family lose 3 sons. NDJ 20.12.1917 5d

Also amongst the long list of killed were Cpl.A.Squire from Lynton aged 21 and Pte.S.Morgan of Barnstaple who was just 18. Both were listed as members of the Tank Corps which was now a fully fledged branch of the Army. Morgan's passing was especially sad as a report in the *Journal* on 13th December recounted how his mother had three letters to her son marked 'Wounded' returned to her on the Saturday - only to receive a telegram three days later to say her son was dead. Again as he was so young it is no surprise to learn that his father Sydney was serving with the Royal Garrison Artillery in Egypt. Another report recorded how 100 men from Bishops Nympton were serving in the Forces – of whom 8 had been killed, an indication of how war could impact one village.

In addition to all these deaths were even longer lists of men wounded with many being treated in North Devon hospitals including this smiling group at 'Craigmore' in Ilfracombe.

3. Smiling wounded soldiers at Ilfracombe.

Even given the high death rate and even higher wound numbers morale still seemed to be high, as indicated by a jaunty poem published this month and used on a Christmas card from local troops in Mesopotamia.

'Tis Xmas '17 A.D.
And still we face the foe,
With that zeal and energy
We did three years ago.

'Tis Xmas '17 A.D.-
And our task is yet undone,
But ere again '18 (D.V.)
The victory will have won.

May Xmas '17 A.D.
Bring joys without regret,
Just whisper round this tip from me –
We're not downhearted yet.

Another Christmas card came from Wilfred Darch from Landkey who had joined the Royal Flying Corps and was stationed at Chingford.

Such regimental Christmas cards were fairly common but the men still found time to make their own as this very simple one from a Bideford man shows.

Some parishes overprinted existing cards and sent them to local men as with this example from Parracombe.

5. A Bideford soldier's home-made Christmas card.

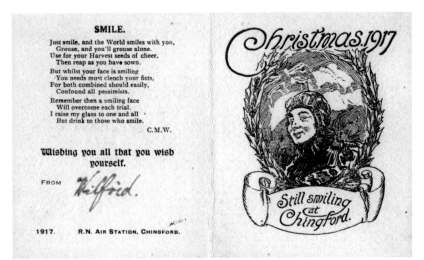

4. A RFC card from Christmas 1917.

6. A Parracombe card.

Servicemen still seemed to be cheerful and it was good that they weren't downhearted as drafts of new men were drying up – with the North Devon Tribunals meeting on very few occasions this month – and when they did they produced just five men for the Forces. Even the Appeals Tribunal only saw two men being ordered to enlist – with the military representative noting that 'the authorities were at present combing out young men from munitions, and those who had entered coal mines' so desperate was the country for new recruits.

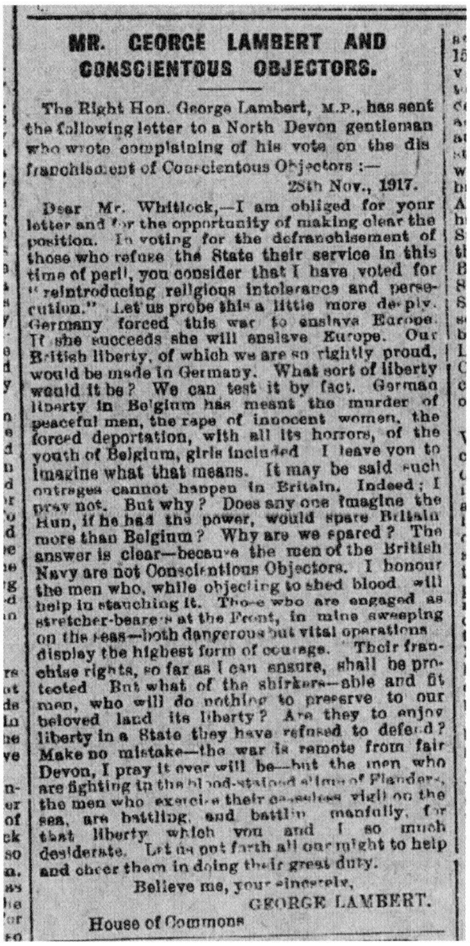

The contentious subject of COs came up again this month when local MP George Lambert wrote to a constituent who had accused him of 'reintroducing intolerance' by voting to disenfranchise COs whose views were based on their faith. His reply was printed in the *Journal* and was followed a week later by this resolution from the Barnstaple branch of the 'Comrades of the Great War'.

MR. GEORGE LAMBERT AND CONSCIENTOUS OBJECTORS.

The Right Hon. George Lambert, M.P., has sent the following letter to a North Devon gentleman who wrote complaining of his vote on the disfranchisement of Conscientous Objectors :—

25th Nov., 1917.

Dear Mr. Whitlock,—I am obliged for your letter and for the opportunity of making clear the position. In voting for the defranchisement of those who refuse the State their service in this time of peril, you consider that I have voted for "reintroducing religious intolerance and persecution." Let us probe this a little more deeply. Germany forced this war to enslave Europe. If she succeeds she will enslave Europe. Our British liberty, of which we are so rightly proud, would be made in Germany. What sort of liberty would it be? We can test it by fact. German liberty in Belgium has meant the murder of peaceful men, the rape of innocent women, the forced deportation, with all its horrors, of the youth of Belgium, girls included. I leave you to imagine what that means. It may be said such outrages cannot happen in Britain. Indeed; I pray not. But why? Does any one imagine the Hun, if he had the power, would spare Britain more than Belgium? Why are we spared? The answer is clear—because the men of the British Navy are not Conscientious Objectors. I honour the men who, while objecting to shed blood, will help in staunching it. Those who are engaged as stretcher-bearers at the Front, in mine sweeping on the seas—both dangerous but vital operations display the highest form of courage. Their franchise rights, so far as I can ensure, shall be protected. But what of the shirkers—able and fit men, who will do nothing to preserve to our beloved land its liberty? Are they to enjoy liberty in a State they have refused to defend? Make no mistake—the war is remote from fair Devon, I pray it ever will be—but the men who are fighting in the blood-stained slime of Flanders, the men who exercise their ceaseless vigil on the sea, are battling, and battling manfully, for that liberty which you and I so much desiderate. Let us put forth all our might to help and cheer them in doing their great duty.

Believe me, yours sincerely,

GEORGE LAMBERT.

House of Commons

7. *George Lambert MP on Conscientious Objection. NDJ 6.12.1917 3f*

CONSCIENTIOUS OBJECTORS.

At a recent meeting the Bar staple branch of the "Comrades of the Great War" the following resolution was passed, a copy being sent to Sir Godfrey Baring, Bart, M.P :—

"That in view of the fact that a large number of conscientious objectors are now allowed to live in the fair county of Devon, this Branch will be pleased if you will impress upon the Government to take the necessary steps to clear them from our midst, and also to disfranchise them both from Parliamentary and Municipal privileges, and to prohibit them from taking any employment under State or Municipality." Acknowledging the receipt of the resolution Sir Godfrey Baring wrote:—"Will you be so kind as to inform the members of your branch that the terms of this resolution shall receive my most respectful and sympathetic consideration."

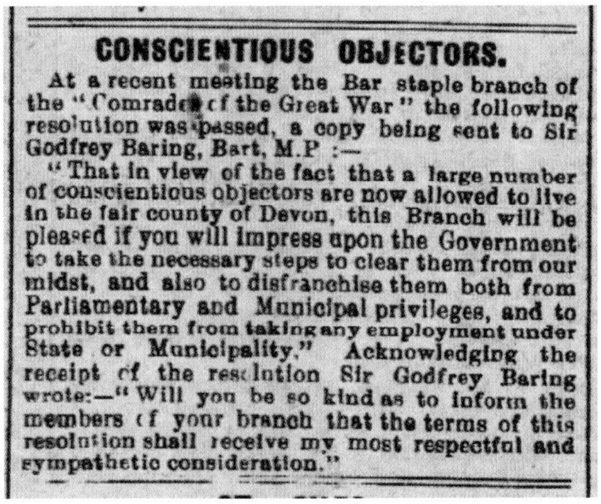

8. *The Comrades of the Great War on Conscientious Objectors. NDJ 13.12.1917 5d*

A fortnight later a very long letter appeared from C.Mortlock-Brown of Braunton who bravely came forward to defend COs. He noted that the 5000 COs in Britain could be split into three groups a) religious COs who followed Christ's teachings, b) political COs 'chiefly Socialists' who saw war as 'an economic mistake' and c) the 'very small group' of those opposed to taking any life – what might today be termed 'vegans'. He further subdivided these into passive/active/aggressive resisters before getting to the point of his letter about disenfranchisement as shown here.

It is interesting that the *Journal* chose to publish this given that it would have been an extremely unpopular view in the earlier years of the war but one wonders if people were now questioning their own views given the never-ending slaughter on the battlefields?

Another possibly unexpected result of the war came this month when Lord Clinton put up for sale 5790 acres of farmland along with many houses and cottages.

As regards their disfranchisement, it is deplorable that the present august Parliament, that constantly exhorts the people to die for noble ideals, that is out to relieve the oppressed, that is the first English Parliament to accord anything like equal political rights to women, that is determined to extend to her humblest supporter equal educational rights, that has treated with Christ-like forbearance her refractory offshoot Ireland—it is deplorable indeed that such a Parliament should disfranchise a conscience-stricken and minute section of the community. This retrograde step is not "towards Democracy." One is tempted to ask "Are we indeed free in England to have a conscience and abide by it?" Yet men are shedding their blood that "Freedom might be free."

To one the long dusty road without a turning; to another the steep hill climb and the glory. Some cannot see the glory of dying for their country: others cannot see the glory of living for it. "What is our life?" Are not some dying and some living for the same ideal, and may there not be many roads unto that ideal of Christendom and Democracy—the durable Peace of the whole world?

Nothing will militate more effectually against a durable Peace than the cultivation and practice of a spirit of intolerance.

I am, Sir, yours faithfully,

C. A. MORTLOCK-BROWN.

Sanfield, Braunton, Dec 18th, 1917

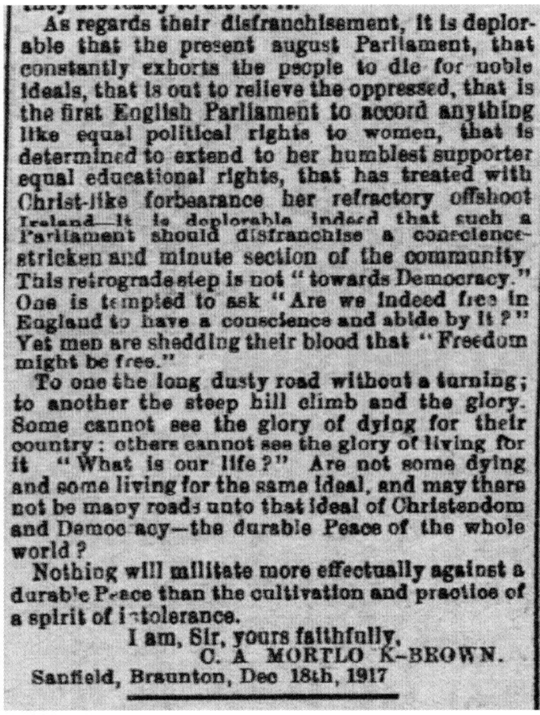

9. *Conscientious Objectors defended. NDJ 27.12.1917 3d*

Presumably, given the high wartime prices being paid for farmland, this was a good time to sell – and many of the lots sold to the sitting tenants. Over the two day auction some £91,000 was realised - equivalent to just over £8 million today. After the war agricultural incomes dropped enormously and many other large estates were put on the market only attracting low prices.

An advertisement appeared this month when farmers were informed of the easy availability of motor ploughs, now termed 'Tractors'.

This was in tandem with the announcement at both the Bideford and Barnstaple War Agricultural Committees that orders would be served on every farmer compelling them to meet a quota of new arable land. Appeals were possible but had to go to the Divisional Agricultural Committee.

Voluntary moves to produce more food were still happening with the Raleigh Cabinet Works in Barnstaple forming an 'allotment holders' society and a poultry keepers' association'. In another move Bideford town council decided to open a 'Municipal milk depot' given that the price of milk had risen to 7d per quart and was becoming too dear for some. At Clovelly Mrs.Hamlyn, the Lady of the Manor, inaugurated a 'Communal School Kitchen' designed to provide nutritious meals to the village children without the use of any flour which was now becoming very scarce.

This month also saw the Workers' Union holding another meeting in Barnstaple where shopping at the Co-operative Wholesale Society outlets was strongly supported as a way of balancing domestic budgets. In the same week a branch of the Union was set up in Ilfracombe and, in a display of pragmatism, Barnstaple town council co-opted T.P.Prideaux, the Secretary of the local Trades and Labour Council, into its membership – a major step change in local politics.

One other event occurred this month which was the forerunner of many especially after the war when men were demobilised. James Irwin, a Royal Navy sailor from Ilfracombe, divorced his wife after 5 years of marriage for her adultery he having been away at sea on 'foreign service'.

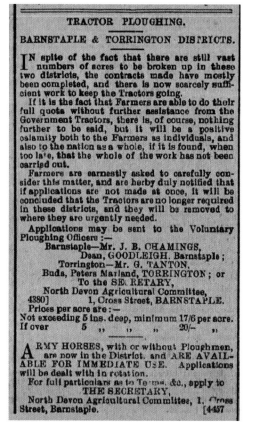

10. Tractors available to farmers.
NDJ 20.12.1917 1e

The First World War in North Devon

January 1918

The New Year opened with a record number of medals being awarded to local men. These included 12 Military Medals, 3 bars to Military Medals, 3 Military Crosses, 2 Distinguished Conduct Medals, 1 Meritorious Service Medal, 1 Croix de Guerre and 2 nursing medals. One of the MM 'bars' went to Cpl.Thomas Langdon from Bideford who in winning it seems to have been so badly wounded that his leg had to be amputated, whilst Sgt. A.Perrymen from Weare Giffard, who won one of the DCMs was only 19. The nursing awards were the Royal Red Cross medal, one going to Annie Barnes of Ilfracombe after she had been a hospital nurse in France for 3 years. Miss Knox, formerly Staff Nurse at the Tyrrell Cottage Hospital in Ilfracombe, received the same honour after 2 years of working at a casualty clearing station behind the Front.

Such decorations were one bright spot in an otherwise gloomy month where another 45 locals were reported as being killed including, as always now, those who had died some time before as, for example, L/Cpl.F.Hill of Barnstaple who had been killed in April 1917. Three men lost their lives in Palestine where the British forces were routing the Turkish troops and revenging themselves for the losses at Kut. Amongst the dead were three sailors, one of them F.Bangham of Torrington went down with his merchant ship – of which he was 'the gunner' which suggests he might have been serving on a 'Q' ship – a disguised armed merchant vessel designed to lure and sink U-boats.

This month saw the *Journal* publish a 'North Devon Roll of Honour' for 1917 over three issues. In total it covered eight columns of this broadsheet paper and is notable for the number of men 'missing in action presumed killed' and 'officially supposed killed'. Reading through the lists of names of mainly young men must have been a chilling reminder to the members of the local Tribunals that the men they were ordering to enlist could well appear in later lists. F.Wilkey, a member of the Northam Tribunal complained this month of being 'publicly insulted' by 'persons at Appledore regarding his duty at the Tribunal' – luckily a rare event. Also at Appledore a public meeting was held to discuss a war memorial for the village's dead – with a fund being inaugurated to pay for one.

This might have been so but the Tribunals still carried on with their work. The first to meet was the Bideford Rural one where it was announced that the War Agricultural Committee had suggested refusing exemptions in 'nearly all the cases' they were aware of – at which Mr.Moore, a farming representative reckoned the Committee 'was not always fully informed of the facts'. Mr.Woodcock, for the Army, immediately protested against this remark – to no avail as the panel granted exemptions to every man appearing before them they all being involved in agriculture. The Ilfracombe Tribunal on the other hand sent all three men appearing before them to the Army. When the Barnstaple Rural Tribunal sat Reginald Parsons, a 21 year old baker classified as 'C3', came before them. Woodcock argued that because the Army was 'taking all high category men' out of trades such as baking and replacing them with 'C3' men he should enlist. He was ordered to be medically examined again to see if he was fit enough to serve.

At South Molton William Sauerzapf, an 18 year old 'A' class horseman appeared. It was explained that his German father had taken British citizenship in 1913. A short exemption was granted 'subject to the Clerk reporting the case to the Home Office' presumably to investigate how patriotic he might be. His case came back before the Appeals Tribunal at the end of the month. The military panel member suggested a stark choice 'if the man had no objection to fighting against the Germans, he should be in the Army, if he had he should be interned.' The other, more pragmatic, members suggested he be kept working on the land which would be of more value than being interned. Another 'foreigner' this month must have puzzled local magistrates. Isaac Berkovitch, a Russian tailor, had opted to join the British Army 'in preference to returning to Russia' but had failed to report to the Exeter recruiting centre. Apparently his request for exemption had arrived too late hence his arrest. He was handed over to the military.

Tribunals were still suggesting that substitutes could take the place of fit, young men – but a case at the Bideford Rural Tribunal showed this wasn't easy. The panel had ordered substitution in the case of one unnamed 19 year old but no substitute could be found – with the same thing happening when his brother reached the age of 18. A panel member remarked on this case 'Where two farmer's sons, Class A men, remain home feeling is getting very bitter.' Another case where substitution didn't work was heard at the Appeals Tribunal when Arthur Burgess, the mate on a ketch owned by John Irwin of Combe Martin came before them. Irwin had appealed on behalf of Burgess and had secured exemption 'on the condition that he advertised for a substitute at 50s a week.' He now appeared again to say he had advertised for a man but got no replies so Burgess was given 6 months exemption with Irwin 'again undertaking to advertise.' At the same Tribunal William Delve, a 42 year old publican of Barnstaple appealed against his call-up which came after he failed 'to get work of national importance'. He pointed out, rather plaintively, that running a pub was all he had ever done and he 'was not skilled in any outside work' – which saw his being ordered to enlist.

It was noticeable that in cases where farmers were appealing to keep their sons at home the local Tribunals were often granting exemption – with the Army challenging them more and more strongly but then being turned down mainly for reasons associated with maximising food production. The spread of tractors was helping here with an article in the *Journal* noting that in the week before Christmas the twelve tractors operating in North Devon ploughed 84½ acres - even though heavy frost cut down their hours of working. In the first week of 1918 some 141 acres were ploughed with the newspaper report noting 'As there is a very large area to be tilled in North Devon, the Government intends to send many more tractors into the district.' It wasn't just the Government bringing in tractors as an advertisement in the *Journal* showed.

1. A ploughing demonstration advertised. NDJ 3.1.1918 4c-d

2 & 3. Tractors working in North Devon this month – note the presence of a soldier.

Farmers were clearly responding to the call for greater food production but civilians were also working hard to grow food and in Bideford a field in Abbotsham Road had been ploughed ready for the allotment holders, whilst local landowner Mr.Stucley had provided another three acres for the same purpose at East-the-Water.

Not everyone was so public minded as was seen when James Mortimer, a Swimbridge farmer, was taken to court under the obscure 'Feeding of Game Order 1917'. P.c.Hunt and Special Constable H.Nott visited Eastacott Wood in Swimbridge and found six lots of corn put down to feed game birds this being illegal under the Order. He was fined £5. Additionally the marvellously named Hamlet Beater Rather who ran the George Hotel in South Molton was fined £3.4.0 for failing to keep a record of food supplied to customers under the equally obscure 'Public Meals Order 1917'.

Clearly the food situation was critical with a new Government order stipulating two 'meatless' days a week in restaurants which was followed by the alarming announcement that appeared at the end of this month under the heading 'The Meat Shortage – A grave situation'.

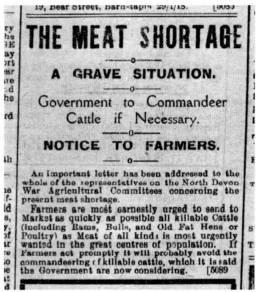

4. *The Meat Shortage. NDJ 31.1.1918 5b*

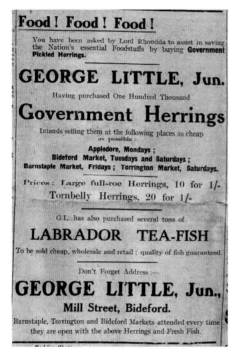

5. *The availability of fish. BG 15.1.1918 2e-f*

Adjacent to this notice in the newspaper was a report that the Barnstaple Food Control Committee had asked the town council to open their 'Soup Kitchen' to supply vegetable soup which 'would help large numbers to observe a meatless day without inconvenience.' Oddly fish seemed to still be relatively plentiful if an advertisement from George Little this month is taken into account. Little makes an interesting appearance before the Tribunal next month.

Some extra mouths had turned up in North Devon from an unexpected source. The South Molton Food Control Committee were informed that 33 Portuguese men were being housed in Chulmleigh, 17 at South Molton with 50 more expected there and another 50 at both Filleigh and Worlington. These men were timber workers brought in to provide wood for the trenches – a never ending demand – at a time when many local forestry workers were in the Army.

One case concerning these men came before the Holsworthy Petty Sessions this month which was not reported in the local newspapers - probably given its propaganda value to the Germans. A Portuguese camp in the Holsworthy area housed 98 men of whom 19 announced they would not work. Thomas Brow, the District Inspector of the Board of Trade Supply (Timber), was summoned from Exeter and calling the men together announced, via an interpreter, that the men were breaking Regulation 42 of the Defence of the Realm Act and were making themselves liable to 'severe punishment'. When he asked why they had stopped work they said they 'struck against the doctor…they were short of food.' Brown pointed out that in fact they got 50% more rations than other such camps – to which one Antonio Continho said 'We have been short of food. We have been without codfish for 3 days – have had beef instead.' The reference to Dr.Kingdon, the camp's medical man, seems to be directed at him passing sick men as fit for work. What appears to have been some cultural insensitivity over diet had turned into this strike. The magistrates sentenced all the men to 14 days in Exeter Prison with hard labour. When 4 more 'strikers' were brought before the same court three days later they too were sent to prison for a fortnight – and fined £2 each.

At Ilfracombe another group of Europeans did make the news when Mrs.Burns, who was 'in charge of the Belgian Home, Inglewood', was presented by the residents with a silver centre-piece and flowers 'in recognition of her great kindness'. Also honoured this month was Frank Jewell, the Mayor of Barnstaple, who was presented with an MBE by the King for his 'magnificent record of public and War work'. This announcement came just before Jewell launched a drive to raise £1000 to buy a YMCA Hut to be erected behind the Front in France for the troops' rest and recreation. A week-long series of events was arranged with even schoolchildren being asked to each give a penny towards the cost.

A similar campaign in Ilfracombe saw an anonymous donor give £1000 which saw the fund-raising group decide to keep going in order to raise enough for a second hut.

At Northam letters began to be received from local men who had been the recipient of a present paid for by parishioners and sent out by the village rector the Rev. Payne-Cook. Unusually he kept all of these and they now form a fascinating collection in the North Devon Record Office. Written on a wide variety of papers they all express thanks for the gifts which clearly meant a lot to them. A typical letter is shown below.

6. YMCA Hut Week. NDJ 17.1.1918 4c-e

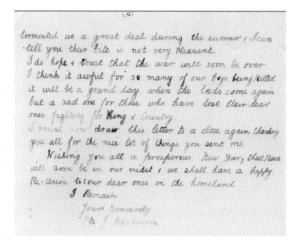

7a & b. A grateful recipient of a Christmas parcel.

The Barnstaple Mayor also chaired a public meeting of the Comrades of the Great War in the Albert Hall where the aims of the group were explained. This Barnstaple group claimed to be the first to be formed in Devon and they already had 140 members. These numbers were outstripped by the Barnstaple Trades and Labour Council who this month reported that they represented 'over 1600 Trade Unionists in the borough.'

Amidst all these 'serious' events there was still opportunities for entertainment even if these were perforce war-related. Thus in Bideford the Palace Cinema was showing 'A Munition Girl's Romance – Founded on Fact' whilst at Westward Ho! a 'Variety Entertainment' was raising funds for a 'Recreation Hut' for the Army.

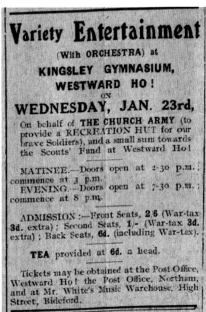

8. The Palace Cinema, Bideford.
BG 8.1.1918 2e
9. A Westward Ho! show.
NDJ 15.1.1918 2c

Doubtless members of both groups and everyone else in North Devon were discussing the appalling murder of a young wife by her husband in Braunton. The man had been working in a munitions factory in South Wales but following a breakdown returned home where he strangled his wife. He was quickly found unfit to plead and sent to Exminster Asylum – two more sad victims of the war.

10. William Lyle of Littleham's medals including his Boer War decorations and his First World War Military Medal.'

The First World War in North Devon

February 1918

Poor weather in Europe at this time seems to have restricted fighting between the combatants with just 17 deaths recorded this month with some of them being 'historical'. Amongst them was that of L/Cpl.H.Isaac of Barnstaple who died of his wounds aged 21 in Palestine. He had been present at the capture of Jerusalem and in a letter home just after being wounded he wrote of 'the great privilege allowed him to have taken part in the capture of the Holy City from the Turk.' He was a typical young soldier so what to make of the death in action of Pioneer William Ashton of Muddiford? Ashton was 54 years old and had enlisted two years before following the death of his son in France. Three of the dead came from Appledore and had all been in the Merchant service – D.Day, S.Screech and _ Parsley, all left widows and children.

One serviceman who did return came home to a hero's welcome. Captain Hackwill came from Langtree and was a pilot in the Royal Flying Corps who took on some German bombers over London and shot down one of them. Arriving on leave at Torrington station he was met by the Mayor and detachments from the town's 'Enderby' Military Hospital and a guard of honour made up of men from the Canadian Forestry Corps who were working in the area. A report this month noted how 170 men of this Corps attended church service at Torrington Congregational church – with a later

1 & 2. Portuguese timber workers at Bratton Fleming.

168

report saying more Portuguese timber workers had arrived in Bratton Fleming.

Such 'imported' workers were becoming vital as by now the local Tribunals were seeing fewer and fewer men and then most were seeking an extension of the exemptions they had already been granted. Occasionally one can see local issues, other than agricultural ones, surfacing at these meetings – as when the Ilfracombe Tribunal heard from Reginald Burton, a dentist. The Army representative Woodcock accepted that no more dentists were needed in the Forces but thought he might be sent to an area where such professionals were scarce. The panel members disagreed, probably not wishing to lose such a valuable man – and, ignoring Woodcock, exempted him. Medical staff were, of course, still required to look after wounded soldiers in local hospitals – such as this group pictured at 'Craigmore' Hospital in Ilfracombe.

3. *'Craigmore' Military Hospital, Ilfracombe – staff and patients.*

The Bideford Tribunal heard 43 cases 'many of them being reviews of exemptions of tradesmen of low medical categories.' All had their exemptions renewed. At Barnstaple a number of bakers and grocers applied all claiming to be doing work of national (and social) importance. Most were exempted or ordered to find substitutes though in the case of Frederick Reeves, a Pilton grocer, he was ordered to enlist in three month's time even though he claimed, by letter, to be a CO. Woodcock said he would go to the Appeals Tribunal to challenge him. Only a few cases were heard at Ilfracombe and when the panel members asked Woodcock for details of the grading of one man he 'said he was not allowed to say' – with the chairman promptly adjourning the meeting until the information was provided.

Two Appeals Tribunals were held this month where, again, many exemptions were granted though only allowed where the men agreed to undertake work of national importance for some days each week in addition to their normal occupation. When George Little, a fish merchant of Bideford, appeared, however, he claimed that he refused high prices for his fish from 'up country dealers' and 'As a consequence the North Devon towns were the only towns in England where herrings were sold for 1½d each.' The panel turned down the military case for him to enlist and granted him an exemption.

As his case showed exemptions based on food were seen as of great importance and this was reflected in many other news items. Weekly figures for acres ploughed in North Devon by tractors continued to be published – 116 acres at the start of the month rising to 172 by the end – although by then 14 tractors were working.

These tractors were backed up by 14 'steam threshing sets' but labour shortages meant that 'the Board of Agriculture were anticipating some little difficulty with regard to the 1918 harvest.' The Barnstaple War

4. *A 25 hp Avery tractor at Mr.Copp's farm, Moortown, Torrington supplied by Heard Bros, Bideford.*

Agricultural Committee in discussing these shortages thought the public schoolboys who came to North Devon in 1917 weren't as helpful as they had hoped, with one member suggesting local 'elementary school boys' would be better, presumably as many came from a farming background. German PoWs could not be used as the district was too near the coast and escape could be possible. The Bideford committee, however, thought the public schoolboys useful and decided to set up a camp when required for the Woolsery and Parkham districts – and German PoWs would be used so long as they were working more than 10 miles from the coast. At South Molton the Unicorn Hotel was being fitted out to house a party of these PoWs.

Whilst these discussions about the production of food were going on consumers weren't forgotten. At Bickington preparations for opening a communal soup kitchen similar to the one at Fremington were being made. Barnstaple town council also decided to open a kitchen with one councillor claiming to have heard that 'great distress prevailed in Barnstaple' although the Town Clerk didn't put much credence in that as virtually no-one had approached the council asking for help. Price control cases were regularly coming to court as when Emily Bright, a grocer of Weare Giffard, was fined £1 for selling margarine at 1d above the fixed price. A trader at Bideford Market was charged with selling rabbits at 2/- each when the fixed price was 1/7 - he escaped a fine on a technicality. A move to evict schoolboys from the allotments they had been working in the Oakleigh Road area of Barnstaple to allow 'working men' to take them over saw a heated argument at the town council with councillors saying it was unfair given how hard the boys had worked. Unfortunately these councillors lost the vote 11-3 and the boys were displaced.

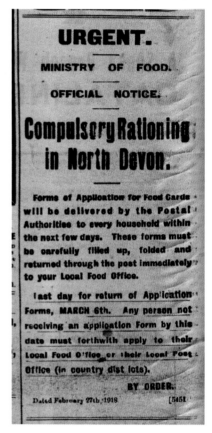

5. *The introduction of compulsory rationing. NDJ 28.2.1918 4f*

The most important news about food came at the end of the month when this advertisement appeared in the *Journal*.

With rationing already in place for some foodstuffs it must have been clear to most that much wider controls would be unavoidable. The impact of this order will become clearer in later months. The food crisis did, if nothing else, boost the importance of farm workers so it is no surprise to learn that when the Barnstaple Trades and Labour Council held a meeting in Kentisbury to establish a branch of the Agricultural Labourers' Union in the district it was well attended, with 22 men enrolling.

It has already been mentioned how the churches were facing difficulties trying to balance Christian teachings with the needs of the war and this month saw what was termed a 'Striking Sermon' delivered at the Ilfracombe Wesleyan church entitled 'Why God does not end the War'. This was an odd mix of biblical references, an attack on brewers and the continuing immorality of the populace and one has to wonder how much impact this had?

On a more practical basis Ilfracombe saw a Children's Pageant being staged to raise funds for the 'War Emergency Fund' of the 'Waifs and Strays' Society' – with over £100 being realised. At Barnstaple the Mayoress started a subscription list to help pay for a Maternity Centre by appealing to those 'who are anxious for the future welfare of our race.' At Lynton the working group making crutches sent more they had made to the 'Central Depot' whilst the Bideford Chamber of Commerce sent £50 to various charities raised by selling waste paper they had collected.

Also at Bideford F.Searle the organiser for Belgian refugees in the town reported that their numbers had fallen from 107 to 64 with many of these being locally employed. All the refugees were now fluent in English especially 'but some

6. *A Belgian refugee family in Bideford.*

of their children were unable to converse with their fathers when the latter came home on leave from France.'

Not everyone liked the Belgians as in Ilfracombe John Renard was fined 10/- for using obscene language to A.Velghe, a Belgian, who was then living in Cambridge Grove.

Entertainments continued with a brand new specially constructed cinema being opened in Bideford. The building still exists as a night club and live music venue.

A more unusual entertainment this month was the announcement that 'La Somna whose powers, it is said, border almost on the supernatural' would be appearing at the Theatre Royal, Barnstaple. She could tell you 'anything about the War, your wife, sweetheart, husband, or friend, lost or stolen property, the whereabouts of missing relatives, your marriage' etc. One wonders how many war widows went to her performance?

THE PALLADIUM PICTURE PALACE,
MILL STREET, BIDEFORD.

This Up-to-date Palace will **shortly be opened**, when the **Finest Films obtainable** will be shown.

The newly-constructed Hall, which will **Seat 500 People,** is well adapted and constructed for Vocal and Instrumental Music. The floor is sloping towards the stage, and is **advantageous to all playgoers**; while the **Exits** are **Three** in number and capable of empting the Hall in two minutes.

All Doors open outwards.

Look out for future Advertisements.

T. WATERHOUSE, Proprietor.

7. A new cinema opens in Bideford.
BG 26.2.1918 2f

The First World War in North Devon

March 1918

This month saw one of the lowest number of war deaths recorded - at 15, with four of these being 'historical'. Pte.E.Cloke from Bideford, for example, died 2 years earlier and two others, Pte.R.Williams from Barnstaple and Pte.E.Short from Frithelstock, who was only 19, had died in May 1917. Not all of these deaths were on the Western Front as when Pte.Alfred Pugsley from Bideford and Sergt.William Huxtable from Berrynarbor were both killed in Salonica. Sadly this low number of deaths was to change after the Germans launched their massive Spring offensive towards the end of this month.

The relatively small number of deaths was matched by the few medals given out this month. Four Military Medals were awarded, along with a DSO, a DSM and a DCM. When Pte.Robbins, winner of a Military Medal returned on leave to his home in South Molton he received a hero's welcome.

Given the manpower shortage a small news item about the Canadian Forestry Corps would have caught peoples' attention. It noted that 200 men of this body who had been billeted in houses in Torrington were moving to huts erected near Stevenstone, just outside the town. Another small item concerned the family of Lemuel Smith of Ilfracombe whose six sons were all serving, with a daughter in the WAAC and four sons-in-law also in the Forces. This was clearly to be compared to those coming before the local Tribunals arguing against their conscription.

The first hearings at the Barnstaple Tribunal this March heard that all exemptions given to workers at the Pilton glove factory had been cancelled as their jobs were no longer deemed to be 'a certified occupation' (i.e. reserved) – and two glovemakers were ordered to enlist immediately. When the South Molton Rural Tribunal met they exempted seven agricultural workers and sent no recruits to the Army. At the Barnstaple Rural Tribunal two interesting cases came up. When Henry Short of Atherington, a road contractor, appeared Woodcock, the military representative, demanded he join the Army as 'Men working on the roads in France at present were nearly as important as men in the

HERO'S WELCOME AT SOUTHMOLTON.

A civic reception was accorded Pte. Robbins, of Southmolton, who was recently awarded the military medal for distinguished service, on his return from France on furlough. The Mayor (Alderman Bush) and members of the town council greeted the gallant young soldier in the presence of a large gathering of inhabitants. Spirited music was performed by the Town Band, under Mr J. Taylor. The Mayor said that Private Robbins, although in years only a boy, had won distinction for himself and for the County. It was a very great pleasure to welcome him home. Alderman Moor expressed the pleasure with which the town heard of the recognition of Pte. Robbins's gallantry in the field.

Sergeant-Major Crang said that when he was acting as recruiting-sergeant at Southmolton, Pte. Robbins was the first who volunteered his services to the Country. Being under age, he (the speaker) refused him; but the lad was so persistent that he was eventually accepted. It was interesting to recall that when Pte. Robbins passed the medical test the examining officer (Dr. Mortimer) remarked, "That boy will yet make a name for himself." (Cheers).

The Mayor and Mayoress afterwards gave a reception in the Assembly Hall, Pte. Robbins' parents and friends and a few soldiers on leave being present. "I have only done my duty, as a soldier should," modestly remarked the young hero in thanking the Mayor and Mayoress for ther kindness.

1. A hero's return. NDJ 7.3.1918 8d

trenches.' The panel disagreed and gave him an exemption. The same panel then saw John Westlake a Combe Martin blacksmith. His village used to have an ironmongery but its owner had enlisted whereupon Westlake had opened a new shop selling similar goods. Woodcock said 'at the present time the Ministry would not allow shops to be opened in this way when tradesmen from the same places were away serving.' Westlake was exempted but was ordered to close his shop. Only a handful of men were secured from the Bideford and Ilfracombe Tribunals though the Appeals body ordered nine men to enlist, only granting exemption in six other cases.

One reason for the shortage of men might be seen in a court case from Ilfracombe. Superintendent Hulland had gone to the Queen's Hotel and noticed a registration form in the name of 'Harry Jones'. When he questioned 'Harry' the man admitted his real name was Claude Andrew, he being a discharged soldier, who claimed he always gave that name when 'on the spree'. Claude's brother Archibald was also there but when he saw the policeman did a rapid disappearance as he was a deserter from the Army. Claude was gaoled for one month with hard labour for lying on the form - with a warrant being issued for Archibald's arrest.

The on-going food crisis saw many more moves to either increase food production or ration out existing supplies. Thus the 14 tractors at work in North Devon ploughed up to 192 acres in a week – a new record. In addition 109 'Government horses' were working in the area with another 70 coming. The Torrington District War Agricultural Committee applied to have 25 German PoWs sent to help their farmers whilst a PoW camp was set up at South Molton with the men being given a good report.

In a sign of things to come, however, the Torrington Workers' Union announced their

> FULL employment for the German prisoners at Southmolton has been booked for weeks ahead. Most of the men are still engaged at Townhouse farm Others go out in parties of four; in some cases with a guard, while in others farmers ride in and take charge of them. The prisoners' readiness to obey orders is marked. Several of them now speak English tolerably well. In their own country they were all either farmers or farmers' men; and though our methods differ from theirs they turn out a good day's work. More than one of them, it is said, wears the Iron Cross. The British guard includes men who have been four times wounded.

2. German PoWs put to work. NDJ 28.3.1918 7c

members would not work with Germans and if local farmers took them 'they will have to put up with the consequences.'

Another way of addressing food shortages was to intensify the battle against German U-boats that were still operating and sinking merchant ships bringing food to Britain. In June 1916 a Royal Navy Air Service airship base had been established at Mullion in Cornwall with a smaller base in Bude. From here slow moving airships cruised up and down the Bristol Channel off of the coast of North Devon searching for U-boats – and then lobbing bombs on to them. Wilfred Darch from Landkey was one of the crewmen and he is shown here wearing his heavy military clothing – very necessary given that the small 'gondola' beneath the craft was unheated and 'sweeps' over the sea often lasted hours.

3. Wilfred Darch in his RNAS uniform.

4. The SST2 airship he flew in – SS stands for Sea Scout.

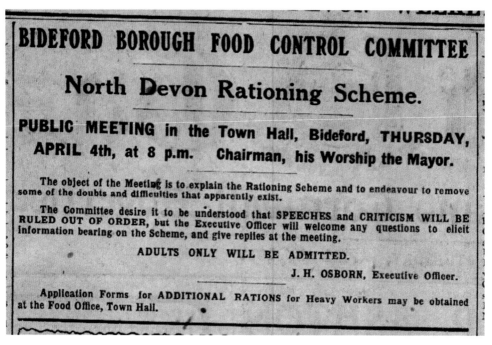

5. Rationing explained. BG 12.3.1918 2e-f

Eking out food supplies was now of major importance with Barnstaple town council opening their Soup Kitchen and the Ministry of Food fixing the price of rabbits. On the 27th of March official rationing was announced being due to come into force on April 8th. A public meeting in Bideford heard an explanation of the new scheme – note the rather draconian 'Criticism will be ruled out of order.'

Traders selling produce over the fixed price were being fined regularly now as when Frank Pierce, a Torrington grocer, was fined £2.10.0 for selling margarine at 1d over the official price. Even more draconian was the fine of £30 plus £20 in costs levied on James Snow of Beaples Barton in Knowstone for failing to cultivate 34 acres when ordered to, such was the vital necessity to produce more food.

6. West & East Buckland and Charles Red Cross workers photographed in Barnstaple.

It wasn't just food that was being targeted. Schoolboys foraging on Exmoor collected enough sphagnum moss to fill, when dried, two bags which were sent to Exeter for use in bandages. Other school children at Chittlehampton collected enough waste paper to sell for £4.11.4 which they sent to the Red Cross. In many parishes it would seem that volunteers came together to raise funds for the Red Cross – as with this group from Charles, West and East Buckland.

The Lynton working group sent 1000 hospital bags for wounded soldiers to keep their personal belongings in to a London depot.

Unions were active this month with the Torrington Workers' Union playing a street organ to raise funds for a YMCA hut in France whilst the Ilfracombe branch demanded an increase in overtime pay. The Braunton branch of the Union heard a speaker from Exeter talk 'on the future of the worker, and what lessons the War had taught the worker.' Builders in Barnstaple went on strike for an extra 1d an hour and won - at the same time as local bakers saw their minimum weekly wage increase to £2.

The movement of women into the workplace continued with a report commenting on the fact that the four female assistants at the Maypole Dairy in Barnstaple served 2240 people with ½lb of margarine each in just 2 hours. Even the Barnstaple Division of the Conservative Party amended its rules to allow women to join – and at the end of the month the *Journal* printed a letter inviting women to join the police – although they would not have police powers.

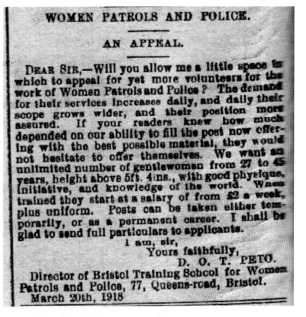

WOMEN PATROLS AND POLICE.

AN APPEAL.

DEAR SIR,—Will you allow me a little space in which to appeal for yet more volunteers for the work of Women Patrols and Police? The demand for their services increases daily, and daily their scope grows wider, and their position more assured. If your readers knew how much depended on our ability to fill the post now offering with the best possible material, they would not hesitate to offer themselves. We want an unlimited number of gentlewomen from 27 to 45 years, height above 5ft. 4ins., with good physique, initiative, and knowledge of the world. When trained they start at a salary of from £2 a week, plus uniform. Posts can be taken either temporarily, or as a permanent career. I shall be glad to send full particulars to applicants.

I am, sir,
Yours faithfully,
D. O. T. PETO.
Director of Bristol Training School for Women Patrols and Police, 77, Queens-road, Bristol.
March 20th, 1918

7. Female police. NDJ 28.3.1918 6f

A court case from Combe Martin saw a Mrs.Ellen Stevens as a witness she 'having left London in consequence of the raids' – the forerunner of many more a quarter of a century later.

Both men and women were being urged to buy War Bonds in order to help the war effort but amidst all this war-related news one curious issue saw feelings running high. A Bill aimed at making divorce easier was being discussed in Parliament following a rise in divorce numbers and pressure from newly enfranchised female voters. Not everyone was in favour with a public meeting in Barnstaple hearing Mrs.Wyndham Bruce attack the Bill on the rather odd grounds that our ancestors had never had the option to divorce and it could lower the birth rate. She also said 'Why upset the whole marriage life of England, because just a few couples here and there were unhappy?' A similar meeting at North Molton also denounced the Bill 'as being contrary to Divine Law, thoroughly demoralising to Society, and a danger to the State.'

The First World War in North Devon

April 1918

The massive German offensive launched last month continued into April but initial successes created by the use of highly trained Stormtroopers were lost as the impetus of the attack faltered. During these attacks, however, the Allies' losses were great – with 32 local men recorded in this month's newspapers as dying, though two of these had been killed as long ago as April 1917. Another man, Pte.Leonard Mills from Barnstaple, a member of the Artists' Rifles regiment, died in October 1917 his body only being identified by 'mementoes found on the clothing'. He had been Registrar of Births, Marriages and Deaths in Barnstaple before enlisting.

As ever, some of the dead were young. Thus L/Cpl Howard of Chittlehampton had only just reached his 19th birthday when a sniper's 'explosive bullet' killed him. Pte.J.Kemp of Braunton died of his wounds aged 20 it being noted that he had been in the Royal North Devon Hussars at the outbreak of war presumably aged just 17. Pte.A.Staddon who had been a Bideford shop assistant died 'from the effects of gas' aged 21. Two PoWs were also reported as dying this month – Appledorian Pte.W.Parkhouse died as a prisoner of the Turks and Sapper W.Hoare from Barnstaple died in Germany. The report on the death of Walter Gammon from Ilfracombe noted 'He was among the first to go to the front with the 'Tanks', when they began to harry the Germans.' Most of these fatalities received only passing mention in the newspapers but when Dr.Alfred Gardner was killed he merited a longer obituary, and note the euphemistic reference to 'recent setbacks on the Somme'.

As noted the German offensive on the Western Front saw large numbers of casualties and the Government in a panic introduced the 'New Man-power Bill' this month – with its features described in the *Journal* for April 11.

As can be seen the Bill raised the age for conscription to an incredible 55 for some men which could never have been envisaged at the start of the war. An attempt by a group of MPs to exclude skilled agricultural workers from the call-up was defeated in the House of Commons by 234 to 74 votes. By now any 18 year old appearing before the local Tribunals had very little hope of exemption especially if fit and healthy. Older men also had to have very strong cases to avoid conscription now. When, at Barnstaple, William Turner, graded 'C2' and father to 10 children appeared he was sent for medical examination to see if he might be upgraded. At the same Tribunal

DEATH OF DR. A. L. GARDNER IN FRANCE.

It was with feelings of deep and widespread sorrow that the townspeople of Ilfracombe learnt of the death of Dr. Alfred Linton Gardner, on April 10th last, while on duty at the front, where the great battle is raging. "Dr. Alfred," as he was familiarly called, was the only son of the late Dr. J. T. Gardner, and was as popular in the town and in his profession, as was his late father. He was born in 1882, and was educated at the Ilfracombe College, under Mr. W Rees He entered as a medical student in Guy's Hospital, following his father in this. Shortly after the lamented death of his uncle, Dr. Ernest Gardner, he settled in Ilfracombe, in association with his uncle, Dr. Percy Gardner, continuing the geniality and personal charm which he had inherited In the autumn of 1916 he entered his name for Army service, and in January, 1917, went to Blackpool for training. After a few weeks, however, he was sent out to France, and was gazetted Captain in the R.A.M.C. Field Ambulance, No. 107. He had charge of several base hospitals at various times, his organising ability being considerable, and he was highly esteemed by the military authorities for his admirable work. During the recent setback on the Somme, he was in the thick of the hose, i a! work, and during this trying time he lost his kit, his personal belongings, and the various mementoes always treasured by the family man. As previously stated, he was killed on April 10th, and it is a pathetic coincidence that on the same date, just one year before, his cousin, Lieut. Eric Gardner (also an only son), of the Somerset Light Infantry, died for his country in France.

Dr. Alfred married a daughter of the Rev. Puilein Thompson, of Chelsea; he leaves a widow and one little boy, about a year old.

He was a very att active personality. Early in his youth, he manifested considerable musical ability, and conducted several of his own orchestral compositions in public. As instructor of various ambulance and Red Cross classes he was very popular, and knew how to teach in a very happy style.

The greatest sympathy is felt by all for his young widow, who has done a good work in the town in connection with the Maternity Centre

1. The death of Dr.Gardner.
NDJ 18.4.1918 5f x 2

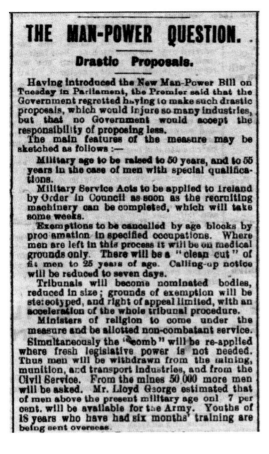

THE MAN-POWER QUESTION.

Drastic Proposals.

Having introduced the New Man-Power Bill on Tuesday in Parliament, the Premier said that the Government regretted having to make such drastic proposals, which would injure so many industries, but that no Government would accept the responsibility of proposing less.

The main features of the measure may be sketched as follows :—

Military age to be raised to 50 years, and to 55 years in the case of men with special qualifications.

Military Service Acts to be applied to Ireland by Order in Council as soon as the recruiting machinery can be completed, which will take some weeks.

Exemptions to be cancelled by age blocks by proclamation in specified occupations. Where men are left in this process it will be on medical grounds only. There will be a "clean cut" of fit men to 25 years of age. Calling-up notice will be reduced to seven days.

Tribunals will become nominated bodies, reduced in size ; grounds of exemption will be stereotyped, and right of appeal limited, with an acceleration of the whole tribunal procedure.

Ministers of religion to come under the measure and be allotted non-combatant service.

Simultaneously the "comb" will be re-applied where fresh legislative power is not needed. Thus men will be withdrawn from the mining, munition, and transport industries, and from the Civil Service. From the mines 50,000 more men will be asked. Mr. Lloyd George estimated that of men above the present military age onl 7 per cent. will be available for the Army. Youths of 18 years who have had six months' training are being sent overseas.

As to Ireland, the Premier said that the report of the Convention had just been laid on the table, and although it was the report of a majority it did not represent a substantial agreement. The Government therefore proped to introduce a measure for Irish self-government that would be carried without violent opposition. The moment had come, however, when it would be illogical and unjust not to apply conscription to Ireland, whose fortunes were as much at stake as ours.

Reviewing the battle situation, Mr. Lloyd George said that the enemy had succeeded for the time being in crippling one of our great armies (the 5th Army). Between it and the 3 d Army a serious gap was created, but the situation was retrieved by the magnificent conduct of our troops. Nevertheless, the Germans had obtained a great initial success, and were preparing an ever greater attack. They were too near to Amiens for our comfort or security.

When the battle began the enemy's strength on the Western front was not quite equal to the total combatant strength of the Allies. Without unity of command we would encounter fresh disasters, and he entreated the nation to support the appointment of General Foch as director of the Allies' strategic operations at the front. Our immediate anxiety had been relieved by the splended and generous contribution with which the United States had come to our aid, but it might be that the men made available by the present Bill would decide between victory and defeat in the great battle, which would probably last for many months. If that battle was won the doom of Prussianism would be sealed ; if it were lost we would not, as long as we had a ship afloat, accept a German place.

2a & b. The 'New Man-Power Bill'.
NDJ 11.4.1918 5e x 2

George Slocombe, Grade 3 and father to 8 children under the age of 12 with a 'delicate' wife was given 4 month's exemption with his case to be reviewed then.

The main impact of the new Bill in North Devon was to remove more young farm workers from the land. Admittedly the 17 tractors now operating in the area were doing sterling work in ploughing farm land even if two of them had broken down. When the Barnstaple War Agricultural Committee met they agreed to establish a camp for schoolboys to help with the harvest as doubtless labour would be short 'particularly when the men of 50 were called up'. It was also suggested that 'civilian prisoners of war' could be put to work this presumably referring to interned Germans and Austrians. The South Molton Committee also wanted to set up a schoolboy camp in the Witheridge/Worlington district to complement the German PoWs now at work it being remarked that the latter 'were very good workers, especially with horses.'

As these concerns were being addressed a variety of new orders concerning food and fuel were being announced which impacted on everyday life including these from just one issue of the *Journal*.

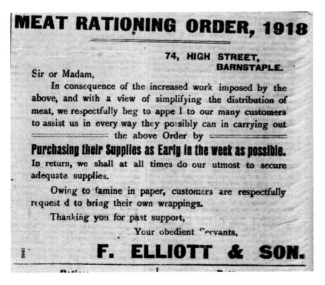

MEAT RATIONING ORDER, 1918

74, HIGH STREET,
BARNSTAPLE.

Sir or Madam,

In consequence of the increased work imposed by the above, and with a view of simplifying the distribution of meat, we respectfully beg to appe l to our many customers to assist us in every way they possibly can in carrying out the above Order by

Purchasing their Supplies as Early in the week as possible.

In return, we shall at all times do our utmost to secure adequate supplies.

Owing to famine in paper, customers are respectfully request d to bring their own wrappings.

Thanking you for past support,

Your obedient Servants,

F. ELLIOTT & SON.

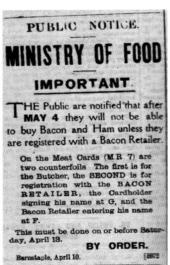

PUBLIC NOTICE.

MINISTRY OF FOOD

IMPORTANT.

THE Public are notified that after MAY 4 they will not be able to buy Bacon and Ham unless they are registered with a Bacon Retailer.

On the Meat Cards (M.R. 7) are two counterfoils The first is for the Butcher, the SECOND is for registration with the BACON RETAILER, the Cardholder signing his name at G, and the Bacon Retailer entering his name at F.

This must be done on or before Saturday, April 13.

BY ORDER.

Barnstaple, April 10.

3 & 4. New rules.
NDJ 11.4.1918 4e-f + 5a

The following week came an announcement that 'heavy workers' would be provided with 'Supplementary rations' if they applied, with the advertisement noting that 'BOYS of 16 and 17 and WOMEN' were eligible if 'wholly engaged upon heavy work'. One wonders how many applications they got given that the South Molton Rural Food Committee had received 1180 applications just for preserving sugar. It probably didn't count as 'heavy' work but this month the Bideford Motor Works issued an advertisement calling on 'Women of Devon' to attend their workshop and train as 'Motor Drivers' to help the war effort – with success guaranteed.

All these new regulations gave rise to more court cases as when Thomas Pearce, a Barnstaple baker, fell foul of the 'Cake and Pastry Order 1917' after he added raspberry jam to buns he had made. He was fined 10/-. Also at Barnstaple Edwin Symons, a Tawstock farmer, was fined a nominal 5/- on two counts of selling butter at 2/4 a pound – 1d over the fixed price. More serious was the prosecution brought against Richard Huxtable of Brayford and John Ware of High Bray. They were charged with buying a rick of oats 'fit for human food' at South Molton several months before and then letting it rot – a crime in these times of food shortage. They were each fined £2.6.0 – an indication of how seriously the authorities were taking the food crisis.

Farmers such as these must have felt themselves under siege what with their labourers having been taken, produce prices fixed and a whole host of new regulations to be followed. On top of all this their remaining workers were flexing their economic muscles with the Braunton branch of the Workers' Union passing a resolution protesting at moves by farmers to increase working hours and lower wages. This wasn't the only Union activity this month. In Barnstaple a branch of the London and Provincial Union of Licensed Vehicle Workers was formed under the auspices of the Trades and Labour Council. This latter body was convening fortnightly it being noted at the first meeting that 'there was a large attendance of members, including many female delegates' – and this event saw them decide to form a Labour Party branch in the Barnstaple Division, with the first meeting scheduled for May 1st.

During this month the 28 men of the Barnstaple Borough Surveyor's staff asked for a wage increase of 5/- per week and after being offered 3/- went on strike. The council then met and by a vote of 6 to 5 informed the men 'that unless they returned to work their places would be filled with the result that all save five (who have

5. A munitions dispute. NDJ 18.4.1918 3c

obtained employment elsewhere) resumed work' on the council's terms. Also in Barnstaple female workers at the Newport Glove Works left their benches after the forewoman told off one of the girls.

One event concerning 'Trades Union Girls' ended up at the Exeter Munitions Tribunal. The munition works at the centre of the case is not identified though it was probably the Bideford one but the details of the dispute are fascinating and indicate the growing power of organized labour.

6. *Female workers at the munitions works in Bideford.*

One wonders if worries about strikes were behind the swearing in of ten Special Constables at Ilfracombe this month? Very little appears to be known about such 'Specials' but many areas seem to have had them – as shown with this group from the West Buckland area.

7. *'Specials' with a regular Police Officer at West Buckland.*

More positive items of news came from Torrington and Barnstaple. At the former the large mansion known as Sydney House in the centre of town was to become a Red Cross Hospital joining the existing Voluntary Aid Detachment one at 'Enderby'. Barnstaple town council met to examine the plans for a new shipyard to be built by the British Construction Company on the site of the old Westacott's shipyard – which would see shipbuilding revived after many years.

8 & 9. Wounded soldiers pictured in Torrington.

The First World War in North Devon

May 1918

Given both the slowness of communications between the battlefields and Britain and the chaos of wartime this month saw many reports of deaths occasioned by the German Spring offensive launched at the end of March. Some 62 local servicemen are recorded in this month's lists of deaths – the second highest number in the war. The usual mix of very brief mentions and fuller obituaries appeared including these.

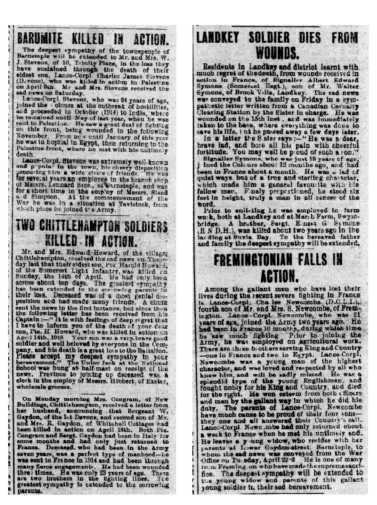

1 & 2. Obituaries. NDJ 2.5.1918 5f

Notice that Signaller Symons was only 19 – as were other soldiers killed this month. They included Pte.G.Parkhouse of High Bickington, Pte.Albert Darch of Torrington and Pte.S.Norman of Charles – whose older brother was killed just 4 days before him. Pte.R.Summerwill of Ilfracombe who enlisted on reaching his 18th birthday, was sent to France on the 5th April and was dead 9 days later. The oldest fatality seems to have been Pte.William Harris of Barnstaple who died in Italy aged 'about 42'. Four men died in captivity – Pte.S.Sluman from Bideford, Pte.L.Deering from Hartland and Berrynarbor's Pte.A.Trump who died as Turkish PoWs whilst Pte.W.Lewis from South Molton died in a German camp.

Almost certainly as a direct result of the German advance the number of men being reported as being PoWs was noticeably higher this month than at any other time – with 21 men noted as now being in prison camps. Often their parents or wives had been told their menfolk were 'Missing' so a brief postcard from them saying they were now prisoners was a relief. There were also a high number of deaths from medical causes this month. Thus Pte.L.Beardon from Chulmleigh died of tetanus, W.Hales of Bideford and F.Davie of Goodleigh both succumbed to pneumonia in France. Pte.S.Hocking from Westleigh died of dysentery and Pte.S.Fulford of Northam died following an operation for appendicitis whilst Pte.S.Sanders from Barnstaple had 'heart failure' – all reminders that sometimes the Germans weren't the only enemy.

SYDNEY FULFORD.

Son of Samuel and Mary Jane Fulford. Corporal – M. A.s. Tank Depot. Died – Mont Idoon ~ Treport ~ May 18. 1918.

3. Cpl.Sydney Fulford.

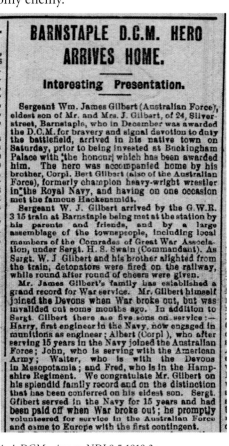

BARNSTAPLE D.C.M. HERO ARRIVES HOME.

Interesting Presentation.

Sergeant Wm. James Gilbert (Australian Force), eldest son of Mr. and Mrs. J. Gilbert, of 24, Silver-street, Barnstaple, who in December was awarded the D.C.M. for bravery and signal devotion to duty the battlefield, arrived in his native town on Saturday, prior to being invested at Buckingham Palace with 'the honour] which has been awarded him. The hero was accompanied home by his brother, Corpl. Bert Gilbert (also of the Australian Force), formerly champion heavy-wright wrestler in the Royal Navy, and having on one occasion met the famous Hackenschmidt.

Sergeant W. J. Gilbert arrived by the G.W.R. 3 15 train at Barnstaple being met at the station by his parents and friends, and by a large assemblage of the townspeople, including local members of the Comrades of Great War Association, under Sergt. H. S. Swain (Commandant). As Sergt. W. J Gilbert and his brother alighted from the train, detonators were fired on the railway, while round after round of cheers were given.

Mr. James Gilbert's family has established a grand record for War service. Mr. Gilbert himself joined the Devons when War broke out, but was invalided out some months ago. In addition to Sergt. Gilbert there are five sons on service :— Harry, first engineer in the Navy, now engaged in munitions as engineer; Albert (Corpl.), who after serving 15 years in the Navy joined the Australian Force; John, who is serving with the American Army; Walter, who is with the Devons in Mesopotamia; and Fred, who is in the Hamp-shire Regiment. We congratulate Mr. Gilbert on his splendid family record and on the distinction that has been conferred on his eldest son. Sergt. Gilbert served in the Navy for 15 years and had been paid off when War broke out; he promptly volunteered for service in the Australian Force and came to Europe with the first contingent.

4. A DCM winner. NDJ 9.5.1918 3c

These were the unlucky ones but at the same time others were being given honours. Five more local men were awarded Military Medals this month with three officers being given Military Crosses whilst Barnstaple's Commander C.Chichester of the Royal Navy won the Distinguished Service Order for organising the evacuation under fire of an aerodrome. When Sergt.William Gilbert of the Australian Imperial Forces, who had won a Distinguished Conduct Medal, visited his parents in Barnstaple he was given a hero's reception.

This article appeared in the *Journal* just inches away from a report on an inquest into a Barnstaple suicide. Walter Thorne, a tailor, had cut his throat, with various witnesses recounting how he had been called up for medical examination three times, being first rejected and then twice passed 'C3'. One witness William Thorne reckoned 'They kept on worrying the poor little fellow to death' with the Coroner commenting 'This continual calling up of a sensitive man would be enough to unhinge him.' The inquest jury reckoned he had been 'temporarily insane' at the time of his death,

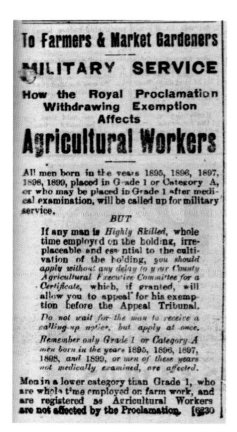

5. The cancellation of most Agricultural Exemptions. NDJ 2.5.1918 5a

Whether this gave Tribunal members pause for thought is unknown – but they continued to meet and adjudicate cases – having to take on board the order affecting agricultural workers as explained in an announcement published in the newspapers at the start of the month.

The Government may have promulgated this order but North Devon's Tribunals continued to exempt many agricultural applicants always reckoning they were 'indispensable.' This infuriated the Army man Woodcock who found his claims turned down time after time – often along with other tradesmen being exempted though some of these had strong cases. Thus when the Lynton panel sat and R.Jarvis, a plumber, appeared before them they heard that he had been in the Army but was discharged as unfit and then had been rejected by the Forces on three further occasions – he was given an exemption until October 1. An even more extreme case was heard in Barnstaple when William Harris, a foreman carpenter, applied. He had first been rejected then medically re-examined and classed 'C2' and then, following another medical, passed as fit for military service which was remarkable given he only had a thumb and forefinger on his right hand. He was exempted.

One interesting case heard at the same Tribunal was that of William Davie, the 49 year old manager of the Derby lace factory. It was pointed out he oversaw 430 workers who were operating 96 machines for 14 hours a day producing mosquito nets for the Army. Notwithstanding this he was told to be available to the Army on September 1. It is worth noting that at this sitting 29 cases were heard with 21 of these being of men aged in their 40s with only two aged 18 plus one in his twenties.

Given Woodcock's frustration over having so many agricultural workers exempted it is not surprising to find that at the end of the month the Appeals Tribunal met with 'regard to young men in agriculture coming under the 'clean-cut' proclamation'. The meeting began with Captain Stirling (he had been promoted) for the Army stating that Devon had to find 950 men 'from agriculture at once' going on to suggest that farmers employ 'women from the Land Army, or prisoners'. Apparently some 367 cases in North Devon had already been looked at with 181 men identified as recruits with another 98 being available if substitutes could be found. Even so many of the exemptions granted to 'indispensable' men were challenged by Stirling, he succeeding in a few cases.

This stricter approach to agricultural labour was reflected in the ever more onerous rules governing rationing with new orders being announced all the time as shown by these advertisements.

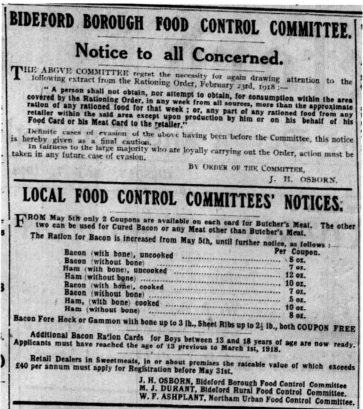

6. More Food rules. BG 7.5.1918 2d-e

Tractors continued to plough fields in North Devon whilst more and more allotments were being made available with Bideford town council announcing they had 27 acres of allotments being cultivated by 342 people. At Barnstaple a public meeting heard Professor Douglas from the Ministry of Food explain that the town was to be the first outside of London to be the site of a factory utilising 'blood and other by-products' from sheep for human and poultry food. This food was the black pudding which was then worth £80 a ton. Another new factory was opened at Sticklepath, Barnstaple when the Combe Martin Jam & Preserve Company leased premises used by Woolaway and Sons to produce their 'high class' products. At Woolacombe the inhabitants decided to establish a 'communal or national restaurant' run by volunteers to supply hot and cold food to both locals and tourists.

In an effort to help with labour shortages West Buckland School agreed to make 30 boys available to farmers during their holidays whilst at Bideford the School Managers extended the Summer holiday to five weeks to allow children to help with the harvest. Of more lasting impact was the increase in the Women's Land Army with a 'Recruiting Rally' advertised to be held in Barnstaple along with a Government film on the WLA being shown at the town's Theatre Royal.

7. A Women's Land Army rally. NDJ 9.5.1918 4d-e

8. An appeal for cooks. NDJ 30.5.1918 4e-f

At the rally Miss Calmady Hamlyn 'said to every women and girl who was not using every ounce of her strength for her country at present that they were not playing the game.' At the conclusion of the very wordy speeches which were reported verbatim in the *Journal* twenty recruits were enrolled. A week later a meeting of the Devon Women's War Agricultural Committee at Exeter heard that 253 recruits had been accepted into the Devon WLA – but another 479 had been rejected – and of those accepted 57 had subsequently withdrawn.

If women didn't want to work on the land they could have gone into the Queen Mary's Army Auxiliary Corps as this advertisement in the *Journal* at the end of May showed.

Also this month the Barnstaple Maternity Centre opened at 113 Boutport Street offering both clinics and a creche which allowed women to work during the day. On a lighter note over in Bideford magistrates were asked to issue a license for a new 460 seat cinema constructed behind the Heavitree Inn in Mill Street which had 'every modern requirement'.

This month also saw more Union activity starting with a public meeting in Barnstaple Market held by the British Workers' League. This group began as a breakaway organisation from the Labour Party - which then became anti-socialist and pro-British Empire. Their appearance did not stop the establishment of a Labour Party branch in Barnstaple committed to standing a candidate in the General Election. The group, which had 'a goodly sprinkling of women' went on to hold another meeting in Barnstaple where the questions of post-war housing and unemployment were discussed with a warning that there would be 'a social cataclysm' if these issues were not addressed. The Barnstaple Brotherhood, a church group, discussed 'The League of Nations', deciding that such a body was essential following the war.

One problem that wasn't touched on was the continuing spread of venereal disease. The Barnstaple Board of Guardians responsible for care of the poor did support the setting up of a 'National Council for combatting venereal disease' though the chairman did not like discussing the topic in a 'mixed assembly', the Board having several female members. This was odd as the Women Citizens' Association was active in North Devon – one of whose aims was the 'study of political, social and economic questions'. Clearly a 'social cataclysm' was coming following the granting of votes to women.

The First World War in North Devon

June 1918

The halting of the German offensive saw a period of relative quiet on the Western Front and now that 650,000 American soldiers had arrived, with 10,000 extra arriving every day, it was clear that the end of the war was probably in sight. Nevertheless 16 more men had their deaths recorded in the *Journal* this month though this total included Pte.R.Beagen of Barnstaple who had died 'on or since' September 1915 and L/Cpl.Mitchell, also of Barnstaple, who was killed in October 1917. Another young soldier who died was L/Cpl.Archibald Passmore of Torrington who was only 19 when he was killed in action in March 1918. Two more prisoners of the Turks died – Pte.J.Penhorwood from Appledore and Pte.J.Hoyle from Torrington. One soldier who died away from the battlefield was Cpl.Frederick Rhodes of the Canadian Forestry Corps. Aged 48 and working near Torrington he was 'engaged in blowing up a tree by means of fuses when an explosion occurred before he could get out of the way' and he died instantly. His Canadian compatriots clubbed together to purchase an impressive gravestone for him which can still be seen in the Torrington cemetery.

1. The gravestone of Cpl.Frederick Rhodes in Torrington cemetery.

News has this week reached Barnstaple of an act of noble self-sacrifice on the part of a Barumite who risked his life by consenting to the transfusion of blood in order to save a wounded comrade. The hero is Pte. Arthur Ralph Easton, of the Australian Imperial Force, son of Mr. and Mrs. A. R. Easton, of Victoria-road, Barnstaple. In a letter (dated June 14th) to his father from Edmonton Hospital, Pte. Easton says:—"After the hurriedly written postcard I wrote in the Red Cross train en route for this hospital, I know you will be anxious to know how it is I am here. Well, I was sent out of the line at ———— with a septic hand to a casualty clearing station, where I was detained. Just as I was about to be discharged, an Australian came in and had to have his leg amputated. Next morning he was dying through loss of so much blood, so I volunteered to be operated on so that I might endeavour to save his life. I am delighted to say that on my leaving the hospital he was hopefully pulling through. I gave about two pints of my blood; I cannot say I am feeling very ill, but I am feeling very, very weak. On my card I am classed as a 'blood donor,' and papers following me read something like this, ' Pte. A. R. Easton volunteered to act as blood donor in view of saving a dying comrade,' and I am strongly recommended for leave by my Colonel and the doctor who did the transfusion." After leaving the casualty clearing station, Pte. Easton proceeded to England, and is now doing well in Edmonton Hospital. The gallant soldier has recently gone through very heavy fighting.'

Happier news came when Pte.Arthur Easton, a member of the Australian forces from Barnstaple, wrote about how he had saved another man's life.

2. An early blood transfusion. NDJ 20.6.1918 5e

Other 'good' news came from men captured during the German offensive who wrote home from prison camps in Germany to say they were alive and safe, there being 27 of them. Also good news was the award of medals to 15 local men. These included a Distinguished Conduct Medal to Sergt.C.Morgan of the Royal Engineers for his work in France laying telephone and telegraph lines he being an 'Old Contemptible'. Astonishingly only a few weeks later he was awarded the Meritorious Service Medal for similar work in Italy. One civilian award was an OBE to Mrs.Edith Curzon of Watermouth Castle for her work in organising the Officers' Hospital at Berrynarbor. After the war a small pamphlet was published giving the history of this hospital which included a list of all the officers treated.

Although the Front was 'quiet' the work of the Tribunals continued with farmers becoming ever more restive – so much so that Earl Fortescue was forced to write to the newspapers cautioning them not to over-react.

The Narrative.

Promptly after the outbreak of the Great War, Major and Mrs. Penn Curzon offered the use of Watermouth Cottage as a residence for convalescing wounded soldiers, and as promptly was it taken advantage of.

Watermouth Cottage is situated in what Arthur Norway (" Highways and Byways in Devon and Cornwall ") describes as that grand and beautiful domain that lies among sweet woods low down by the shore of a rocky cove.

On 28th October, 1914, it was opened for the reception of wounded Belgians, but other arrangements were soon made on their behalf, and before the end of the same year, they were being replaced by non-commissioned officers and men from our own Army.

These latter occupied the Cottage onwards through 1915 and until March, 1916, and in the memory of all of them, " Watermouth was the gem of the journey."

But the War, like Virgil's description of Fame, was growing by going, and by the early months of 1916, the salvage of its slaughtering had developed into such a large and lamentable establishment, that it demanded concentration in larger groups for the purpose of receiving closer inspection, with more varied and systematic treatment, and

Watermouth Castle instead was put in commission for the care of convalescing Officers from the British Forces, and was opened about the middle of May, 1916. From then until now, September, 1919, more than six hundred officers have been admitted and discharged from its roll, and as the one prosperous industry of Watermouth Castle is the production of **longevity**, to which both nature and art contribute lavishly, there are certainly hundreds of unpublished iliads in the fond recollections of those whom Fate included in that fortunate crowd.

There are others, many others, alas! who, notwithstanding achievement gained, decorations won, and even the addition of disabilities more or less permanent, nobly replied to the overseas call again, and as soldiers, like soldiers, fell. Men like Capt. Howard Lister, D.S.O. and M.C. (with two bars) were amongst them. Peace to their brave hearts and a silent thought to their great sacrifice,

3. A page from the history of Watermouth Castle Hospital.

A WARNING TO ANGRY FARMERS.

Earl Fortescue writes :—Sir,—It has been reported to me that some farmers who anticipate that they will be seriously inconvenienced by the calling up of sons or labourers under his Majesty's Proclamation of 20th April, are saying that they will put their cattle into the fields they had laid up for hay.

People suffering from a sense of grievance are apt to say more than they mean, and I hope there is no occasion to take threats of this kind at all seriously; but if there should, unfortunately, be any farmers in this County who in resentment at steps made necessary by the requirements of National Defence have forgotten their duty to provide all they can for the food of the nation and its fighting men and their animals, I would remind them that under the powers entrusted to Agricultural Executive Committees by the Defence of the Realm Act, they can be compelled to farm as directed and are liable to £100 fine and (or) imprisonment if they fail to do so.

Yours faithfully,
FORTESCUE, Chairman.
Devon Agricultural Executive Committe, 50, Queen-street, Exeter. May 30th, 1918.

4. A letter from Earl Fortescue. NDJ 6.6.1918 3c

The Bideford Tribunal was the first to meet this month where they heard that two men, E.Leonard and Ewart Ellis, long-time members of the Volunteer Training Corps, had agreed to enlist in the Regular Army after a call went out for 15,000 Volunteers to step forward. The panel chairman thanked them, adding that they were unlikely to be called up for another month. The Barnstaple Rural Tribunal began its proceedings by reading a letter from Colonel S.Harding, head of recruiting in Devon, 'enforcing the great need, in view of the grave news coming from the Western Front, of using every endeavour to obtain Grades 1 and 2 men, whatever their ages.' Unfortunately this meeting only had four cases – and only one was ordered to enlist – the same number as the Rural Tribunals of Bideford, South Molton and Torrington and the Ilfracombe Tribunal found. The Lynton panel did slightly better managing to find two men.

All these Tribunals met in the first half of the month but on June 11 all agricultural certificates granting exemptions were cancelled with the chairman of the Barnstaple Rural body saying 'Tribunals would finish with agricultural cases.' From then on any men seeking exemption would have to go before the local Agricultural War Executive Committee. Because of the new ruling this Tribunal identified only 4 new recruits with several other farm workers ordered to act as substitutes to free up fitter men. The Barnstaple Tribunal saw 2 new recruits one being 45 years old whilst Bideford sent 7 men to enlist though all were in their forties.

Some applicants didn't turn up to the panel – they being ordered to enlist immediately in their absence.

One case was sad. Charles Braunton, a Barnstaple lace worker, had originally been rejected by the Army and was then regraded as 'C2' and then again regraded as 'Grade 1'. He pointed out that of his eight brothers six were in the Forces and two were on work of national importance and he asked, plaintively, 'that one should be left at home with the old people.' The Tribunal chairman 'appreciated what the family were doing' but he was still ordered to enlist.

With young agricultural workers now being taken the use of German PoWs became ever more important but when the Torrington War Agricultural Committee met it heard that the local Workers' Union members 'would refuse to work, directly or indirectly, with them.' Labelled as 'shortsightedness' an editorial in the *Journal* emphasised 'the permanent need of subordinating individual preferences to the common weal in the present crisis' going on to note the magnificent work of the Women's Land Army which 'has already melted away the prejudice of the past.'

When the Barnstaple War Agricultural Committee met they had no similar threat to face but rather heard that 40 Wandsworth Naval Cadets were coming to North Devon to help with the harvest along with 'some boys under 14 years of age' who would be put to hoeing potatoes. They also heard that under new regulations men over 45 and in low medical categories 'instead of being called into the Army, could volunteer for work on the land.' Members thought this would see 'an overwhelming number of men applying'. That they were needed was shown at the South Molton Committee's meeting when figures for acreages of crops in the district were given with comparisons to earlier figures.

	CORN	**POTATOES**
1916	14796	573
1917	16356	777
1918	25442	1323

These figures were heartening but they weren't enough to stop bakers being ordered to add potatoes to flour when making bread to eke out supplies. This made the bread 'dark' and rather sour to taste but it had to be done. Better news came with the temporary relaxation of rationing of bacon and ham.

The argument over German PoWs and local workers wasn't the only dispute. Samuel Pugsley wrote to the *Journal* denouncing local farmers for the low rates of pay their workers were getting and went on to suggest nationalising the land. W.Crook also wrote to defend the Workers' Union and their efforts to improve wages. An anonymous correspondent signing himself 'Landworker'

FOOD CONTROL.

NOTICE.
SALE BY CATERERS OF BACON AND HAM
FREE OF COUPONS.

(1) The Ministry have sanctioned from June 10th, the supply by registered Catering establishments, of Bacon and Ham as part of a meal, without the detachment of coupons.

(2) Caterers may obtain additional supplies of Bacon and Ham for this purpose from their authorised supplier or suppliers, and in excess of the amount shown on their respective Demand Notes.
   The Official Order form must be used for this purpose, and each order form so used should be marked "additional supplies" in RED INK.

(3) Retailers are authorised to sell surplus stocks of Bacon and Ham to registered catering establishments who are unable to obtain sufficient Bacon and Ham for this purpose, from their authorised suppliers.
   This concession is not to be used for the purpose of enabling any catering establishment to obtain choice cuts which they are unable to obtain from their authorised suppliers.

(4) The above relaxation in the rationing scheme is a temporary concession only, and is liable to be withdrawn any moment.

June 12th.   **BY ORDER.**

5. A relaxation of rationing rules. NDJ 13.6.1918 8a-b

replied suggesting Pugsley was 'simple minded' and 'mischievous' reckoning his views would lead 'to anarchy and the miseries of Russia'. Pugsley replied calling on every agricultural worker to join the Union noting that 'Two full-time organisers will be in Devon shortly' which indicates how active these bodies were becoming.

Whilst this exchange of views was occurring the 'rival' Unions were holding meetings in North Devon. The

British Workers' League held open-air ones beneath the Cross Tree in Braunton, at the bottom of Cross Street in Barnstaple, near the Collingwood Hotel in Ilfracombe and on Bideford Quay. At the latter the speaker said the group was formed 'to oppose the programme of pacifism which it was felt was creeping into the ranks of Trade Unionism.' Against this burst of activity the Workers' Union could only present a meeting at the New Inn, Muddiford where 'a good number of new members were enrolled' and their opposition to working alongside German PoWs.

The Union members did not seem to be opposed to the increasing numbers of Portuguese workers arriving in North Devon – although serious concerns were raised about the 'rudimentary' sanitary conditions at one of their camps at Arlington whilst the stench at the Fremington camp was 'enough to kill anybody' and the Braunton camp was 'in a deplorable state.' One wonders what a particular group of women thought of these conditions? The Women's Land Army had established a small sub-group known as the Women's Forestry Corps who were employed on felling timber but seem to have spent more time on measuring timber. A rare pair of photographs show them at work with Portuguese labourers probably in North Devon.

6a & 6b. Members of the Women's Forestry Corps at work with Portuguese men probably in North Devon.

One group of non-Union members who got a raise were the police in Barnstaple who, at this date, were still run by the town council. Their 'War Bonus' went up from 6/- to 11/- per week but one councillor thought they should receive more as he pointed out they worked 9 hours a days, 7 days a week and that 6 constables were now doing the work of 11. The council decided to keep with their original offer.

Another rather unexpected group who were given a cash boost were soldiers from Northam who were languishing in Turkish PoW camps. The Northam rector the Rev.Payne-Cook had been very active in organising Christmas and New Year gifts to men from the parish who were serving abroad and in this month he seems to have extended these gifts to PoWs. In return he received a postcard thanking him from W.Craner complete with Ottoman Empire censor marks – though whether 10/- in Sterling was much use in a Turkish prison camp is debateable.

7a & b. A PoW's postcard.

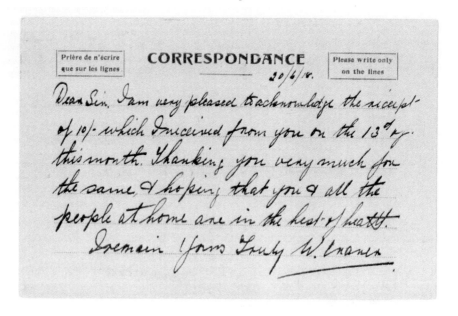

An unusual war memorial was presented to Horwood church this month by Lt/Col.H.Dene in memory of local men killed in the war. It came from Arras in France and was a crucifix 'being entirely made of machine gun bullets, and the figure and halo made out of bits of shrapnel having been made by French soldiers.'

One event that didn't get publicly reported at the time was the crash landing of a DH4 aeroplane on Lundy on 4 June. The pilot Lt.Charles Oldfield and his observer were flying near the island when their engine failed, but they managed to land on a grassy field. Unfortunately the aircraft hit a bump and turned over though both men weren't too badly hurt. The observer quickly returned to Ilfracombe whilst Oldfield stayed for a short time on Lundy being nursed back to full strength before travelling to Milford Haven. Relics of the aeroplane are apparently still kept on the island.

The First World War in North Devon

July 1918

With 20 deaths amongst local servicemen being recorded this month it seemed again that the Front was quiet. Of those reported two had died 10 months before and four were teenagers. Amongst this group was 17 year old Hubert Braddon from Barnstaple, a Royal Navy boy, who died of an unspecified illness on a hospital ship. Two 18 year olds, Pte.Frederick Stanbury and Pte.Thomas Shaxton of Shirwell, both died of pneumonia but one wonders if this was due to the influenza pandemic that was beginning to be noticed with pneumonia often following the initial flu infection. An older soldier, Sergt.F.Chugg of West Down, is also listed as dying of pneumonia along with two more men dying of unidentified 'disease'. Certainly the *Journal* was carrying advertisements for influenza cures at this date.

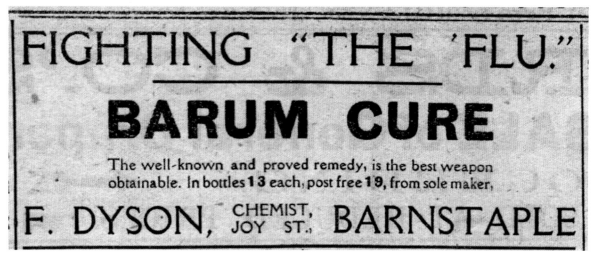

1. Influenza begins to make itself felt. NDJ 25.7.1918 6b-c

Local newspapers rarely reported German successes but this month saw one such when they claimed to have captured 191,454 prisoners since March 21st of whom 94,939 were British. Certainly this month 12 local men were named as being PoWs in Germany, almost certainly captured during the German attacks earlier in the year. Rather more positive news was the award of medals to twelve local men. Four Military Medals, three Distinguished Conduct Medals, one Conspicuous Gallantry Medal and two Military Crosses were given out with, in two cases, the medals joining one the man had already received. Thus when Pte.G.Coles from Bishopsnympton won a Military Medal it joined the DCM he already had. If this was impressive what are we to make of RSM George Pearce of South Molton who had already won the MC and DCM and was now awarded the French decorations the Medaille Militaire and Croix de Guerre with palms?

By now the local Tribunals were seeing fewer men than ever with many only appearing before them to renew existing exemptions. In other cases concerted moves were made to retain men seen as important to the community as was the case with Alfred Roach of West Down – although things were very different when Harry Bedford, a CO, came before them.

2. Harry Roach at the Tribunal. NDJ 4.7.1918 2b

3a & b. Harry Bedford a CO at the Tribunal.
NDJ 4.7.1918 2b-c

At the first Bideford Tribunal three men were refused exemptions though all were in their forties. At its second meeting 41 year old Frederick Beer was ordered to enlist but asked 'why farmers' young sons of the district who were put in the same grade as himself at the same time were not brought before the Tribunal' – to which he got no answer. The South Molton Rural Tribunal exempted virtually all of the agricultural workers who came before it though 'The Military are appealing against the decisions in the majority of the above cases.' The Torrington Tribunal met twice this month but sent no-one to the Forces.

The Barnstaple Tribunal met four times this July and reviewed some forty cases with the military pressing for as many men as they could, often unsuccessfully, though one wonders how useful some of them might have been to the Army. John Parminter, for example, was a 48 years old 'discharger' at Barnstaple Quay and part-time fisherman. He was ordered to produce 'time sheets' showing how much time he spent in each job. The two meetings of the Ilfracombe Tribunal produced no new recruits and indeed in two cases men claiming CO status were granted exemptions as the panel members were satisfied that their beliefs were 'genuine'.

When the Barnstaple Rural Tribunal convened they heard their Clerk refer to a local 73 year old member of the Volunteer Training Corps from Bickington who regularly drilled with a full pack and rifle – which saw the military representative Woodcock applaud him - clearly with the implication being that age was no impediment to serving.

Doubtless Woodcock was horrified to read that the, admittedly small, parish of Creacombe had not provided a single man for the Forces as highlighted in a report in the *Journal*. Perhaps the oddest claim for exemption came when Mrs.C.Bevan of the Lyn Valley Hotel at Lynton applied on behalf of her porter/gardener 49 year old W.Slee. After listing all the various jobs he did she also added as an afterthought that she herself had 'some little time since...volunteered as a motor transport driver in case of invasion.' He was given an exemption.

The North Devon Appeals Tribunal met twice this July with the Army representatives challenging virtually every man. When the case of Augustus Ayre, foreman at a Torrington glove factory, came forward a letter was read out from the Workers' Union urging he be exempted as if he went 'very serious hardship would be caused for large numbers of female employees, including war widows and wives of men serving.' The panel chairman didn't accept this adding that the 45 hours a week Ayre worked 'was small in war time'. At its second meeting of the twenty men whose ages are given seventeen were aged between 41 and 48. One, Henry Guard, a

4. An older man's record of service.

schoolmaster from Northam appealed 'against any kind of combatant service' – with his appeal being rejected though he later became a cause celebre when the local Education Board refused to continue employing him after the war. Men being conscripted now still had to be trained – with Salisbury Plain as ever providing the space and accommodation needed as shown on this postcard sent home to a Bideford man's family this month.

5. Codford, Salisbury Plain.

Whilst these hearings were occurring the food crisis was continuing with new orders regarding meat rations being published on July 1st.

MINISTRY OF FOOD.

Value of the Meat Coupon after July 14th.

As from the introduction of the new Ration Books on July 14th the following changes will take effect:—

(A). Three Meat Coupons (those marked a–a, b–b, and c–c) in the Adult Ration Book will be available for the purchase of Butchers' Meat, including pork.

(B). One Coupon only in the Child's Ration Book (that marked a—a) will be available for the purchase of Butchers' Meat.

(C). The value of the Meat Coupon will be 7d., instead of (as at present) 8d.

The value of the Coupon in terms of Bacon and Ham will remain as at present.

Consequential amendments are necessary in the table of equivalent weights, and a revised table will shortly be issued.

CATERERS.—As from the 14th July catering establishments and institutions will be required to account for Butchers' Meat purchased by them at the rate of 6 and 2-5ths ounces (i.e., 2-5th lb.) per coupon instead of 8 ozs., as at present.

BUTCHERS' MEAT.—As from July 14th Butchers will be permitted without the issue of fresh permits or notes of requirements to purchase quantities representing an increase of 25 per cent. in value of Dead Meat and an increase of 25 per cent. in amount of Live Stock over the weekly figures shown in their existing permits. This increase allows for (a) the increased number of coupons valid for Butchers' Meat on the Adult Ration Book, and the increased proportion of their total supplies of Meat which Caterers and Institutions may take in the form of Butchers' Meat; and (b) the decreased value of the coupon and the reduction of the number of coupons valid for Butchers' Meat in the Child's Ration Book. Butchers should ascertain from Institutions and Caterers they are supplying whether their requirements of Butchers' Meat will, in fact, be raised to the full extent permitted by the new concession.

BY ORDER.

July 1st, 1918.   [6992

6. Instructions as to meat rationing. NDJ 4.7.1918 8a-b

OCCASIONAL NOTES.

Considerable commotion was caused in Bideford Pannier Market on Tuesday by the arrival of two Food Inspectors, who expressed dissatisfaction with the general want of facilities for dealing on the spot with the rationed quantity of butter, which since May last has been five ounces instead of four ounces per head per week. The butter is mostly brought into the market in half pound rolls, already weighed, and very few bring scales. In some quarters umbrage was taken at the activities of the Inspectors, and individuals threatened that if there was going to be such interference they would not bring butter to the market at all. We understand that the condition of affairs in regard to butter found at Bideford is common to other markets in North Devon, and vendors at these Markets should take note that steps must be taken to ensure that the regulation amount of butter is supplied to customers. It is not permissible (as has been done in some cases) to supply four ounces one week and six ounces the next, making an average of five ounces per week; the supply must be confined to 5 ounces per head per week.

7. A food commotion at Bideford Market. NDJ 18.7.1918 8c

The maximum price of milk was then fixed at 6d per quart with bass at 1/- per lb. Local supplies of meat were being augmented by frozen imports but at Barnstaple it was found that much 'was unsound and unfit for human food' – with some 400 lbs being condemned. At Bideford two 'Food inspectors' visited the Pannier Market and discovered anomalies which caused ructions among the dealers.

A later letter from one of the women denounced the 'officials' as 'a lot of shirkers that could be better employed in the trenches fighting for their King and country....instead of frightening the farmers' wives.'

Further news came of the proposed 'animal by-products' factory scheme when it was announced that the old ice factory at the Lion Mills at Bradiford in Barnstaple was to be taken over to house the operation. More meat-related news emerged when the South Molton Rural Food Committee heard from Mr.Selley, a butcher of Witheridge, that 'in consequence of the last of his six sons having been called to join the Colours he was compelled to close down his business.' He went on to point out he had been supplying 717 adults and 150 children. The Committee unanimously decided to 'take steps' to obtain the last son's release from the Army to ensure locals got their meat ration. This month saw the issue of new ration books, with retailers advertising their products in line with the new orders.

Complaints regarding coal rationing came from the Barnstaple Trades and Labour Council who considered the 'inadequacy' of supplies was due to 'coal merchants having been called up to the Colours'. The group also complained when it was announced that Barnstaple Post Office would be closing every day from 1 to 2.30 p.m. – presumably owing to a shortage of staff. This wasn't the only Union activity as at South Molton the Workers' Union held an inaugural meeting and signed up 21 new members.

The on-going correspondence between S.Pugsley, secretary of the Workers' Union, and 'Landworker' continued at great length in the *Journal* each attacking the other with Pugsley accusing his opponent of 'misquotation, jibes and futile attempts' to prove him wrong. Other correspondents became embroiled in the debate which became heated and reflects the rapidly changing status of the worker/employer relationship at this time of social dislocation.

While this interchange of views went on other groups met under more harmonious conditions. In Barnstaple the newly established branch of the National Federation of Discharged and Demobilised Sailors and Soldiers met and heard a report on the work already done to help members. The Bideford Emergency League, who ran the Belgian Relief Fund, met and heard how the 60 Belgians recently in town were now reduced to 23 whilst subscriptions had fallen below expenditure. As a result the 'London Committee' was to be asked to take over the financial care of the remaining refugees.

On a more personal level when Miss Beatrice Westacott left the Derby lace factory to become a clerk in the RAF her fellow workers presented her with a gold watch. Several weeks later the same workers presented a gold ring to Miss Mabel Taylor when she left to join the Women's RAF. They weren't the only female workers noted this month as when two women agricultural workers were sent to work on Lundy this also made the news. Further collections of sphagnum moss by school children were recorded at North Molton and Twitchen – with a Government circular arriving in North Devon asking that fruit stones and nut shells be collected by children 'for urgent War purposes'.

Two stories concerning women came to prominence. The Barnstaple Board of Guardians decided to support a Devon county council proposal for 'the compulsory detention in Workhouses of all mentally defective women who might, from time to time, enter the maternity wards in the county, and who, as well

8. *A retailer and rationing. BG 9.7.1918 4e-f*

as being a recurrent source of expense, were a danger to society.' This harks back to the eugenics debate of the late nineteenth/early twentieth century though the placing of expense before society is telling. The second story concerns an inquest at Alverdiscott on the body of a 13 month old 'keep child'.

The report clearly hints that Mrs.Squire was a 'baby farmer' i.e. someone who took in babies who then died thus relieving the, probably unmarried, mother of an embarrassing child. Notice that the cause of death, 'pneumonia' could be another example of an influenza-related death.

Just to round off the month the men of the Canadian Forestry Corps, who had been working at Pegham Wood for 10 months, were leaving – and staged a 'farewell dance' in Torrington Town Hall. Two war memorials were put on foot. At St.Giles in the Wood a 'wayside cross' was being erected 'to the memory of Captain J.O.Clemson' and all from the parish who had died fighting. At Combe Martin the village's Friendly Society was being wound up after 60 years with much of the remaining funds in its account given to form 'the nucleus of a War Memorial Fund'.

INQUEST AT ALVERDISCOTT.

The Deputy Coroner for North Devon, (Dr. Ellis Pearson) and a jury, of which Mr. J. T. Lyle was foreman, held an inquest at Abbaton Cottage, Alverdiscott, on Thursday, on a thirteen months' old keep child, son of a domestic servant. A Bideford witness spoke to acting on behalf of the mother and placing the child out to keep with Mrs Annie Squire in September last. Six shillings per week was paid, and the mother provided the clothes. She last saw the child about a month ago, when it was in good health. She saw it frequently, Mrs. Squire bringing it in to Bideford. It was a healthy child, and Mrs. Squire had never complained of its being otherwise. No message was left on Saturday that it was ill, and it was then perfectly well as far as witness knew.—By the Foreman; Witness was satisfied with the manner in which the child had been kept.—Mrs. Annie Squire, of Abbaton Cottage, said the child had good health. It was all right on Sunday. On Monday it was a little fidgety, as children were when teething. It slept well Monday night, and was fed as usual, but about 8 o'clock on Tuesday morning she noticed a change, the infant breathing hard, being unable to keep its head up, and a little feverish. She put up poultices and telephoned for Dr. Toye, of Bideford. He was attending an urgent case and could not come, and then Dr. Ackland was 'phoned for. He could not come either, and a telephone message was sent to Dr. Grose, Bideford, the reply being given that he would come as soon as he could. These messages were sent about 9 30, and she was waiting all day for the doctor to come. The child died about a quarter to five—the Coroner: Are you in a habbit of taking children to nurse?—Witness: Yes, but I don't think I shall take any more now, sir, I have finished with it.—Why won't you take any more?—Because I think there is trouble enough as it is.—What trouble do you mean? I think this is trouble now, sir,—Have you had a similar thing before?—Yes, you had been here once before, sir.—How many children have you had died suddenly?—Only this one and the one back in January, when you were here.—Witness added that she was properly registered to take in children.—Dr. E. J. Toye said in his opinion death was due to syncope consequent upon an acute attack of pneumonia.—The jury concurred, and returned a verdict of death from natural causes.

9. An inquest at Alverdiscott. NDJ 11.7.1918 2e

The First World War in North Devon

August 1918

This was both the fourth anniversary of the start of the war and also the month when the Allies launched a massive offensive along the River Somme which shattered the German Army both in terms of the numbers of prisoners taken (30,000 on the first day) and the morale of their soldiers. The battle, which began on August 8, saw victory looming – but as usual local men died during the fighting, but news of their deaths only really started arriving in North Devon towards the end of the month. Indeed of the 23 non-historical deaths this month 11 were reported in the last week of August with 4 being those of teenagers. They were Pte.Jack Osmond from South Molton (19), Pte.James Bendle of Barnstaple (18), Cpl.C.Perrin also of Barnstaple (19) and Cpl.Harry Ridge of Wrafton (19). Three other men died in prison camps and two were accidentally drowned. Further news came of men captured earlier in the year with 25 North Devonians being recorded as being PoWs in Germany with another 3 being held by the Turks. In an interesting sidelight PoWs were added to the area's Voter's Lists when the electoral lists were drawn up this month suggesting that their early release was expected.

Although very late in the war the local Tribunals continued to meet but not before news was published of the Court Martial of six COs at Exeter for disobeying military orders. They included Frederick Mitchell of Langtree and Harold Holmes of 'North Devon' who were both sentenced to 112 days in prison with hard labour. The North Devon Appeals Tribunal saw a CO Samuel Balman, the telegraphist at Ilfracombe Post Office, exempted from combatant service.

The Barnstaple Tribunal met twice this month seeing three men in their fifties one of whom was ordered to be available for the Army. In contrast to these they also saw 19 year old James Sanders a fellmonger who had a permanently damaged right hand but worked buying wool at South Western markets for 'army clothing

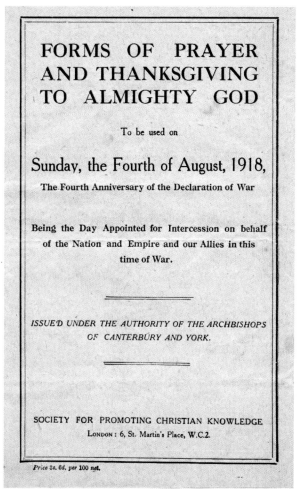

FORMS OF PRAYER AND THANKSGIVING TO ALMIGHTY GOD

To be used on

Sunday, the Fourth of August, 1918,

The Fourth Anniversary of the Declaration of War

Being the Day Appointed for Intercession on behalf of the Nation and Empire and our Allies in this time of War.

ISSUED UNDER THE AUTHORITY OF THE ARCHBISHOPS OF CANTERBURY AND YORK.

SOCIETY FOR PROMOTING CHRISTIAN KNOWLEDGE
LONDON : 6, St. Martin's Place, W.C.2.

Price 3s. 6d. per 100 net.

1. The church asks for God to intercede on behalf of the Allies.

and for airmen's jackets'. Woodcock, the Army representative, wasn't impressed saying he 'did not think any officer or soldier over 40 years of age would like to think a young single man of 19 was home buying the wool with which their jackets were lined.' He was ordered to enlist.

The Ilfracombe Tribunal saw eight men and of the six whose ages are noted four were in their fifties and two in their late forties. One, Thomas Watts, a fishmonger, claimed to be a CO but hadn't put that on his form that went to the Tribunal – his case was adjourned. At the Barnstaple Rural Tribunal Samuel Brown, a 45 year old 'Grade 1' road contractor applied for an exemption but Woodcock demanded he enlist with one panel member the Rev.J.Dene suggesting he volunteer as 'To be able to see different countries in the Army would be much more interesting' than staying in North Devon – to which Brown replied 'he had seen different countries already, having been in the United States, for example.' He was ordered to enlist in a month's time.

As in previous months the Appeals Tribunal was noticeably more exacting when judging cases thus when James Broom, a restaurant proprietor of Barnstaple appeared he brought various medical certificates saying he 'suffered from gastric catarrh, had had an attack of sunstroke and also suffered from insomnia'. Captain Stirling the Army representative reckoned Broom was 'one mass of complaints from start to finish' – and the panel rejected his application. When Thomas O'Donnell, a marine store dealer and licensed hawker of Hartland, appeared he was told to enrol in the Volunteer Training Corps even though he had applied to enlist in the Regular Army in 1892, 1893 and 1897 'to be told he was absolutely unfit for service.' At one Appeals Tribunal hearing it was announced by a panel member that 'Tawstock has been very patriotic throughout the War, and there is not an eligible man left in the parish' which gives an indication of the success of the Tribunals.

These panels could order a man to enlist but the Police had to deal with deserters as a case this month showed. Mrs.Louisa Jeffery and Thomas Clow both of Barnstaple were charged with failing to get their lodgers to fill in an official form giving personal details. Both claimed ignorance of the law but the forms had been mandatory for two years. The need for these forms came out when the Chief Constable R.Eddy explained that 'At present men were going from place to place in order to evade military service, and the military authorities had the greatest difficulty in tracing them.' They were both fined 10/-.

All through August further notices regarding rationing were being published such as these.

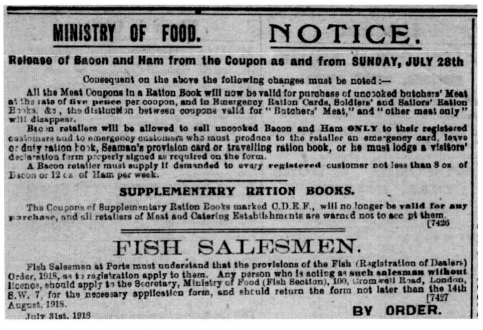

2. Meat and fish rationing. NDJ 1.8.1918 8a-b

Supplies of some foodstuffs seem to have been rather haphazard as when the South Molton Rural Food Control Committee heard that an extra allocation of 7¾ cwt of sugar for jam making had been distributed amongst 192 applicants – with another 1 lb for preserving blackberries and whortleberries if the applicant had collected the fruit themselves. This year was a good one for soft fruit and at Parracombe over 300 people turned up to pick whortleberries including 200 who came by train, even though rail tickets had doubled in price since 1914.

The Barnstaple War Agricultural Committee opened its 'Schoolboy Harvest Camp' for boys from the Wandsworth Naval Cadet Corps. The boys were to 'take a short march through the town and Cattle Market…so that the farmers can see for themselves what is the type of labour available to assist.' The Bideford Committee opened three camps at Hartland, Parkham and Woolsery.

In addition to these boys two groups of 10 German PoWs arrived in Shebbear and Dolton to help local farmers. The labour shortage was being experienced across North Devon so it was no surprise when the Northam Manor Court heard that 'potwalloping' or the throwing back of stones onto the Westward Ho! pebble ridge had not been done 'as people could not be got to do the work, except at a prohibitive price.'

Exacerbating these shortages was the fact that a lot of local men had enrolled to work at the newly built shipyard at Barnstaple – and their employment was guaranteed when it was announced that the Admiralty had signed contracts with the British Construction Company who owned the yard to build five 'reinforced concrete barges' and 'five concrete tugs'. This unexpected shipbuilding material was being used rather than steel owing to the shortage of the latter due to the demands of war.

3. School boy harvest camps. BG 23.7.1918 2c

4. North Devon tourism. NDJ 22.8.1918 8a

Another industry doing well now was tourism as people tried to forget the war, if only for a week or two - with an editorial in the *Journal* waxing lyrical over the area's attractions.

One group of visitors to North Devon were US and 'Colonial' troops here on leave. Earl Fortescue wrote to the newspapers requesting that local people offer to host these men, who, it was noted, would bring their own ration cards.

Another letter was one from the Prime Minister David Lloyd George, which was read out by the Mayor of Barnstaple at the Theatre Royal Picturedrome, in which he called for the country to 'Hold Fast!' as we were winning the war – a sentiment greeted with applause and the singing of the National Anthem. The Mayor also officiated at the Barnstaple 'Remembrance Day' service in Rock Park, with a similar event being held in South Molton with that town's Mayor present. On a less serious note in Northam the RAF Concert Party from the local aerodrome staged two concerts in aid of the 'Commons' Hospital, with a reviewer in the *Bideford Gazette* commenting on 'The spirit and go of the Air Service'. At Bideford the Palace Cinema was showing a film of 'The Raid on Zeebrugge'. This had occurred in April 1918 when the Royal Navy attempted to block the harbour at that Belgian port to prevent its use by U-boats.

It wasn't successful in military terms but it did boost civilian morale coming as it did originally at a time of defeats on the Western Front.

Not all was positive, however, with more letters filling the newspapers from S.Pugsley and his detractors. The Barnstaple Comrades of the Great War joined in by supporting a speaker at one of their meetings who denounced the recent strikes by workers in the West Midlands as unpatriotic. When the British Workers'

BEFORE Barnstaple Borough Bench on Thursday, Edward Norman, aged sixteen, of Bear-street, was charged with sketching an indecent figure on the shutter of a High-street establishment on July 20th.—The Chief Constable (Mr. R. S. Eddy) stated that whilst in the police station at 8 30 p m. he noticed defendant pencilling something on the shutters of an unoccupied shop opposite. Defendant was covered by two or three other boys, and the street was packed with people. Complaints were received of these indecent sketches being drawn on walls and premises in all parts of the town. Offenders were difficult to detect, and he asked the Bench to make an example of defendant. —P.C. A. Hill, who, on orders from the Chief Constable, stopped defendant outside the shop in question, bore out Mr. Eddy's statement.—Defendant had nothing to say except that he had seen other boys drawing on the walls.—The Mayor (Mr. F. A. Jewell) said this was no excuse, and such acts showed a very depraved nature Defendant was fined 10s., and the Bench trusted it was the last time he would appear before them.

5. *Youthful graffiti. NDJ 8.8.1918 5d*

League met at Barnstaple they heard a speaker proclaim 'Let the Trade Unions be led by trade unionists, and not by pro-Germans.'

Two odd items also appeared this month. At Bideford a 'wooden temporary cross' as used in France and supplied by the Army was placed on the grave of Gnr.H.Brett in the town's cemetery – the first seen in Bideford. At Barnstaple 16 year old Edward Norman was taken to court for something that might be covered by the phrase 'boys will be boys'. It reads as shown.

The First World War in North Devon

September 1918

The Allies may well have been seeing the Germans in full retreat but even successful armies lose men and this month saw 36 deaths reported amongst local servicemen – with 19 in one week. They included three teenagers and several men who were the second or third in their family to die. Most were Privates from a wide range of regiments but one man showed how the war had hastened the development of technology. First Class Air Mechanic Cyril Shute from Northam was 35 when he died of malaria in Italy on September 14th.

If there were fatalities there were many more reports of men being wounded and others being invalided out of the Army following hospital treatment.

With the Allies advancing there were few notices of PoWs but one was a reminder of a rather unfortunate band of 'prisoners'. In 1914 a British naval division was part of the force defending Antwerp. Overwhelmed by the Germans some 1750 British troops escaped to neutral Netherlands where they were interned for the remainder of the war. As the end of the war approached some of the British were allowed to return home for short periods on parole – and this month saw Lt.J.Chanter allowed to visit his parents in Barnstaple.

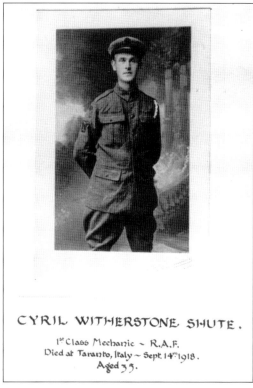

CYRIL WITHERSTONE SHUTE.
1st Class Mechanic – R.A.F.
Died at Taranto, Italy – Sept. 14th 1918.
Aged 35.

1. Cyril Shute – a new technician.

Although it was clear to most that the fighting was drawing to a close the Tribunals kept meeting though many of the men appearing before them had become War Agricultural Volunteers and thus were not subject to call-up. In other cases strong arguments were advanced to prevent a man being taken. Thus when Walter Ellis from Bideford was summoned to

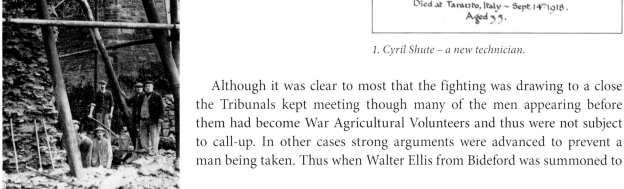

2. Workers on Bideford Bridge at this date.

the Appeals Tribunal it was pointed out that he was the 'sole contractor for the Bideford bridge, the piers of which had been under renovation for the past six years' with the work expecting to continue for some years. Nevertheless he was told to be available to join the Army on December 1st.

Another case before the Appeals panel attracted 30 farmers who had attended to oppose the conscription of George Hearn 'an unregistered veterinary'. Woodcock, the military representative, 'strongly objected to an attempt to intimidate the Tribunal in this way' – but he lost the case 'amid great applause and jubilant exodus of the farmers.'

When the Barnstaple Rural Tribunal met they lamented the fact 'that men had gone into the local shipyard where they were recciving such high wages.' The panel also saw William Spear of Marwood who was described by the Tribunal chairman 'as one of the few genuine conscientious objectors'. He agreed to do Red Cross work, this coming just a week after the vicar of Chittlehampton, instead of delivering a sermon, gave his views on COs, quoting Biblical texts 'showing the shallowness of what they represented at the Tribunals.' The same panels then heard one of their members, H.Isaac, decry the young, single men working 'in the woods' as lumberjacks who were in a 'protected' occupation and who 'crow[ed]' about their protection to married men who had to enlist. The difficulties associated with labour shortages following the mass call-up were highlighted by the Torrington Rural District Council when they wrote to the Admiralty seeking the 'release from service' of a local plumber called Eastwood. They pointed out 'that plumbing in the town and district was absolutely at a standstill, there being no-one in the town to do this work.'

The biggest local story this month was the launch of the first concrete barge – an event heralded by a long article published in the *Journal* under the heading 'Revival of shipbuilding at Barnstaple'. The first two paragraphs are shown here;

This was followed a fortnight later by an announcement on the front page of the paper about the actual launch.

REVIVAL OF SHIPBUILDING AT BARNSTAPLE.

CONCRETE SHIPS.

The building of concrete ships is in progress at Barnstaple, and so the borough is once more associated with the shipbuilding industry, which was prior to about 1870 a leading feature in the industrial life of the ancient borough for centuries. "Westacott's" yard, located on the site of the present Raleigh Cabinet Works, dated back to the 16th century, and the last ship launched at Barnstaple was built by the late Mr. John Westacott. It is quite a romance of industry that a grandson of this gentleman is responsible for the revival of the shipbuilding industry at Barnstaple. From an interesting article on this revival which appeared in the "Western Morning News" of Saturday last we take the following:—

'The war has resurrected Westacott's yard. Barnstaple is again a shipbuilding centre—one of a score or more which have been established in different parts of the country for the construction of the new type of concrete ship. As recently as March last the site of the present vibrant energy was a grass-grown waste through which at low tide the sandy bottom of the Taw gleamed golden in the sunshine. Now works covering 25 acres have been established there, with a river frontage of 1,000 feet, and a wharf 300 feet long for the purpose of fitting out the vessels when launched. Numerous buildings cover the ground, and there are seven slipways whereon at the moment of writing four 1,000-ton-sea-going barges and three tugs are already nearing completion. It is expected that the first launching will take place about September 21st. Barnstaple retains some of its old and prized distinction at the opening of its new career, for among the new yards it is one of the largest. An even more interesting fact is that the yard which is officially described as the Barnstaple branch of the British Construction Co., Westminster, has been opened by Mr. P. Westacott, engineer, London, who is a descendant of the old proprietors, and who was especially requested by the Admiralty to start one of these yards. Gossip has it, too, that there are shipwrights working at the new yard who served their apprenticeship at the old Westacott yard.

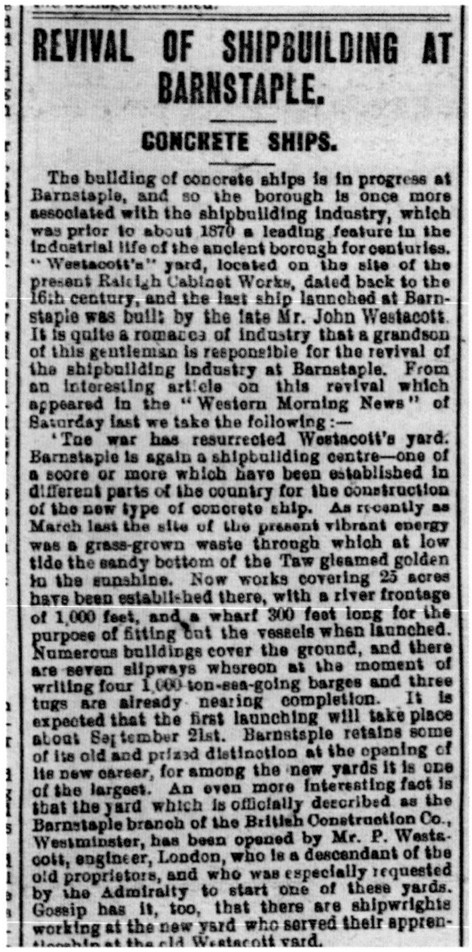

3. Shipbuilding returns to Barnstaple. NDJ 5.9.1918 7b

LAUNCH

From the BARNSTAPLE SHIPYARD on SATURDAY MORNING, September 21st, 1918, at 7 o'clock.

THE BRITISH CONSTRUCTION COMPANY regret that owing to inadequate accommodation, and Admiralty restrictions, they are unable to invite the general public to the Launch of the first of the Concrete Ships which they are building for the Government.

SPORTS have been arranged for the FIRM'S EMPLOYEES in the field adjoining the Shipyard, commencing at 2.15 p.m. on Saturday the 21st, and the public will be admitted at their own risk. A BAND OF THE DEVONSHIRE REGIMENT will play selections during the afternoon.

THE BRITISH CONSTRUCTION COMPANY,
39, Victoria Street, LONDON, S.W. [7929

(Designers and Builders of Concrete Ships up to 10,000 tons deadweight).

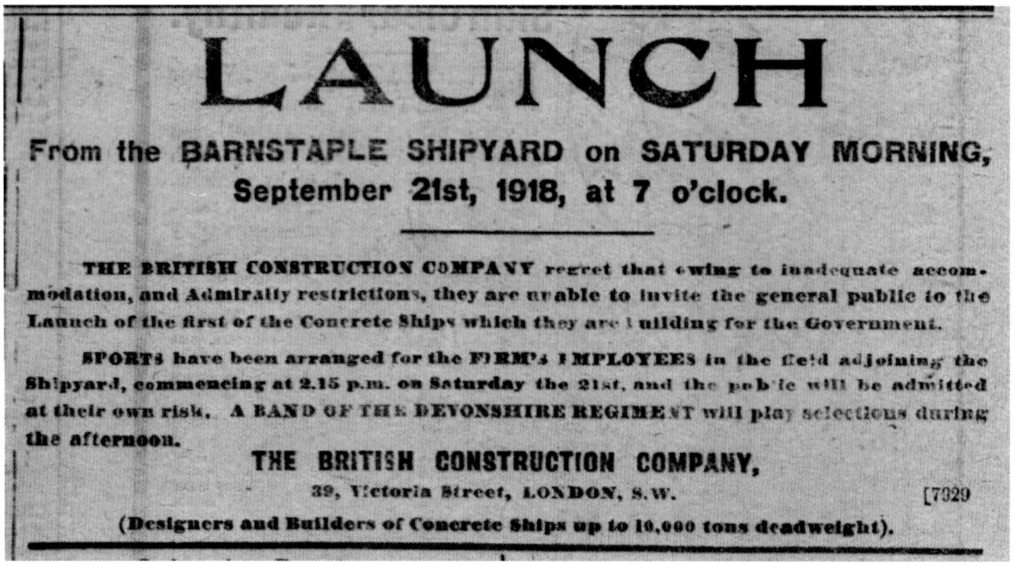

4. The announcement of the launch. NDJ 19.9.1918 1e-f

The event was covered at great length in the *Journal* which even included three photographs, with a short film recording the work being taken.

5.6.7. The building of the first concrete barge.

Named *Cretpath* its naming was viewed by the Mayors of Barnstaple and Bideford, an Italian Admiral as well as Admiralty and Army officers. As the barge slid down the stocks into the River Taw the band of the Devon Regiment played 'Britannia Rules the Waves' whilst a huge number of spectators cheered. Two ceramic models of the vessel were made by local potters C.H.Brannam Ltd., one going to the Admiralty and the other presented to Mrs.Goring Kerr who carried out the christening. She later presented it to the foreman of the yard and his family still possess it.

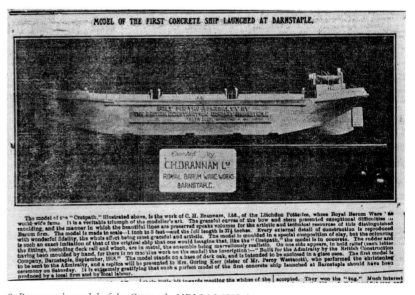

8. Brannam's model of the Cretpath. NDJ 26.9.1918 6a-c

More good news came in the form of medals presented to 11 local men. Sergt.Adkins of Woolacombe was awarded the newly instituted Distinguished Flying Medal – this being in addition to the DSM and bar he already possessed. Sergt.F.Knill of Barnstaple who had been one of the men involved in the Zeebrugge operation was awarded the Conspicuous Gallantry Medal and the Croix de Guerre this month. For 'gallantly performing his duty in charge of a 4-inch gun on HMS *Mary Rose* in action against superior forces' Lt.J.Freeman from Northam won the DSC, the report on this noting laconically 'He had been torpedoed twice before.'

Whilst men were away fighting women were just as busy at home. A rally in Barnstaple by the Queen Mary's Army Auxiliary Corps saw 30 members march through the town headed by the band of the Devon Regiment with a banner at the front reading 'Join us and release men for fighting'. Lots of speeches were made including one from Captain the Rev.Welby-Pryer who noted 'There was no conscription for women, but they were expected to roll up and say "We have come to help our brothers and shorten the war"'. At the close of the rally ten women had enrolled.

A letter in the *Journal* a fortnight later called attention to 'the urgent need there is of more women in our aeroplane factories', going on to claim that women were now working 'not only at the simple operations with which in the earlier days of the War they were entrusted, but at the more complex work in munition and aircraft factories.' In the same issue of the paper where this appeared also came a short report on a presentation to a retiring worker at the Barnstaple Cabinet Works by Frederick Thompson 'a member of the Aircraft Committee' which suggests at least one aeroplane factory was local.

That more aeroplanes were needed is shown when a DH6 reconnaissance aircraft flying out from the Northam Burrows aerodrome was forced to land on Lundy on 19th September. This time the plane did not turn over and the pilot was unhurt – indeed a photograph of the aircraft on the island with St.Helen's church in the background appears to show the pilot with his arm around a young woman.

9. *The DH6 on Lundy this month.*

The compilation of Voters' Lists was completed this month with the Registration Officer for North Devon reporting that they totalled 33,000 names - including those women who were now eligible to vote. Additionally there were 8000 absent voters which indicates roughly how many local men were still abroad with the Forces. Further analysis showed that Barnstaple, for example, had 2300 males and 2495 female voters with 1450 absentees.

Women were at last taking their rightful place in society but that didn't stop the *Journal* printing an extraordinarily detailed story about a Barnstaple war widow with 6 children, her case being characterised by 'immorality, drunkenness and disease.' Her husband had been killed in 1916 when her eldest child was 9. The NSPCC Inspector had visited her house to hear her admit that she 'was suffering from a certain disease' (VD) this being 'the result of her wickedness' she commonly bringing home wounded soldiers after an evening spent drinking in local pubs. The woman was sentenced to 3 months in prison for the neglect with the children being taken into care. With demobilisation looming one has to wonder if this story was printed as a salutary warning to other widows and to highlight the prevalence of VD?

This report had, in an adjacent column, a letter from Earl Fortescue outlining plans for the 'organised collection of blackberries' with collectors being paid to deliver the fruit to jam factories – with a list of 'Local Agents' being published the next week. At Combe Martin 'several tons' of fruit had been delivered to the local factory – with large quantities arriving every day 'from villages many miles distant.' In addition the corn harvest this year was good – with German prisoners having cut 300 acres of the crop in the South Molton district. Rationing was still in force and was to continue for some months – with new Ration Books being regularly issued.

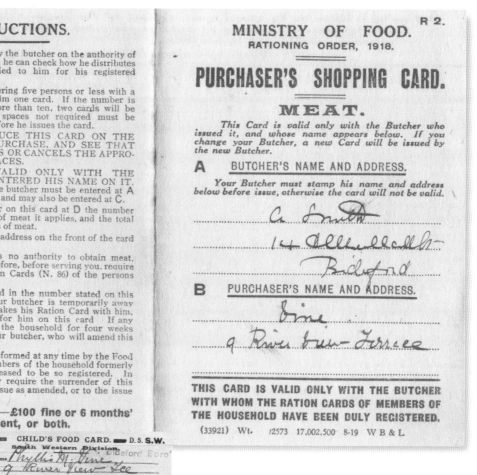

10 & 11. Examples of local rationing paperwork.

More cheerful news came when the RAF Concert Party from the Northam Aerodrome staged three shows in the Bideford Pannier Market. The events raised some £70 for the Bideford Hospital and the District Nursing Association.

Another war memorial was unveiled this month when a 'Parclose screen' was dedicated in St.Mary Magdalene church in Barnstaple. This was in memory of Pte.A.Hewish who had died from his wounds in October 1917.

12. The RAF Concert Party show.
BG 3.9.1918 2c

The First World War in North Devon

October 1918

The war was now virtually over with the German army disintegrating rapidly, but still local men were dying on the battlefield – with 47 being reported this month. As usual some were young with Pte.F.Peters of Barnstaple being just 18 along with two 19 year olds; Pte.W.Colwill of Bideford and Pte.T.Lamey of Appledore. Several obituaries make it clear that the men were under-aged when they enlisted. Thus Trumpeter Harold Swain from Barnstaple would have been 17 as was Pte.G.Glyde from Ilfracombe. In two other cases parents received new that they had lost a third son – Pte.William Short from Atherington and Pte.L.Paskey from Barnstaple being the men. Three more died of influenza with others noted as dying of 'disease'. In many cases the condolence letters from officers or chaplains are quoted – with the men they are writing about having died 'instantaneously' and 'feeling no pain' the writer often closing with an uplifting sentence. Thus when Frank Heywood of the Royal Flying Corps was shot down and killed this month a chaplain wrote of his part in the advance 'These victories, won at such terrible cost to so many, seem to be hastening the end of the War, and a victorious end too,'

One man who escaped death was Signaller L.Burgess of Lynmouth who lived due to his parachute opening in time.

A Lynmouth lad, Signaller L. Burgess, writing to his parents, Mr. and Mrs. R. Burgess, thus relates his first parachute descent :—" I have just had a very thrilling experience. I was in the balloon with an officer when we were attacked by a Boche 'plane ; we at once knew that his intentions were to set us on fire, so we immediately dived over the side   Am pleased to say my parachute opened all right and I made a good landing, and also the officer. The Boche was successful and set the balloon on fire, but a lucky gust of wind blew it away from us. I could not describe the sensation one has when dropping from the basket until the parachute fully opens. I fell over a hundred feet head first before the shute opened, but still, ' all's well that ends well,' and I am now quite O.K."

1. An early parachutist. NDJ 3.10.1918 6b

Many more men are noted as having been wounded, in lots of cases for a second or third time. Thus when Pte.F.Mock from Barnstaple was reported as being in a London hospital 'in a very critical condition' he suffering from wounds to his head, stomach and right arm it was noted 'Pte.Mock has been wounded three times, (on one occasion a cigarette case saving his life) besides having suffered from trench feet.' North Devon hospitals were still doing sterling work in treating these wounded men.

2. The Ilfracombe Voluntary Aid Detachment pictured in October 1918.

Along with the high number of fatalities went a large number of decorations awarded – with 17 Military Medals, 5 Military Crosses, 4 Meritorious Service Medals, 2 Distinguished Service Crosses and 2 Distinguished Conduct Medals given out this month. One unusual award went to Cpl.Arthur Copp of Barnstaple who had served for four years in the Royal Flying Corps he being given the 'Grecian military medal' as well as being mentioned in despatches. In another case a Croix de Guerre 'with Gold Star' was won by Sergt.C.Greenslade.

In this closing period of the war the Tribunals continued to meet but by now virtually no men were being ordered to enlist with most receiving exemptions that would take them past the Armistice. In quite a few cases the men had enrolled as War Agricultural Volunteers which removed them from the liability of 'call-up'. This was just as well as in one case the Ilfracombe Tribunal heard about – that of J.Richards who had enrolled as a WAV – the man was 57 years old. Two deserters were arrested this month, one Charles O'Brien a 'travelling optician' from Plymouth who had no registration card when stopped by the police in Barnstaple, he then admitting 'moving about from place to place'. He was fined £2 and handed over to the Military. The other was Henry Bickles, a Yorkshire soldier arrested at South Molton, he being remanded until the Army came to collect him.

Whilst this 'normal' wartime news continued the civilian population of North Devon were deep in the throes of the influenza pandemic. What had started with just a few cases was now affecting life across the whole of North Devon. In Bideford the schools were closed with the 'unusual spectacle' of a 'large queue outside a chemist's shop waiting for medicine.' Other shops closed as their staffs were depleted by the illness. In addition several deaths occurred in the town and 'such an epidemic of sickness has not been known in the borough for a great number of years.'

At South Molton the closure of schools for five weeks was announced whilst at Appledore the 'influenza epidemic is reaching alarming proportions' with nine deaths recorded and 'practically every house' being affected. Apparently there was no doctor resident in the village with District Nurse Watkins and the vicar's wife doing the best they could to help sufferers. Here again the schools were closed and 'all meetings of every kind' postponed. At Marwood 'influenza is raging' and 'in some instances all the family are affected'. Torrington saw three deaths including that of a Mrs.Cole of New Street who had only been married a week. In Barnstaple schools were closed and children were banned from cinemas although in Braunton the epidemic 'is not quite so bad...as in other North Devon towns.' By this date the disease had acquired the name it has gone down in history with – 'Spanish flu' – as shown in an advertisement in one of this month's *Journals*.

No-one knew how to tackle the pandemic but at

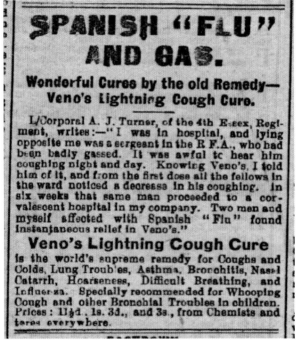

3. 'Spanish flu'. NDJ 31.10.1918 3d

Northam town council some members apparently 'believing in the efficacy of tobacco as an influenza preventative' smoked through the meeting.

One of the assumptions about the severity of this disease is that rationing introduced after nearly four years of war had weakened the population thus

4. An advertisement for dealers in jam.
NDJ 10.10.1918 8a-b

allowing the virus to make such inroads. Certainly food was still a topic of interest to the newspapers with ever more notices appearing about rations, such as this one concerning jam.

In the same issue of the newspaper carrying this announcement, and indeed in the same column, was the news that 'Enormous quantities of blackberries have been gathered in North Devon this season' – with the Combe Martin Jam Factory alone buying-in 30 tons of the fruit. On the other hand this month also saw the butter/margarine ration reduced from 6 to 5 ounces per person per week. At Ilfracombe the price of herring was fixed at 7d per lb and in Barnstaple potato prices were similarly fixed at 1¼d per lb. German PoWs were now working on many farms with suggestions they could also be used to trim hedges along roads as with farmers concentrating on planting and harvesting crops they had become very overgrown.

One interesting idea was floated by Earl Fortescue in a letter circulated throughout the county – not so much 'houses fit for heroes' as 'fields fit for heroes', though the idea does not seem to have been developed to any extent.

Such a scheme was clearly aimed at defusing any post-war unrest – but strong feelings as to wage rates and politics were already running high in this area. Thus a mass meeting of railwaymen at Barnstaple expressed their dissatisfaction with their employer's wage offer whilst 'A Trades Union demonstration' was staged a week later at the Albert Hall in Barnstaple where those attending heard speakers from two furniture unions. A week after this a small advertisement

LAND FOR DISCHARGED SOLDIERS.

We have been requested to publish the following circular which has been addressed to land-owners by Earl Fortescue as to discharged soldiers and sailors from country parishes. A large number of favourable replies have been received :—

Castle Hill, Southmolton,
25th July, 1918.

Dear Sir,—The Central Land Association, under the Presidency of Lord Selborne, have formulated a scheme with the object of enabling discharged sailors and soldiers from the country parishes on their return to their former homes to obtain a piece of land for cultivating on a voluntary basis.

It is not suggested that the holdings should be "small holdings" in the technical sense requiring buildings and capital, but plots or a little field of five acres or thereabouts conveniently accessible to the cottage in which the demobilised sailor or soldier lives.

While having full sympathy with the object, I considered that the scheme required modification in certain particulars ; but on receiving the assurance that it was to be considered only in the light of a suggestion, and that each county could modify it as it thought fit, I undertook to write to the principal landowners in this county to ask them if they would be willing to meet the wishes of discharged men returning to their homes by endeavouring to provide a piece of land by agreement if they so desired.

It is thought that an excellent impression will be produced if the men of the Navy and Army understand that there is a general willingness on the part of landowners to do what is in their power to meet the wishes of discharged men from their own parishes, who desire to obtain a piece of land to cultivate, and are capable of cultivating it.

5. Land for returning Servicemen. NDJ 24.10.1918 7c

appeared in the *Journal* offering membership of the local Labour Party at 1/- a year for men and 6d for women. At the end of the month the Barnstaple & District Trades and Labour Council met and passed a resolution demanding 'equal pay for equal work by women workers'.

On a happier note the Barnstaple Theatre Royal was showing a film of the launch of the *Cretpath* whilst W.Buchanan, the foreman of the engineering department of the shipyard that built it, was presented with a silver watch by the men in his section. In addition a framed photograph of the shipyard's joiners was presented to Captain H.Jewell, son of the Mayor of Barnstaple, as a mark of appreciation for his interest in the men's welfare. To round off the month the RAF Concert Party 'from the North Devon Air Station' on Northam Burrows staged a show at Barnstaple's Albert Hall to raise funds for 'The Flying Services Fund' which proved very successful. References to this air base are very rare but two are shown here.

6. A page from a local autograph book with an entry by a Northam Burrows RAF man.

7. A photograph of an Northam Burrows RAF man from the same book.

The First World War in North Devon

November 1918

This may have been the month when the Armistice was signed but men were still dying in numbers as the fighting continued up to the moment of cessation. Some 34 deaths of local men were reported this November which must have been doubly tragic for relatives given that the men had survived so far – only to be killed in the last days of fighting. Thus Mr & Mrs.Rodd of Ilfracombe heard that their son Driver Jack Rodd, who had been attached to the Royal Field Artillery in France 'since the beginning of the war' was killed in late September, the second of their sons to die. Another 'Old Contemptible' to die was Pte.Edgar Willis of Dolton who had survived being wounded, gassed and frost bitten he also being the second son to be lost to his parents. Signaller F.Trute of Braunton but late of Swimbridge died in Palestine after serving for 2½ years whilst 21 year old Lt.Frank Puddicombe, who had enlisted aged 18, died in action in Italy. One of the saddest cases was when 'Mr.Cole, gardener of Fremington, had just returned from attending a thanksgiving service held on Tuesday in the Parish Church to mark the signing of the Armistice when he received an official message stating that his son, Sergt.Cole R.E. was killed in action last week.' Another 'late' death was of Mark Hedden who died of his wounds two days after the Armistice – though there were to be many more with some surviving until the 1930s before dying of wounds, both physical and mental, they received during the war – yet their names do not feature on war memorials.

One death that made the news was that of Lt.George Moor VC, MC from Braunton. It will be recalled that he won his VC aged just 18 in June 1915. Sadly he died of influenza as did at least eight other soldiers recorded this month including First Class Air Mechanic Llewellyn Pengilly RAF whose body was brought home for burial in his home village of Clovelly. The world-wide nature of the pandemic is clear when one considers that Drummer A.Passmore of Barnstaple died of

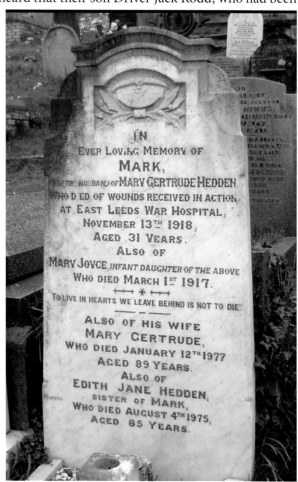

1. A death after the Armistice recorded on a grave in Appledore churchyard.

the disease in India whilst Pte.W.Dennis from Wrafton succumbed to flu 'while on his journey home from German East Africa where he had been since the outbreak of War.' North Devon civilians were still suffering with the illness it being 'very prevalent' in Chittlehampton whilst in Barnstaple 'most of the police constables' were ill with 'Specials' standing in for them. At Clovelly 'most of the school children have been afflicted.' The most serious effects were experienced in Appledore where 22 people died, this being due to the 'difficulty of obtaining medical services' there as alluded to last month though the District Nurse sent a letter of thanks to those who helped to the *Bideford Gazette.*

Another 13 had died in Northam whilst at Croyde 'influenza, is heavy upon the village'. One death at the latter place shows the virulence of this particular strain of influenza. Pte.George White of Fig Tree Farm came home on leave on a Friday, was 'quite bright' on the Saturday, took to his bed on Sunday and died on Tuesday with his funeral on Saturday – though none of his immediate family could attend as they were 'all too ill', with his sister dying of the disease shortly afterwards. A particularly sad death this month was of Doris Drodge a Voluntary Aid Detachment volunteer from Instow who died, probably of influenza, aged just 16. She is buried in Instow churchyard.

On a more positive note the last meeting of the North Devon Appeals Tribunal was recorded on November 13 where it was announced that 'all cases should be suspended pending further notice'. Their clerk noted that this was the 88th sitting of the panel they having dealt with some 1951 cases at these hearings. Given that these were only the appeals against decisions by lower tier Tribunals one gets some idea of the number of men who had challenged conscription.

Of course, the biggest news item this month was the signing of the Armistice and the cessation of fighting at 11 a.m. on the 11th of November. The *Journal* published a special editorial which reckoned 'The German beast of militarism is safely caged' which reads rather ironically today given our knowledge of what was to happen 21 years later. Another article reported on how the news reached parts of North Devon.

Various spontaneous displays of joy broke out when the news did reach the area. At Barnstaple the newly-formed band of the Comrades of the Great War played in the town and Pannier Market. At South Molton on November 11 the

2. A letter from the Appledore District Nurse. BG 12.11.1918 4b

3. The grave of an Instow VAD worker.

4. The joyful news arrives in North Devon. BG 12.11.1918 2dd

town 'was gay with flags' with the Mayor and corporation attending a thanksgiving service in the parish church in the evening.

5 & 6. Peace celebrations in South Molton.

Church bells were rung in celebration in many places with the vicar of Woolacombe marshalling the local school children who 'carrying the flags of the Allies, paraded the village, cheering en route.' At Braunton the news arrived in the morning and 'almost at once, as if by magic the town was bedecked with flags and decorations' with similar displays coming at Combe Martin and Bideford. At Northam the Square was crowded with excited people.

Along with this good news came the welcome report that 'A large contingent of North Devon soldiers arrived home on Monday on leave from Mesopotamia.' One assumes they were not sent back following the Armistice.

There may have been peace on the battlefields but here at home labour disputes were still being reported.